EARLY CHILDHOOD EDUCATION SERIES

Leslie R. Williams, Editor

ADVISORY BOARD: Barbara T. Bowman, Harriet K. Cuffaro, Stephanie Feeney, Doris Pronin Fromberg, Celia Genishi, Stacie G. Goffin, Dominic F. Gullo, Alice Sterling Honig, Elizabeth Jones, Gwen Morgan

---

(continued)

Culture and Child Development in Early Childhood Programs

PRACTICES FOR QUALITY EDUCATION AND CARE

Carollee Howes

Foreword by Louise Derman-Sparks

Teachers College, Columbia University
New York and London

Published by Teachers College Press, 1234 Amsterdam Avenue, New York, NY 10027

Library of Congress Cataloging-in-Publication Data

Howes, Carollee.
  Culture and child development in early childhood programs : practices for quality education and care / Carollee Howes ; foreword by Louise Derman-Sparks.
        p.   cm. — (Early childhood education series)
  Includes bibliographical references and index.
  ISBN 978-0-8077-5020-9 (pbk : alk. paper)
  1. Early childhood education—United States.   2. Child development—United States.
I. Title.

LB1139.25.H68 2010
372.21—dc22

                                                                    2009031589

ISBN: 978-0-8077-5020-9 (paper)

Printed on acid-free paper
Manufactured in the United States of America

17   16   15   14   13   12   11   10   8   7   6   5   4   3   2   1

Contents

PART II
ECE Programs Within Cultural Communities

Foreword

IF YOU ARE READING this foreword to decide if you want to buy *Culture and Child Development in Early Childhood Programs*, run, don't walk, to your computer or local bookstore. If you already own the book, prepare for an exciting voyage. I found the book exhilarating—just ask my husband, who listened to a stream of enthusiastic remarks as I read it. Here, at last, is an illuminating way to think about cultural communities as contexts for learning and about what really makes up quality early childhood care and education.

The relationship between quality and cultural context is one of the core, and often fractious, conversations in early childhood education. However, this book sheds a new and very promising light on the topic. Instead of posing culture and quality as two distinct dynamics that are in contradiction, or at least require a good conflict resolution process, the author begins with the premise that the two are undivisible. It is not a question of either/or, but rather of how the two interact in programs' and teachers' missions and practices. The author's diverse and talented team, with her leadership, created a breathtaking research approach that allowed its participants, and, now, us, to explore, see and analyze the many-dimensional factors that make up the integral relationship between culture community and quality.

The discussion of the research methods in Part I is fascinating (and I often find those kinds of chapters a bit tedious). From the beginning, researchers partnered with community advocates for children in each of the cultural communities where they carried out their study. For example, they collaborated in defining the elements of quality programs and in choosing early childhood care and education settings in the four different cultural communities that became participants in the study. The author likens their research approach to playing with a kaleidoscope—by turning its lens, numerous different patterns appear among the same pieces of glass. Similarly, a diverse and collaborative team, using its multiple research methods, was able to see many more variables and to identify many more patterns than does most research about quality in early childhood programs. Don't skip the chapters that explain all of this in detail—they are inspiring!

Part II provides wonderful details about the missions, practices, activates and interactions in each of the early childhood programs that were observed. I often felt that I was actually seeing the programs myself because the descriptions are so vivid. Moreover, the multiple lenses the research team used to gather the data enabled them to uncover the many layers underneath the children's and teachers' observable behaviors and the teachers' comments about their work. Thus I felt that I was understanding what makes up the quality of a particular early childhood education program in new ways—where the viewpoints of the cultural community and the early childhood profession work in collaboration to get closer to the program's core. The great value of observing through a variety of lenses and paying attention to patterns of practices, activities, and interactions rather than to single actions on the part of teachers or children becomes very clear (the kaleidoscope metaphor at play again). It is stunning to realize how much more we learn.

By choosing to research early childhood care and education settings that both community advocates and early childhood professionals agreed were quality programs, and by using a kaleidoscopic analysis of the data, this innovative study richly portrays how there are numerous paths to good early childhood care and education programs . It also sheds light on how teachers in various cultural communities construct their versions of what the ECE field considers to be best practice in relation to the cultural community's beliefs and behaviors. Equally important, the book gives us a framework and vocabulary to hold conversations about quality and culture that avoid false dichotomies between the two. Indeed, this stunning book ought to lay to rest the use of such dichotomizing.

I urge all higher education faculty, in-service teacher trainers, accreditation observers, researchers, textbook writers, and policymakers of standards to read this book. It will give you new and more proactive ways to continue the discourse about what quality really means, and how it really looks and how to nurture multiple ways to achieve it. I wish I were at the beginning of my teaching and writing career so that I could have used this book in my own work and with my graduate students. I hope you, the reader, will do so.

Now, settle in for an enlightening, enjoyable read!

—Louise Derman-Sparks

Acknowledgments

I AM GRATEFUL for the generous contributions of the project participants: the program directors and teaching staff, the children, and the many members of the research team. Special thanks to Dick Clifford and Sharon Ritchie for their thoughtful insights into the processes involved in teaching and learning for diverse young children and their families. The analysis and writing of this book could never have been accomplished without the generous and loving support of my life partner, Karen Brodkin. Thank you.

This work was supported by grants to the National Center for Early Development and Learning under the Educational Research and Development Centers Program, PR/Award Number R307A60004, as administered by the Office of Educational Research and Improvement, U.S. Department of Education.

Overview

EARLY CHILDHOOD EDUCATION programs (ECE)[1] are expected to provide exemplary care for all children—poor children as well as affluent; children of color as well as White children; and children who speak English as a first, second, or third language. They also are expected to adapt care to children's families and cultures so that experiences within programs are meaningful, relevant, and respectful (see, e.g., Bredekamp & Copple, 1997). These two sets of expectations, of both exemplary and culturally adaptive standards of care, are difficult for teachers and programs to conceptualize and to implement. All too often they have been presented as contradictory; ratings of child care quality are considered race- and class-biased, and practices are assumed to be of high quality if they are culturally appropriate.

This book argues that high-quality (and low-quality) programs come in many different cultural contexts, and that quality needs to be and can be measured in culturally specific ways. In the chapters that follow I describe multiple dimensions of a small number of ECE programs (Table 1.1) considered by adult advocates from the programs' geographic communities to be exemplary for low-income children of color. The participants in this project came to understand that to meet dual expectations of universally sensitive care and culturally adaptive care, child development constructs had to be embedded within cultural contexts. That is, the program directors and the teachers in the ECE programs used practices derived from their cultural communities to implement universal standards of child care. This integration required awareness of universally agreed-upon program standards, for example, sensitivity to children's social communications, as well as awareness of practices—ways of doing things—rooted within culture.

Defining exemplary and culturally adaptive standards of care has been difficult for the scholarly fields of child development and early childhood education. Postmodern education scholars assert that the statements on practices of the National Association for the Education of Young Children (NAEYC) are rooted in White middle-class assumptions of child competence and fail to place children's and teachers' behaviors within class, race, and ethnic contexts (Lubeck, 1998; New, 2005). Developmental psychologists argue that practices for providing emotionally safe care to children are universal, not culturally specific, but dependent on adults' sensitivity to children and their awareness of discrimination, bias, and

Table 1.1. The ECE programs.

Name	Larger Cultural Community	Age Group	Size
South Central	African American in LA	Preschool	24
Nickerson	African American in LA	After-school	112
Ready to Learn	African American in LA	Pre-K	90
Love and Learn	African American in LA	2-14 yrs.	60
El Peace	Latino in LA	2-8 yrs.	114
Pierce	Latino in LA	Pre-K	32
Mission Hope	Latino in LA	Preschool	32
Coast	North Carolina	2–6 yrs.	120
Mountain	North Carolina	2–6 yrs.	80
Therapeutic Preschool (TPS)	Diverse Families in LA	Preschool	16
Moms	Diverse Families in LA	Toddlers	32
Down the Hill	Diverse Families in LA	2–6 yrs.	45

exclusion (Baker, Dilly, & Lacey, 2003; Howes & Ritchie, 2002; Johnson et al., 2003).

  Particularly contentious in this scholarly debate is the construct of quality in ECE programs. Applied developmental psychologists, like myself, who began studying child care environments in the 1970s initially focused on children's social development and on practices that potentially could harm children (Rubenstein & Howes, 1979). We devised the construct of quality to address policy concerns about distinguishing between good enough child care and harmful child care (Phillips & Howes, 1987), that is, distinguishing between programs that do and do not jeopardize children's development. In the intervening years distinctions between child care and more traditional education programs—preschool, nursery school, and prekindergarten—have become blurred (Kagan & Kauerz, 2007). The term *quality*, used in all of these contexts, has taken on a variety of disparate meanings beyond adult–child interaction, including whether teachers do or do not have BA degrees, whether children are ready for school, and whether ECE can prepare future workers (Dahlberg, Moss, & Pence, 2007; Kagan & Kauerz, 2007; Lee & Walsh, 2005). While the preponderance of ECE programs in the United States that do not serve children well remains troubling (Howes, Burchinal, et al., 2008; Pianta et al., 2005; Polakow, 2007), quality as a universal construct for evaluating ECE programs, particularly programs for low-income children of color, needs further examination (Dahlberg et al., 2007; Lee & Walsh, 2005; Wishard, Shivers, Howes, & Ritchie, 2003).

This book is about a collaborative project between advocates and researchers around the construct of quality care. It was designed to answer the question of whether there are commonalities in good early childhood programs for young children that are shared across class, race, and ethnic communities, that is, whether there are ways of understanding common themes that are interpreted in culturally specific ways. This collaborative project took place in the late 1990s, before NAEYC revised its performance standards document to include culturally adaptive standards (Copple & Bredekamp, 2009; Bredekamp, 1987; Bredekamp & Copple, 1997; NAEYC, 2005) and before the latest push to include academic standards and content in preschools (Bracken & Fischel, 2006).

At the time the project was designed, research reports, media attention, and many of the day-to-day experiences of people in programs concurred that poor children and children of color were most likely to experience ECE that was not optimal for their short- or longer term development (Bowman, Donovan, & Burns, 2000). In the shorthand language of policymakers, this care was of poor quality. Subsequent research only added validity to these concerns, suggesting that on average the quality of ECE in the United States for poor children and children of color was lower than for the children of well-educated and affluent parents (Burchinal, Peisner-Feinberg, Bryant, & Clifford, 2000; Peisner-Feinberg et al., 2001).

In 1995, as a member of the larger Los Angeles community concerned about child care, particularly for poor children of color, and after several decades as a researcher examining children's experiences in child care, I saw programs that did a wonderful job of providing care for children in poor communities as well as the more common poor job.[2] I was exhausted and disheartened by the task of reporting findings of poor care for poor children of color from large-scale studies that I had participated in designing and implementing. Therefore, I enthusiastically agreed to participate with a group of researchers at the University of California, Los Angeles, and at the Frank Porter Graham Child Development Center at the University of North Carolina, Chapel Hill, who proposed to study, in depth, ECE programs for young children that were doing a good job of serving poor communities and communities of color.

BUILDING A NEW CONCEPTUAL FRAMEWORK FOR STUDYING CHILDREN'S EXPERIENCES WITHIN ECE PROGRAMS

At the time it seemed relatively simple. We would ask community advocates in Los Angeles and rural North Carolina to find the good programs and then we would use our research tools to describe them.[3] We then would be able to write a book about practices that worked in programs that did a good job of serving poor children and children of color. And on one level it was simple. Community advocates, if not able to completely agree on the definition of quality, selected 12 programs that had high scores on our late 1990s measures of quality (Wishard et al., 2003). But not long after the project began it was clear that our quality framework was not sufficient. Instead, as this book describes, I developed a theoretical framework that integrates theories of development within context and theories of culture. I have adapted Rogoff's (2003) framework for examining practices as ways of doing things within cultural communities as our theory of culture and Bowlby's (1982) theory of attachment to form a new theory to explain how children's experiences with forming relationships with adults and other children are shaped by cultural practices. Because Rogoff's theory may be less familiar to the ECE community than Bowlby's, in the next section I discuss how the construct of cultural communities permitted description of ECE practices within programs.

CULTURAL COMMUNITIES AND PRACTICES

A cultural community is defined as a grouping of people who share goals, beliefs, and everyday practices (Rogoff, 2003). Cultural communities are influenced by participants' race, ethnicity, and home language but are more dynamic than simply an ethnic or racial label (Rogoff, 2003). In each location, Los Angeles and North Carolina, the board members knew one another or knew of one another because of their activities. The community advocates on the advisory boards formed a cultural community—a group of people participating together to make sure that there were good early childhood programs for the families in their geographic area. These participants paid attention to programs, funding, regulations, and legislation having to do with ECE. Our advisory board members' participation in specific ethnic communities and in a statewide advocacy community gave them two angles of vision and the ability to think across cultures. As well as participating in cultural communities around ECE, the advisory board participants were simultaneously participants in other cultural communities based on shared values and/or shared history. For example, several members of the Los Angeles advisory board simultaneously participated in city and statewide advocacy for children and programs, as well as another cultural community identified by participation in advocacy for African American families and children. Thus the advisory board participants were members of cultural communities nested within larger cultural communities.

The participants in each selected ECE program also were part of program-level cultural communities in providing good services to their children and families, as well as participating in a larger cultural community marked by geography or ethnic identity. The North Carolina programs shared participation in a rural cultural community with strong regional identification. Because of the salience of race, ethnicity, home language, and region in Los Angeles, there were three larger cultural communities represented there. Several of the programs in Los Angeles shared participation in larger cultural communities based on racial identity: the larger African American and Latino cultural communities. I grouped the other Los Angeles programs into a larger cultural community, also based on the salience of racial identity, but in this case the similarities included historical roots in groups of White, relatively affluent people in leadership positions in the programs who were committed to antiracism and providing good early childhood programming within a multicultural and economically mixed context.

Within our theoretical framework, practices and culture are mutually constructed (Rogoff, 2003). Understanding the practices used in early childhood programs requires attention to the mutual contributions of individuals, interactive partners (e.g., teachers and children), and the community and institutional traditions of the program participants. Culture in this framework is defined through practices—that is, patterned configurations of routine, value-laden ways of doing things that make sense only when they occur together.

A large part of this project involved developing tools to describe the activities, goals, and practices of the program participants and to examine how these activities, goals, and practices were developed within the cultural community of the program. At first we assumed that teachers, and certainly program directors, could explain to us what they were doing and what they intended by what they were doing—their goals, activities, and practices. This assumption was based on work done with elementary school teachers (Ladson-Billings, 1999). But the teachers in the ECE programs we studied were different from the teachers described by Ladson-Billings. Both teachers and program directors had less formal education and more autonomy in their classrooms than elementary school teachers; the practices of early childhood education at this time in history were not codified and as a result teachers had little experience in articulating what they were doing and why they were doing it. We found that to describe practices, we could not just ask teachers why they were doing what they were doing and record their behaviors.

We were surprised to find something similar happening among our researchers. We thought observers who shared the cultural perspective of the program participants would likely see something different, when describing practices, than would an observer who did not. Therefore, from the start of the project we had carefully matched the racial backgrounds and languages of the researchers who observed each program. But as time went on, we came to understand that this matching, while advantageous in beginning program participation and developing project relationships, was not enough to articulate particular teaching practices and their rationales, for reasons I will explain shortly.

We also found that even if we could describe a practice, we were not sure what it meant for us or for the practitioners. And we were very sure from our discussions of our observations among and across programs that a practice in one program could have very different meaning in another. For example, we found that a specific practice, for example, grouping children with one teacher for more than a year, was effective in one program but not in another.

Our research team's experiences with describing practices led us to think about practices as particular to cultural communities. This discovery came out of a team meeting where we were challenging ourselves to think about how to write about the best practices that we were finding in each of the programs. At one point, we were trying to make sense of a set of practices that seemed to many on the research team to be antithetical to the high sensitivity rating that observers gave to the program. That conversation produced an epiphany, and subsequently a more sophisticated model for understanding how sensitivity and adaptive practices are linked across cultural contexts. The following quote is drawn from the transcript of the meeting.[4]

> I will make a for-an-example argument, that we decide that what makes the best practice at Love and Learn is not that they are emphasizing academic achievement at a very young age but that they are emphasizing academic achievement in a manner that is consistent with a community value of fiercely taking care of the children of the community and getting them ready for school. So I'm saying what may look on the surface at Love and Learn [like a] specific skill drill for academic achievement is, in fact, a different practice.

This practice at Love and Learn, using a skill-based, back-to-basics curriculum with very young children, was perhaps the most controversial practice in the project. Rote learning of math facts and vowel sounds, while sitting quietly in circles listening to the teacher, was not among our preconceived best practices. In fact, in our initial days of reporting on the project, we often were told, politely and not so politely, that by including this program we had violated quality standards. Yet observer after observer who spent time in the program commented on the positive emotional atmosphere: "It is so clear that all the kids feel loved." We also knew that this program's scores for teaching interactive tone and teacher–child relationship quality were extremely high, based on data collected by our reliable observers. As the transcript above illustrates, we found that we could not think about academic preparation practices without also thinking about the warmth of the teachers. And we believed that the combination of the academic preparation practices and the warmth in this program made sense because it was within a cultural context of fierce determination that the children be prepared for school. Based on Patricia Hill-Collins's (1994) work in describing child rearing, I came to hear the Love and Learn program director's passionate comments on the importance of providing academics for her children as an instance of other-mothering within the African American cultural community. I believed that she was telling us that she had taken on the responsibility for making sure that the African American children in her program came to school exceeding the expectations for achievement of a system that did not do well with making the children feel successful and valued.

THE RESEARCH TEAM

Our research team was composed of people who brought many relevant experiences to the task of describing practices within programs. Richard Clifford in North Carolina and Carollee Howes in Los Angeles served as principal investigators throughout the project. We senior researchers brought complementary strengths to this work—experiences in research design and instrument development, experiences in long-term working relationships with low-income communities of color around issues of child care quality and provider training, experiences with the lives of immigrant monolingual Spanish-speaking families, and experiences with policymakers and public administrators of programs. Perhaps most important, both of the principal investigators had years of experience working in the space between researchers, advocates, and policymakers. We personally had argued, collaborated, and worked with the members of the advisory boards in our home locations.

In each geographic location, there was a team of researchers, headed in Los Angeles by Sharon Ritchie and in North Carolina originally by Jana Fleming and later by Gisele Crawford. These project directors also had considerable experience working within programs for children and in community coalitions to make lives better for children. Once a program had agreed to be part of the project, we assigned it a research partner. These researchers-in-training, primarily graduate students, conducted ethnographic interviews, collected observation data, and brought their field notes to team meetings.[5] The research partners were ethnically and racially similar to the program participants, and many were former teachers. We assigned Spanish–English bilingual and bicultural research partners to all programs with any Spanish-speaking children. They shared their observations within a group of researchers diverse in race and home language, but also diverse in experience with the research process and status within the project.[6]

Like the advocates, these researchers were members of more than one cultural community that was pertinent to the project—that of the program in which they observed, and that of the community of ECE research. This was not a simple relationship; even researcher partners who "matched" the programs were outsiders to the programs by virtue of having a foot in the research community. As it turned out, both advocates and researchers were positioned to serve and did serve as cultural translators at key points in the research process and in engaging teachers and program staff in it. Here the interaction across cultural communities—research, advocacy, and program communities—was key. Because practices are ways of doing things shared by cultural community participants, they may be more visible to outsiders than to insiders, but their meaning may not be apparent to outsiders, who help insiders explain what they take for granted.

Our different responsibilities and contacts with the participants, as well as our own identities, meant that we had different points of view on the meaning of the data we collected. We had to learn how to listen to and understand one another, and we had to learn how to describe programs in multifaceted ways.

In doing this work, we had intended to form a research partnership with the participating programs. We initially articulated that this project would succeed only if we were able to construct positive and respectful participant–researcher relationships. We based this in part on the experiences of Carollee Howes and Sharon Ritchie as we worked on a prior project about early childhood programs that succeeded in helping children trust their teachers and programs (Howes & Ritchie, 2002). We also knew ahead of time that this was hardly going to be the kind of research project in which the researchers randomly selected programs, visited for a day or two to collect data, and then disappeared from the sight of the programs until the final report on the project. The process of collaborating with participants was neither participatory research nor experimenter-driven (Kirk, 1995). We wanted to do something in the middle of this particular continuum, forming positive and respectful relationships while keeping researcher–research participant boundaries in areas of research design.

To implement this project, we also needed to construct positive and respectful researcher–researcher relationships. The research team met more often than I had expected—weekly for the several years of active participation with the programs. In these weekly meetings we shared our field notes, our different perceptions, and eventually our common understandings of how our own participation in cultural communities organized by race and class shaped our understandings of what we saw (and didn't see).

Also, the research project deliberately was positioned between extremes of research methodology. We used many different methods from different traditions: participant observation and case history, clinical interviews and focus groups, and naturalistic observation with predetermined categories and standardized assessments of children. This book is an integration of the evidence we gathered from all of these divergent techniques. This diversity of methodology was necessary to describe participation in cultural communities and children's development.

THE KALEIDOSCOPE: EXAMINING BOTH INDIVIDUAL
CHILD DEVELOPMENT AND PARTICIPATION
IN A CULTURAL COMMUNITY

As we modified our methodology and our analytic strategy to understand child development as embedded in children's participation in specific cultures with their own practices, I found the concepts of insider and outsider and the image of a kaleidoscope to be extremely important. Early childhood educators and researchers who study ECE may see more easily as a "good" school one that looks like a university early childhood education laboratory classroom and less easily one that has a different configuration. The meanings of the practices within a program with a different configuration require an analysis that incorporates the perspectives of both the insiders and outsiders. Going back to our example of basic skills at Love and Learn, as outsiders the researchers could "see" children being directly taught basic skills and forming trusting teacher–child relationships, and that all the children and the teachers were African American. The insiders—teachers and program director—could tell the researchers that they had determined that their children would do better in school if they had this type of beginning, and that they understood that the official NAEYC developmentally appropriate practice was not appropriate for their children. Using both the insider and outsider perspectives and theoretical perspectives that include culture and race as significant influences on program and child development, I could interpret these practices as cultural participation. The key to our research process was to constantly shift perspectives and bring all of them to bear in analyzing both sets of expectations—sensitivity and cultural content.

Because practices are, by definition, the way things are done, the intention of the practice and perhaps the practice itself are less available for reflection by insiders. This understanding of insider and outsider perspectives helped the research team understand and modify our methodology so that we could help teachers articulate their cultural practices. We initially designed a clinical interview for the teachers. As I indicated earlier, these interviews did not yield the nuanced descriptions of practices we had hoped for. For example, when we asked teachers to explain how they understood school–home transitions, they typically replied something like, "We respect the families." We found that if we instead asked a group of teachers to discuss how they handled the first few days of school, particularly the issue of bringing transitional objects (favorite toys, blankets, etc.) from home, we received a variety of very specific answers: "The children may bring them but they are to remain in the cubbies until naptime"; "They are not allowed at school; it is too hard to keep track of them"; "We encourage the children to bring them"; and "We use these objects to help the children understand what is collective property and must be shared and what is personal and does not need to be shared."

Moreover the focus group leader and the other teachers in the group then had openings to ask about intentions and results, for example, "But how do you help the children become a group if they are fussing with each other about their lovies or keep going to their cubbies and holding their blanket?" The specificity and variety in these discussions permitted us to create more complex understandings of practices.

As a developmental psychologist interested in how children develop within the context of their ethnic and cultural communities, I am most familiar with the Bronfenbrenner-derived approach (Bronfenbrenner & Morris, 1998), which interprets children's development as a series of concentric circles. This concentric circle image implies that the developing child is embedded within a series of widening influences, that is, home, child care, teacher–child relationships, and culture. The analytic strategy in such research is to predict the child's development from the varying levels of context. I initially brought this perspective to the current project. For example, the contextual variables of teacher and child ethnicity, teacher and program practices, and classroom quality all did predict children's learning activities and interactions with peers (Wishard et al., 2003). Likewise, we could describe alternative pathways to effective teaching for the staff of the programs (Howes, James, & Ritchie, 2003). But this concentric circle analysis obscured an understanding that all of the programs were different in configuration of practices *and* were good developmental environments for children *and* were nested within particular cultural communities.

As we set out to describe in more detail the practices of these outstanding programs, I found the image of a kaleidoscope to be very useful. Kaleidoscopes have two important attributes. They always have the same elements regardless of the arrangement of the elements, and when turned they provide different perspectives on a whole by shifting the components so that the observer sees the pattern from a different angle of vision. Using the kaleidoscope image, I can consider as a whole all the details of our descriptive analysis of the children, their experiences, the teachers, their intentions and behaviors, the programs and the ways that they provide care, and the cultural communities of the participating families, teachers, program directors, and community advocates. It is impossible to really focus on all of these details at one time. But if we use the kaleidoscope, we arrange the details so that one set is in focus and the rest are in the background. If we turn the kaleidoscope, we put another set of details in the foreground. And so on. Continuous turns of the kaleidoscope give different angles of vision and eventually a sense of how the parts and whole are related. By shifting our focus we can describe, for example, both the cultural community of the program and the teacher–child relationships of the program, recognizing a bidirectional relationship between them without having to quantify influences. The shifting kaleidoscope approach recognizes that interpersonal relationships can be understood only as being shaped by the practices of the cultural community, as well as both the child's and the adult's participation in the cultural community leading to the construction of the interpersonal relationship. This kaleidoscope image is consistent with Rogoff's (2003) notion of foregrounding and backgrounding of different aspects of human activity.

In our project, the kaleidoscope was more than a way of interpreting data. It was also a way of organizing the research process. The work of turning the kaleidoscope was done by the practice of shifting cultural perspectives, whether initiated by those with a foot in several of the cultures—local community, child care advocacy, research—or learned by those with both feet in one of them.

ORGANIZATION OF THE BOOK

There are two parts to this book. In Part I, the 12 ECE programs are considered together. Chapter 2 describes the theoretical framework of the project. The framework seeks to articulate the tension between core universal developmental processes and the shaping of these developmental processes by cultural practices. I do this by integrating the constructs of cultural communities and practices with the developmental construct of the formation of attachment relationships. Culture is defined as groups of people who have common practices and activities. Participation in cultural communities both at home and in early childhood education provides adults and children with practices or "ways of doing" that they use to engage in interactions with others and, in the case of teachers, provide activities for children designed to help them learn. Chapter 2 also provides an organizational framework for the book, since in order to understand the programs, we need to describe multiple aspects: the consistencies and variety in the cultural communities within which each of the programs is embedded; the institutional dimensions of the programs, specifically dimensions of quality and practices; the interpersonal relationships within the programs; and children's activities, engagements, and development. In Chapter 3, I turn to the ongoing controversies within ECE over quality and school readiness. In this chapter I describe and analyze how different points of view on these constructs within and between the advisory board, the research team, and the program participants can be resolved. I also provide evidence that despite these contested ideas about quality and school readiness, all of the children were prepared for school and did well in school. Chapter 4 focuses on commonalities and differences in practices, activities, and teacher behaviors enacted within the ECE programs. The final chapter of Part I, Chapter 5, is an analysis of how race and ethnicity grouped the 12 ECE programs into four cultural communities. In this chapter I describe and discuss differences in practices, activities, and teachers' engagement across these communities against the background of high quality and teacher responsiveness in all the communities.

The second part of the book focuses on similarities and differences within each of the four larger cultural communities. I use this material to describe how this research project is an example of using the construct of cultural community to understand how the adults in a child care program integrate practices from their home cultural communities with their understandings of "best practices" for early childhood programs to create and implement a set of practices to care for children. The five chapters in this part describe each of the cultural communities across the dimensions discussed in Part I and in the theoretical framework, followed by a concluding chapter.

The discussion of how we did this work is in Appendix A. Definitions of our methodology and coding categories are in Appendix B.

Seeing ECE Programs Through a Kaleidoscope: Lenses and Descriptions

Kaleidoscope: an instrument containing loose bits of colored material between two flat plates and two plane mirrors so placed that changes of position of the bits of material are reflected in an endless variety of patterns.

Multiple Lenses and Elements

HOW DID THE PROGRAMS provide good early childhood education for low-income children of color and their families? To address this question, we must describe many elements of programs—children, their activities, and their experiences; teachers and program directors, their goals, activities, and interactive behaviors; and the programs, their services, and their social-historical context. We also must examine how race, ethnicity, home language, and the participants' interpretations of the meaning of these factors shaped these programs.

The theoretical framework for this work is my theory of relationship development within cultural communities. In this theory I assume that the most proximal influences shaping children's experiences are their interpersonal interactions and relationships with others. I also assume that participation in a cultural community shapes the kinds of activities and practices that surround and give meaning to the interactions of the participants, in this case, adults and children in ECE programs. In constructing this theory I draw from two different theoretical traditions: Rogoff's (2003) theory of the cultural nature of human development and Bowlby's (1982) theory of attachment. From an attachment theory perspective, children's experiences in the program can be understood through their interpersonal relationships with adults. When teachers and children have warm and caring relationships, children are able to use these trusted relationships to explore other interpersonal relationships and learning opportunities (Howes & Ritchie, 2002; Howes & Spieker, 2008; Pianta, Hamre, & Stuhlman, 2003).

Following Rogoff (2003), I assume that the practices of the program are derived from the goals and activities of the program participants, which in turn are developed within the cultural community of the program. In my theory of relationship development within cultural communities, I argue that participation in cultural communities both at home and in ECE programs provides adults and children with practices or "ways of doing" that they then use to engage in interactions with other ECE participants and, in the case of teachers, to provide activities for children designed to help them learn to live well together and be ready for school. This research project is an example of using the construct of cultural community to understand how the adults in a child care program integrate practices from their home cultural communities with their understandings of "best practices" for early childhood programs to create and implement a set of practices to care for children.

ANALYZING CONTEXTUAL INFLUENCES:
KALEIDOSCOPES AND CIRCLES

A kaleidoscope is different from a circle. There is a long tradition beginning with Bronfenbrener (Bronfenbrenner & Morris, 1998) for developmental psychologists to understand development within context by placing the child within concentric circles of environmental influences, family, community, and society. This concentric circle framework was used in the Garcia-Coll and colleagues (1996) integrative model for examining developmental competencies in minority children. And in our own earlier analysis we used the circle as a framework for analyzing layers of contextual influences on children enrolled in the programs described in this book (Wishard et al., 2003).

I selected the kaleidoscope image instead of a circle because in this book I am not concerned that each element in our explanatory framework be independent of the others. Independence of elements is useful when the goal is to explain bidirectional influences or causation between elements. My goal in this work is not to determine which practices in which program best predict which children's outcomes, or which practices best predict quality ratings. Instead, it is to understand how the participants in early childhood education programs from different ethnic, racial, and cultural groups interpret and implement early childhood education, that is, to understand how early childhood education is shaped within different cultural communities. In order to fully describe, and therefore understand, the complex patterns of practices embedded in these programs for young children—programs that are nested within larger communities based on racial and geographic identifications—I continuously must shift the described element. By shifting the focus, I am not creating independence but rather preserving the whole while focusing on a part.

CULTURAL SHAPING OF EARLY CHILDHOOD PRACTICES

Through participating in cultural communities by engaging in common practices and activities, people create culture—for our purposes, the culture of early childhood practices (Rogoff, 2003). Practices are everyday ways of doing things such as what and how to share in circle time, how much rough-and-tumble activity can happen indoors, or what happens when the children discover a worm in the playground.

Participants in a cultural community engage in practices and activities that make sense to them in terms of their experiences and social history. Directors and teachers in the participating early childhood programs therefore interpreted and implemented prescriptions for good programs by engaging in practices and activities that they understood as consistent with their goal of providing good care for the children in their community. These practices may have looked different from external prescriptions such as NAEYC's developmentally appropriate practice (Bredekamp & Copple, 1997) because of intentional variations, disagreements with the goals of the prescriptions, or unintended variations in meaning and interpretation. Only by describing practices and activities can we understand how these variations became cultural shaping of early childhood practices.

Children, teachers, and directors in an early childhood program are participants in the cultural community of that program. Not every participant in a cultural community has exactly the same goals, practices, or activities. In part because of these differences and in part because of social and historical influences, the goals, practices, and activities within a cultural community are not static; they are renegotiated over time. In ECE programs, practices and activities may change as the participants change. As children from very different home cultural communities enter a program, their and their parents' ways of doing enter the mix of goals, practices, and activities and as a consequence the program changes. Thus, early childhood education practices are embedded within culture.

DESCRIBING EARLY CHILDHOOD PROGRAMS

The elements of ECE programs are (1) children and their interpersonal relationships, (2) the cultural-institutional community of each program, and (3) the larger cultural communities to which the program belongs.[1] Describing children and their interpersonal relationships relies heavily on attachment theory. Describing the cultural communities of the programs requires using a multiplicity of descriptors often considered outside the realm of developmental psychology: the social-historical context, racial and ethnic identities, and the imposition of regulations that govern who may teach in programs and what may be taught.

Any theory of culture and ECE programs must describe what goes on in the daily life of participants in the program. In line with Rogoff's (2003) work I have called this daily life the activities of the program. Activities in ECE include learning opportunities designed by teachers with the intent of assisting the children's learning. Although, as we will see, in this project there was great variation within and across programs in how teachers understood children's learning, all of the programs served young children. Young children tend to use a lot of materials as they learn. Therefore, in all of the programs children met in small groups, either by choice or by teacher request, to jointly participate in using blocks, letter cards, dress-up clothes, real cooking materials, paint, clay, sand and water, and so on. Activities also include routine care. These children were all too young to be left unsupervised; most were too young to put on their own shoes or wipe their noses; and some were so young that they were in diapers. Some activities in ECE programs are created by children themselves without teacher instigation or interference, for example, children clustering around a snail that made its way onto the playground, a child hiding in a cubby with a stuffed toy, or a running chase game of Wonder Woman. All of these activities are both the context of interpersonal interaction and shaped by the practices of the program.

Children and Their Interpersonal Relationships

Within every ECE program, children engage in interaction and construct relationships with others—teachers and peers. Children's interpersonal experiences with teachers are how they participate in the cultural community of the program as well as a reflection of how the adults in the cultural community organize children's behaviors. From the research team's first encounters with the programs, differences in descriptions of how children engaged with teachers and peers were striking.

Because we were watching very young children with their teachers, there was an informality and intimacy to the interpersonal interactions. Children needed their noses wiped, their hands washed, and their hands held when they were near a street. Children also fell down, got their feelings hurt, and ran fevers, and generally needed an adult to make them feel better. Children sometimes asked to be read to, sat attentively as adults read, or needed guidance to sit quietly and listen to another child share. Children ran to the far end of the yard, played at being a wild thing, and needed an adult to come after them to keep them safe. Children made paintings and took them to share with the teachers. They played endless games of making cakes in the sandbox, dressed up as firefighters and ran through the yard, and acted out Billy-Goat Gruff in the classroom. As children and adults interacted, we recorded the tone, the content, and the structure of the interactions. For example, did the adults respond in a warm or hostile fashion, did they encourage language arts activities, and did they take the interactional opportunity to elaborate a child's rudimentary language and ideas? Did the children take turns in their play, or engage in social conversation or pretend play?

Attachment theory assumes that these observed routine and mundane caregiving interactions with adults are internalized by the child to form a working model of relationships (Bretherton & Munholland, 2008). Mundane interactions within ECE programs might include being greeted by the teacher and saying good-bye to parents, eating and toileting routines, seeking comfort (or not) after taking a spill on the playground, being told to sit still during circle time, and cuddling with a teacher as she reads a story. When these interactions are warm and sensitive, children come to trust that the teacher will take care of them and that they are worthy of being taken care of (Bretherton & Munholland, 2008; Howes & Ritchie, 2002). Children who feel emotionally supported by teachers in ECE programs will be willing to approach peers in a friendly manner and therefore have opportunities to construct complex play sequences and build friendships (Howes, 2008; Howes & James, 2002). Emotionally supported children also are more willing to engage with classroom learning activities, in part because of self-confidence and in part because they can rely on the teacher for help if they need it (Hamre, 2007).

Teachers in ECE programs differ widely in their practices for forming relationships with children. Some teachers ask children to use honorific titles, for example, Ms. Jones, and insist on manners and proper school behavior. Other teachers are quick to hug and insist that children talk about feelings and comfort one another. Within my framework, any specific practice can be sensitive or insensitive. Sensitive teachers are emotionally available and attuned to the individual cues of children in their classrooms (Hamre, 2007; Howes & Spieker, 2008). Children are more likely to form positive attachment relationships with teachers independently rated as sensitive (Howes & Spieker, 2008), and children with sensitive teachers are more engaged and self-reliant in the classroom (NICHD ECCRN, 2003).

Children in programs that are diverse in race, ethnicity, and home language have teachers who share and those who do not share their racial, ethnic, or home language. For some children, sharing a heritage appears to assist in forming a positive teacher–child relationship (Howes & Shivers, 2006). Sharing a heritage with a teacher may be particularly important for minority children (Garcia-Coll et al., 1996). Adaptive competence is the ability to negotiate multiple realms of experience in the face of racism and discrimination (Garcia-Coll et al., 1996). Children who are helped by trusted adults to achieve coping skills manage to repel the internalization of negative experiences derived from racism. Instead of internalizing negative representations based on racism, sexism, and other bias, children—again if helped by trusted adults—may learn to move comfortably between dominant cultural experiences and within-group cultural experiences.

Attachment theory also suggests that previous relationship history influences children's approaches to new relationships with adults (Howes & Spieker, 2008). Children who enter ECE classrooms with positive and trusting relationship histories are most likely to assume that teachers will be positive and trustworthy as well. When children act in a positive and prosocial manner toward teachers, a positive teacher–child relationship is more likely than when children approach teachers by whining and demanding or acting out (Howes & Ritchie, 2002). Children who have had difficult life circumstances, for example, domestic and neighborhood violence or foster care experiences, find it hard to construct positive relationships with teachers, in part because their previous relationships do not lead them to trust new adults. We were able to identify the children in our sample who came from difficult life circumstances, and we expected that these children would be less likely than others to construct positive attachment relationships with teachers. Several of the programs had a predominance of such children, and we examined differences in their practices for engaging children in positive relationships.

In every participating ECE program, children engaged with peers, primarily age-mates. We observed these interactions because our framework assumes that children who are successful in negotiating complex play are able to both meet their own social goals with others and be sensitive to social communications from others (Howes, 1988; Rubin, Bulowski, & Parker, 1998). Pretend play is an excellent place to observe this meeting of one's own goals without disregarding the goals of others, because it requires collaboration on the script, the roles, the nonliteral meaning of objects, and fantasy.

Cultural Institutions: Program Practices

When we shift the kaleidoscope to a lens that focuses on cultural institutions, we describe the programs for young children in terms of practices. It is important to remember that the program participants and their relationships with one another are still in the larger frame but now in the background. The construct of practices is drawn from Rogoff (2003) and can be defined as ways of doing. Program practices are the ways that directors and teachers intend to achieve their goals of having children be safe, loved, and learning. They are enactments of goals for children that are deeply rooted in social, cultural, and historical values associated with race, ethnicity, and home language within cultural communities (Coll et al., 1996). Practices in this sense are what early childhood programs, their directors, and their teachers intend to do and actually do as they participate in the cultural community of the program. In addition to describing what is done within classrooms, practices include which families and children are served, as well as the roles and responsibilities of the program relating to culture and home language differences, to children with disabilities and special needs, and to teachers and families.

Practices can be articulated as isolated and contested particular ways of doing, for example, testing children or lining them up in separate lines for girls and boys. But our theoretical frame suggests that isolating particular practices from the pattern of practices and from the cultural context of the practices reduces the meaningfulness of the practices (Rogoff & Angelillo, 2002; Rogoff, Matusov, & White, 1996). Therefore, in this work we focus on the patterning of individual practices rather than attempting to isolate the variables responsible for the observed patterns. To continue the example above, the practice of how children are arranged in lines may or may not fit into a larger pattern of practices about gender; for instance, the same program (Love and Learn) that makes separate gender lines for 2-year-olds also has rituals for developing girls' sense of self-worth.

> Twelve 4-year-old girls immaculately dressed in red and gray plaid uniforms stand and say in unison: "Focus and self-discipline are the keys to success. A clear vision and a decision work best. I am centered. I know my intention. I am focused. I direct my attention."

We assume that the pattern of practices, in this case socialization around issues of gender (both lining up and promoting self-worth), is more important for understanding children's development than each individual practice. We assume as well that the patterns of practices of a cultural community are nested within the particular race, ethnicity, and home language of that community. The particular combination of separate gender lines and using spoken affirmation to increase self-worth could have had a different meaning in a context other than the Afro-centric program in which it was embedded. And it would have been unimaginable in another of our programs, Moms, which placed a high priority on never using gender as a category to define children.

In organizing our descriptions of practices within programs, we identified six areas of practices:

- Teaching and learning of pre-academic material
- Social competence
- Language and culture
- Disability and special needs
- Teacher development
- Involvement with parents

In the following sections we define and describe these areas of practice using excerpts from our field notes to illustrate the large variations found in these programs in enacting the practices.

Teaching and Learning of Pre-Academic Material. There are several reasons for an emphasis on practices designed to enhance children's pre-academic learning. There is renewed interest in the value of early experiences for children's school success, particularly with research that directly links processes within programs to success (Bowman et al., 2000; Shonkoff & Phillips, 2000). Within the early childhood field there is considerable debate about practices that emphasize children's individual needs over collective experiences, and child-initiated learning over didactic learning (Kessler & Swadener, 1992). Finally, many teacher preparation institutions emphasize Piagetian-based, child-initiated strategies for teaching, although emerging theories of teaching and learning emphasize the role of teacher scaffolding of learning (Rogoff et al., 1996). Reflecting this "state of the art" in early childhood education, there was considerable diversity in teaching and learning practices in the selected programs.

At Nickerson, a wraparound, after-school program for kindergarten children, the teacher intentionally shies away from teacher-directed, teacher-centered activities. Instead, she wants children to have a place to learn without the "classroom" expectations that they may encounter in their regular-day classes.

The Ready to Learn program is designed to prepare monolingual Spanish-speaking children for kindergarten conducted in English. Children spend their time in highly structured activities that encourage speaking, pre-reading and prewriting.

The Love and Learn program expects children to learn basic reading and math skills. Teachers are expected to follow, quite precisely, a Christian-based, basic skills curriculum. Phonics is stressed, as is very neat printing and cursive writing. Math is taught in a didactic fashion, and rote memorization is valued.

Social Competence. Historically, early childhood programs have emphasized socialization experiences—learning to get along well with teachers and other children. The current renewed emphasis on pre-academic skills creates a tension with practices designed to enhance social competence. Some parents and practitioners express concerns that children no longer have opportunities to play if they are busy learning numbers and letters. Others suggest that if kindergarten is structured like formal school, then a responsibility of early childhood programs is to teach children how to behave in a school setting (i.e., lines, desks, and not talking). Another concern driving programs to implement strategies to enhance social competence is perceptions about violence in families, neighborhoods, and schools, and desires to have early childhood programs help children learn alternative ways to resolve conflicts. The activities we found within our selected programs reflected these various controversies and concerns.

At Nickerson children are to respond to adults in authority in a respectful fashion. Manners are important.

Children at Pierce spent a great deal of their time in dramatic and creative play. They build elaborate block structures and invent games to go with them. Children dress up in costumes and play a variety of roles.

Children at Moms are helped by teachers to write their own books to help them with problems, whether they have hurt themselves, something scary happened at home, or they are mad or sad.

Language and Culture. The children served and, increasingly, the teachers in early childhood programs are not from the dominant White affluent culture, and this was particularly true for the programs we studied. Programs have the opportunity, and perhaps the obligation, to include as part of their practices attention to cultural legacies, sociopolitical history, and migratory experiences of these children and their families. The National Association for the Education of Young Children has endorsed an Anti-Bias Curriculum (ABC) (Derman-Sparks, 1989). This curriculum gives legitimacy to multiculturalism practices. An alternative set of practices suggests that it may be more appropriate for children who do not come from the dominant culture to have practices that are congruent with those of their homes rather than to be exposed to more than one tradition (Chang, 1993). The programs represented these polarities well. Our sample included several programs designed to serve only one racial or ethnic group, and a director who had been part of the original program that developed the ABC and some 20 years later had brought it into one of the participating programs (Moms). Again excerpts from field notes demonstrate a variety of practices around issues of language and culture.

> At Nickerson we often observed or saw evidence of stories centered on African Americans. A visitor might leave with a feeling that Black history month happens all year round due to the children's artwork around the room that reflected stories the children had heard.

> Mountain teachers incorporate mountain culture into the classroom. Kids quilt (using paper). The science center was devoted to home canning.

> At Moms the children's toys include tiny wheelchairs for dolls with physical disabilities, the books are about different kinds of families, including gay and lesbian parents, and are also bilingual; there is regular, age-appropriate conversation about gender and racial stereotyping.

> At Coast there are some creative and sensitive efforts to help the children understand and grasp the civil rights movement. It is fun to watch children at free play incorporate a toy bus and a tiny Rosa Parks figure!

Disability and Special Needs. Early childhood programs and early childhood special education or intervention programs often are quite separate, with different pathways of practice, research, funding, and agency sponsorship. The lines between these programs are blurring, with movements to include children with special needs in regular educational settings, as more and more mothers, including mothers of special needs children, must contribute to family finances and therefore need full-time child care. By design we included programs that intended to include special needs children with typical children, as well as one program designed to serve only special needs children.

> Several children at Down the Hill have shadow aides in the classroom. There are several children in wheelchairs, and children with autism and behavior problems.

> At El Peace there is a full-inclusion special education class. Ten children receive school support from a special education teacher. The children are

autistic, have developmental delays and speech delays, and experience behavioral and emotional problems.

All of the children at Therapeutic Preschool (TPS) have been diagnosed with special needs. Half of the children have been prenatally exposed to drugs and half have diagnoses that include posttraumatic stress disorder, attachment disorder, expressive/receptive language delay, oppositional defiant disorder, and autism.

Professional Development of Teaching Staff. The high turnover rate and poor compensation of early childhood teachers mean that when they begin their work in programs many teachers are ill prepared to teach and do not stay long enough to enhance program stability. Faced with this dilemma, some programs institute practices to help teachers become more effective (Whitebook, 1999). We were particularly interested in guidance provided for new teachers and in teacher supervision in general. Early childhood education has a long tradition of training teachers through participation in lab schools or other model programs in order for novice teachers to learn from more experienced ones (Spodek & Saracho, 1990). As novice teachers work directly with children, they are observed, supervised, and mentored by more experienced teachers, and they have ready models for teaching behavior. All of the programs used some form of guidance and supervision.

Love and Learn teachers are trained on site to use the program's curriculum. There is a director of teacher training and supervision who spends a good deal of time offering training and support.

The Nickerson kindergarten teacher serves as the wise elder in the community. The teaching staff throughout the program looks to and respects this teacher as their mentor.

All of the Down the Hill teachers have educational backgrounds in early childhood education. The program sends three or four teachers each year to early childhood conferences in the local area.

The initial teachers at Mission Hope were neighborhood mothers who attended child development classes. The program served as the classroom and internship. This meant that teachers had very little educational background and no experience when they came to work. They worked for short periods and then new interns took their place. There was one hired teacher, but the rest of the staff was all novices. In the second year, there was a decision to hire more qualified, more experienced staff.

Supervision and mentoring are practices that programs can use to provide professional development for their teaching staff. The National Research Council Report on early childhood pedagogy (Bowman et al., 2000) suggests that early childhood programs positively influence child learning and development when the teachers in these programs have ample opportunity to meet with supervisors for reflection on their own practice and on the responsiveness of children to the program. There was little variation within programs on this reflective dimension.

> Most of the Nickerson teaching staff knew the project director from her previous job as a counselor/instructor at a job-prep training program. She continues to serve as their mentor and supervisor.

> At TPS case conferences, weekly supervision, and consistent informal conversation provide daily opportunities for reflection, sharing, and learning among the teaching staff.

> The teachers at Ready to Learn all have elementary teaching credentials. The staff meets on a daily basis to talk about children, families, and activities.

Parental Involvement. All early childhood programs must institute practices around families. The decision to provide services, either full- or part-day, explicitly or implicitly implies a different set of expectations and responses to working parents' needs. Within our selected programs we had part-day programs and programs that were open from earliest daybreak into the early evening.

> In order to participate, Nickerson parents need to be working or in school, and the center is open from 6:30 a.m. until 7:00 p.m.

> Since the program is a half-day program at TPS, Pierce, and Ready to Learn, other arrangements need to be made for children for the afternoon.

Many practitioners believe that good practices include knowing the home context and having relationships with children's families (Powell, 1989). The selected programs were noteworthy for the depth of knowledge and understanding they demonstrated about the lives of the families they served.

> The small, stable population of the county gives the Mountain staff another advantage in building good relationships with kids and families—shared history: "Oh, he reminds me so much of his great-grandfather. Old Mr. J. was quite a character."

One of the teachers at South Central has been at the program for 28 years. She has watched children she taught years ago grow up and bring their own children to the center.

The teen mothers at Moms have the opportunity to meet individually with the program director two times each day to discuss their issues as adolescents as well as their issues of parenting.

Parental or family involvement practices often are included in lists of advocated practices for early childhood programs. However, practices within the rubric of parental involvement can be extremely varied, for example, requiring parents to work in the classroom, providing case management services to parents, or asking parents to participate in parent–teacher conferences. When both the program and the parents care for the children, there is a complex dynamic between programs and families. Parents may be seen as deficient and/or in need of intervention, as partners with teachers, or as the primary source of information about the children. The selected programs included the full continuum of family involvement.

At South Central all parents are required to attend an 8-week-long Mother Read course during which they learn to read to their children, recognize themes of development, and talk about their own childhood. The program is designed so that the parents of the children in their second year in the program orient, support, and educate the parents of children in their first year. Training and education in child discipline, development, and issues of abuse are offered, but the processing of that information and real adaptation to the home are done through parent-to-parent contact.

Parents must attend a 10-week course at the Ready to Learn program. Topics of the parent education include nutrition, discipline, and normal child development. Parents must volunteer classroom time. Many of the fathers come early to get out the yard toys and to sweep up; mothers help out in the classroom. Parents put together the homework packets and also collect and check them off.

Love and Learn does at least two elaborate public programs of music and dance each year. Parents help with costumes, sets, and extra practices. But parents are not welcomed into the classroom.

Cultural Communities

Following Rogoff's (2003) theoretical perspective, we assumed that each program was a cultural community through its own practice and history *and* that the programs also were nested within larger cultural communities. Because of the radicalized socially and politically segregated history of Los Angeles, and because we intentionally selected rural North Carolina programs to contrast with the urban programs of Los Angeles, the 12 programs were nested within larger cultural communities that had important underlying similarities based on sociohistorical contexts, as well as distinct racial/ethnic and geographic identities. In Los Angeles, the ten selected programs belonged to three larger cultural communities: African American heritage, Latino/a heritage, and a cultural community not defined by racial identity but by an antiracist stance. In North Carolina both programs were defined initially by being part of rural cultural communities.

Rogoff (2003) argues that a description of a cultural community can and should include dimensions including home language, religion, national origin, generations since immigration, and ethnic heritage. In order to classify programs into cultural communities, we had to research, understand, and consider the historical and geographic contexts of the programs. These understandings took us across the usual boundaries of data collection in developmental psychology. Our descriptions of the programs include these dimensions.

Participants within a cultural community are not expected to be homogeneous because cultural communities are nested within larger cultural communities with their own goals, practices, and history. Among the participants of a cultural community there will be both central tendencies and variations. Participants have some common agreement in beliefs, goals, behaviors, history, and meanings within a cultural community, and they also may have strong disagreements. For example, the participants in the early childhood programs we assigned to the larger African American cultural community had a common strong belief in academic learning, but there was disagreement over the role of play in early childhood programs. Again, following Rogoff (2003), we do not expect cultural communities to be static entities. Instead, by their participation in cultural communities and other external events, including participating in a research project, individuals change the practices that constitute the community.[2]

Quality and School Readiness:
Promises, Controversies, and Definitions

AT THE TURN of the 21st century there was a flurry of public attention devoted to quality early childhood education in the United States. The NICHD study of early child care (NICHD ECCRN, 1996, 1997) and the Cost Quality and Outcome (CQO) Study (Helburn & Howes, 1996), both nationally representative studies of community-based child care, reported that most children experienced only mediocre care. Two reports from the National Academy of Sciences pointed to the importance of high-quality ECE in children's development (Shonkoff & Phillips, 2000) and in preparing children for school (Bowman et al., 2000). States responded by adding prekindergarten, a year before kindergarten, to the public school system. By 2007 the majority of states had prekindergarten programs and all had established criteria to ensure that the programs were of high quality (Barnett, Hustedt, Friedman, Boyd, & Ainsworth, 2007).

This chapter addresses an issue that remained unresolved in the midst of this flurry of attention to quality ECE: How is quality defined? As discussed in the introduction, the definition of quality is contentious in the ECE field (Dahlberg et al., 2007; Early et al., 2007; Hamre, 2007; Pianta, 2007). The starting point for quality in our study was our funded mission: find high-quality programs for low-income families and children of color and describe activities and practices enacted within these programs. The researchers, coming from the CQO study, began with a definition of quality derived from that study. The community advocates who actually selected the programs were equally certain that they knew what were good programs. And as we fairly quickly found out, these two groups did not have exactly the same definition of quality. In this chapter we discuss the process of collaboration and consensus making about definitions of ECE quality between the researchers and the advocates. We also present evidence that these programs were of high quality using both sets of definitions.

Along with quality, the construct of school readiness penetrates and organizes the public and researchers' discussion around ECE and quality: Are children ready for school? Are schools ready for children? Within the more contemporary era of school accountability there are numerous statistics to suggest that the answer to both of these questions is no. Large percentages of low-income children of color do not do well on standardized measures of pre-academic school achievement (Brooks-Gunn, Rouse, & McLanahan, 2007). Likewise, schools—preschool and early elementary schools—generally are not places that support the learning of young children (Hamre, 2007; Howes, Burchinal, et al., 2008).

As we will discuss, the community advocates and program directors in our study also were concerned about school readiness and the transition between their programs and "real" school. Early on in the project, advocates and program directors asked the researchers to design and conduct standardized assessments on children enrolled in the program and to follow them into elementary school. In the second half of this chapter I discuss this process and address the question of whether the children from these programs were indeed ready for the schools in their neighborhoods.

DEFINING QUALITY BY SELECTING
AND ASSESSING ECE PROGRAMS

A unique contribution of this book is that it represents a collaboration among community advocates and researchers in defining quality of ECE. Generally, advocates, parents, and researchers agree that good ECE gives children warm and positive relationships with teachers, a safe and healthy environment, and opportunities to learn (Hofferth, Shauman, Henke, & West, 1998). Disagreements between advocates and researchers often arise over how to measure these attributes. We approached this issue by asking advocates to serve on our advisory boards and to identify programs that they and the communities they represented believed were good programs, high in quality and providing exemplary services to the children and families of particular communities. Were these programs of high quality in the eyes of both the advocates and the researchers? I begin this discussion with definitions of quality by the advisory boards. Next I describe how the research team thought about ECE quality and the research team's assessments of ECE quality in the programs using standardized measures drawn from previous studies on ECE quality. Finally, I examine the extent of agreement between these assessments by the advisory boards and the research team.

The Advisory Boards Define Quality

We began our advisory board meetings by asking the board members to first describe themselves, their interests in early childhood, and the communities they felt they represented. We then asked them to describe exemplary programs in the abstract, and gave them the charge of identifying programs that they, or other advocates and community representatives they talked with, knew well enough to nominate as representing exemplary programs.

The list of components in a high-quality program that was generated by the advisory boards was different from the lists we were more accustomed to as researchers (e.g., ratios, teacher qualifications, and positive child–adult relationships) (Phillipsen, Burchinal, Howes, & Cryer, 1997). The meetings were animated, as the following excerpt of the first California meeting minutes shows, and the members suggested that even more passion and less politeness were needed in the next meeting:

> What we really need to be looking at are alternative pathways to positive outcomes for children and families, and child care/school staff and administration. These pathways must include making a partnership with parents; no violence; a sense of organization, a plan; building mutual respect between children, staff, and parents; recognizing that working in programs is hard work, and must be validated; that teaching is about key moments and about knowing when just the right interaction has taken place; and providing staff with times and places to describe and reflect upon teaching. . . . There was interest expressed in a longer meeting, a more relaxed atmosphere, a time when we would be less polite and more passionate. (advisory board minutes, October 14, 1999)

As researchers, we found this list daunting. How would we operationalize *a sense of organization, a plan*? Is this the same as what we defined as *reflective supervision*? What about *no violence*? Surely the literature on child discipline suggests that committed compliance is more effective for internalized self-control (Kochanska, 2002), but is *no violence* really the core issue? What does *no violence* mean by itself, separated from the context of institutional racism, poverty, neighborhood violence, domestic violence, and child abuse? *Key moments* sounds like a practice for teaching and learning, what researchers might define as *adults engage with children around materials in ways that extend their knowledge* (Dickinson & Smith, 1994; Neuman & Roskos, 1992; Storch & Whitehurst, 2002; Whitehurst, Arnold, Epstein, & Angell, 1994). But could it simply mean *monitoring child-initiated activities without any extension of knowledge*? And so on. It quickly became clear that more discussion was needed, that exemplars would help define the issue (e.g., this aspect of this program meets my definition for high quality because . . .), and that this process of defining quality was going to be an intellectual challenge.

The advisory boards nominated quite a long list of programs in each location. The research project directors, Sharon Ritchie and Jana Fleming, visited each of the nominated programs. They observed in classrooms and talked with teachers and directors about the purpose and mission of their programs. They used these initial observations and interviews to create descriptive profiles of each program, whom the program served, what it identified as its mission and goals, and what policy-related questions were central to the program, for example, home language and classroom language of children who did not speak English at home.

During subsequent advisory board meetings, the research team presented the program profiles to the board members in order to structure a discussion on the enactment of community-defined ECE quality. Because the policy-related questions were pivotal in shaping the discussions of the advisory boards about the dimensions of the programs to be included in the final selection, I provide a representative list of our discussion questions below:

1. How do we determine what is in the best interests of our children and their families as we work to define and implement bilingual education?
2. How can we maximize success for children as they transition from our program into kindergarten?
3. How do we become a resource for improved-quality care for children in our community whom we do not serve?
4. How do we support adults in our community who are working toward self-sufficiency?
5. How do we motivate parents to get involved and stay involved in their children's education? And how do we support continued parental involvement in schools as children transition to kindergarten?
6. How do we help children and families develop a sense of pride in their culture?
7. What constitutes a program that addresses the needs of special needs children, while at the same time offers them the same experiences as other children?

These meetings of the advisory boards were exciting. Using the profiles of nominated programs was a helpful way for the boards to become more concrete in their criteria for what did and did not qualify as a high-quality program serving low-income families. They came to consensus that the following dimensions must be included in the sample of programs as a whole: racial and home language diversity; programs for special needs children; full- and part-day programs; and variety in approach to parental education and family services.

Furthermore, the following 10 elements were to be included in every program that was selected for this project:

1. The program is responsive to the community, and considers the family's needs and interests.
2. There is a recognizable and consistent connection between what the program purports to do and what really happens.
3. There is consonance between the values and beliefs of the community, the family, and the program.
4. The program is grounded in a philosophy that is articulated and intentional.
5. There is administrative support for staff.

6. The program maximizes opportunities for parents to make informed choices from a number of options.
7. The program supports efforts to teach children academic skills.
8. The program is concerned with the continuity of care.
9. The teacher is considered a change agent, an advocate for children.
10. The program offers comprehensive care. (advisory board minutes, March 20, 1997)

The advisory boards also rank-ordered the nominated programs. In making its final selection of programs to invite to participate, the research staff verified that all of the programs provided services to at least some low-income children if the program as a whole was not designed for low-income children, and that across the sample as a whole there was representation of ethnic groups similar to the larger population of Los Angeles County or rural North Carolina. Within the sample we made sure that there was a mix of programs serving children from predominantly one ethnic or home language group and programs serving children from diverse backgrounds, and that there was representation of children with special needs both included in programs for typical children and in "stand-alone" programs. Finally, we made sure that across the sample as a whole there was a variety of distinct practices, including practices that appeared to be contested within the ECE community (e.g., home language versus English-only; child-initiated versus didactic approaches to teaching).

We extended invitations to participate in the project to 20 programs (10 in Los Angeles and 10 in North Carolina). The research staff met with the program staff to explain the project, answer questions, and begin to form a working relationship with the program. Following these meetings all invited programs agreed to participate. For reasons unrelated to the project, after an initial period the number of programs in North Carolina was reduced to two. The 12 remaining programs became the basis of our study. The programs ranged in size from some very small programs—only 16 children—to very large programs—more than 100 children. There was an ethnic mix of children. There was a mix of full- and part-day programs. Spanish and English were the predominant languages of the programs, but one program also used Chinese. In response to the advisory board's concern with comprehensive services, we included seven programs that offered services only to children and five programs that offered a range of programs to families as well as children. These services included parental education, literacy, mental health services, and case management services.

While we selected the programs without regard for auspice (profit, nonprofit, public, or private), it is noteworthy that all of the programs were nonprofit. Five were private nonprofit programs, four were part of the public school system, and all of the programs received at least some portion of their funds from public sources. Only four programs, Love and Learn, Down the Hill, Mountain, and Coast, received any portion of their revenue from parent fees. All of the nonschool programs in California accepted state alternative payments, a form of vouchers for parents who qualify through child abuse prevention or poverty criteria.

Researchers Define and Measure Quality

Definitions. At the time we began this work there was general agreement among researchers that ECE quality could be defined and reliably measured (Abbott-Shim, Lambert, & McCarty, 2000; Kontos, Howes, Shin, & Galinsky, 1995; Lamb, 1998). Like parents, researchers are concerned ultimately with the well-being of the children: Are they safe and healthy? Do they feel secure that the teachers will keep them safe? Are they learning the skills that they will need to be successful in school? In short, does the ECE environment enhance children's development in a variety of dimensions while they are in the program, and give them a good start on the rest of their lives?

Most research on quality in ECE comes from an ecological theoretical perspective (Bronfenbrenner & Morris, 1998; Sameroff, 1983). Within this theoretical perspective, dimensions of the environment are considered to influence one another in a bidirectional manner—for example, policymakers' ideas about ECE regulation influence ECE classroom processes—and in ways that influence children's development, for instance, ECE classroom processes influence children's social development. Several assumptions are critical within this approach: (1) that children's experiences with learning materials help to shape their cognitive development (Bowman et al., 2000); (2) that interaction with adults around concepts and materials enhances children's learning (Bowman et al., 2000; Shonkoff & Phillips, 2000); and (3) that interpersonal relationships with adults provide (or do not provide) children with the necessary secure base to be able to explore the learning activities of the program (Howes & Ritchie, 2002; Pianta, 1998). Working from these assumptions, researchers' quality assessments consider where learning materials are available, whether adults engage with children around learning materials, and whether adult–child and child–child interactions and relationships are warm and positive.

In ECE research, influence usually is conceptualized as the structural dimensions of the ECE environment that influence process dimensions, which in turn influence children's development (NICHD ECCRN, 2002). Structural dimensions are those features that can be regulated, such as the qualifications of teachers or the number and size of bathrooms that need to be provided, while process dimensions refer to features such as warm, sensitive, and stimulating adult–child interactions that can be observed. As we developed our conceptual framework, we assumed that both structural and process dimensions of ECE could be measured, but that measuring process quality would require close observation and measuring instruments based on what developmental psychological research has defined as warm, sensitive, and stimulating. We further assumed that structural dimensions would predict process dimensions, but not children's development. That is, we expected that structure that supported good caregiving would predict good caregiving, and furthermore that good caregiving would enhance development. These assumptions were tested in two large studies: the NICHD study (NICHD ECCRN, 2002) and the Cost Quality and Outcome Study (Peisner-Feinberg & Burchinal, 1997; Peisner-Feinberg et al., 2001; Phillipsen et al., 1997). In both studies, pathways were found linking structural dimensions to process dimensions to children's outcomes.

Across all of the pathways linking the structural dimensions of ECE to ECE quality and to children's optimal outcomes, three structural dimensions emerge as most predictive of process quality: ECE providers' compensation, their education and specialized training, and adult to child ratio (Shonkoff & Phillips, 2000).[1] ECE teachers with higher levels of compensation, with more advanced education and specialized training in child development, and who work with smaller groups of children are found most often in settings with higher quality ratings, are more effective with children, and are associated with optimal development outcomes in children.

The cornerstone of process quality is the relationship between the provider and children. Children whose ECE providers give them ample verbal and cognitive stimulation and generous amounts of individualized attention perform better on a wide range of assessments of development (Shonkoff & Phillips, 2000). Children who trust the provider to keep them physically and emotionally safe can use their teacher–child relationship as a secure base from which to explore and develop relationships with peers and to explore and develop new understandings from the material environment (Howes & Ritchie, 2002). Teachers—good teachers —understand that they constantly must reflect on their knowledge of children's development and of the particular children with whom they are engaged, and balance the needs of the child, the group, and the child within the group (Ahnert & Lamb, 2003; Ahnert, Rickert, & Lamb, 2000; Howes & Ritchie, 2002).

Measuring Quality. Working from the researcher-generated definition of ECE quality, the research team designed ways to measure both structural and process quality in the 12 programs. We interviewed the directors and teaching staff about their formal education, their experiences in the current program and in previous early childhood programs, and their compensation for working in the programs. We also asked directors about how they staffed classrooms, how often they had to replace staff, and what they looked for in finding teaching staff. Our participant observers reported class sizes, adult to child ratios, and staffing patterns in their field notes. In those few cases when field notes and director reports disagreed, we resolved the disagreement by further interviewing and observation. We measured process quality through a combination of global ratings and naturalistic observation. We defined process quality as including environmental quality, classroom emotional climate, and teacher involvement with the children. Each of these three components was derived from predetermined measures. We used classroom scores on the Early Childhood Environment Rating Scale (ECERS) (Harms & Clifford, 1980) to represent environmental quality and teacher involvement, and we used ratings from the Classroom Interaction Scale (Arnett, 1989) to represent classroom emotional climate.

Dimensions of Structural Quality. In all we interviewed 80 program staff, and 68 of these interviews were conducted with teachers that we watched interacting with children. We also interviewed a variety of other people associated with the program who wished to be interviewed—educational directors, social workers, members of the board of directors, and volunteers. These interviews provided contextual information on the programs.

Overall, 50% of the adult program participants were Latino/a, 29% African American, 14% White, and the remainder Asian American or biracial. Fifteen percent of the staff were directors or teacher-directors of the programs, 38% of the staff were teachers, and the remainder were assistant teachers. Most of the staff in all roles were female. Staff participants averaged 41 years of age, with directors older than assistants.[2] Directors, teachers, and assistants were about a decade older than the respective staff interviewed in the nationally representative CQO study (Helburn, 1995).

Latino/a staff constituted the biggest ethnic category (50% overall). But there was a significant association between ethnicity and teaching role,[3] with many more Latino/a assistant teachers and many more African American and White directors. A Latino/a was equally likely to be an assistant (49% of Latino/a staff) or a teacher (49% of Latino/a staff) but 8 times more likely to be a teacher or an assistant than a director (6% of Latino/a staff). African Americans were the next largest ethnic category (29%). Interestingly, African Americans were only 2.4 times as likely to be a teacher (63% of African American staff) than a director (26% of African American staff) and 2.5 times more likely to be a director than an assistant (10.5% of African American staff).

Overall, staff had more formal education than is usual in ECE samples (Howes, 1997). Twenty-five percent of the staff had a BA and another 19% had an MA/MS or higher. None of the directors had less than a BA and only 20% had only a BA. Forty-two percent of the teaching staff (all teachers) had a BA or MA/MS and only one teacher had no formal education. The average preschool adult to child ratio for these programs was 1:8.2 and the average group size was 21 children. These average ratios and group sizes are within the range recommended by professional organizations (Howes, 1997). All of the teaching staff in the 12 programs had salary or hourly wage levels at or above market rate in their communities. Compensation is closely linked to staff stability (Whitebook, 1999; Whitebook & Bellm, 1999). Average teaching staff annual turnover was 9% over the 30 months of our participation with the programs, and 42% of the programs had no turnover. Several programs had staff that had been with the program since it was founded. These are all positive signs of staff stability.

Dimensions of Process Quality of Programs. Classroom scores on the ECERS (Harms & Clifford, 1980), representing environmental quality, were all higher than five, the minimum score that is considered good.[4] Teacher sensitivity scores were very high, and harshness scores and detachment very low.[5] These scores indicate a classroom emotional climate that is warm and positive. We found no significant differences in process quality among African American, Asian American, White, and Latino/a children taught by African American, White, and Latino/a teachers. These measures of process quality indicate that most programs were near the high point in both assessments. This is further support for the assumption that, in general, the programs are not representative of ECE quality, but instead are drawn from a narrow band within the highest quality programs.

Reconciliation of Definitions of Quality

When we asked community advocates on the advisory boards to define quality in ECE programs, their answers on the surface sounded quite unlike research definitions of process and structural quality. Researchers tend to think of structural quality as policy-related and regulable, and therefore on the minds of advocates. However, these were not the issues on which the advisory boards were focused. They tended to define quality in "softer" terms, for example, "mutual respect between children, staff and parents and the building of relationships/partnerships between all of them." The advisory boards "knew quality when they saw it." The programs identified as exemplary by the advisory boards were programs that met researchers' definitions of high structural (and process) quality. Their professional development of teachers, ratios, and group sizes far exceeded the standards of the NAEYC and their state ECE regulations.

The advisory boards' and researchers' definitions of process quality sound more similar than their definitions of structural quality. This is probably because, in developing the ECERS and the Classroom Interaction Scale, researchers worked to measure reliably and validly the sense that the program provides a warm, safe, positive, and stimulating place for children.

It is important to reiterate that all of the programs met very high standards for structural and process quality, based on their selection by advocates and the criterion of representing good care for families who lived in poverty, not as high-quality programs per se. It is also important to bring back into this discussion the image of a kaleidoscope. Throughout this chapter we have focused on a particular aspect of these programs, their quality as defined and measured by advocates and researchers. As we focus on this dimension we need to remember that the features that were measured as quality were the foreground, but in the background were the larger cultural communities and the practices enacted in them. We did not find different levels of program quality in different cultural communities.

This is not the case for practices, as we will examine in subsequent chapters. There were many different practices represented in the programs. And as we will see, practices, unlike quality, were systematically associated with particular cultural communities. Conceptually this makes sense if we define practices as the ways that participants do things within cultural communities, and recognize that providing good care for children is a goal that all the programs as cultural communities are moving toward. We suspect that if all of the participants in that contentious conversation about how best to provide care for children, particularly children of color, were to agree to distinguish between quality and practices, we might be better able to come to consensus.

In summary, when the focus of this analysis was on ECE quality, against a background of larger cultural communities and the practices articulated by participants in these cultural communities, the picture looks very uniform. According to both the advisory boards that selected them and the researcher team that asked questions and observed in classrooms, all of the programs were of high quality.

SCHOOL SUCCESS: "WHAT IS A PREPARED CHILD?"

All of the programs intended to prepare children for school, but there were large differences in what they meant by this construct. Within the descriptions of children provided by participants in this work, there are several possible responses to the question, What is a "good" child who is served well by the program?

1. A good child is a competent child
2. A good child is a participant within his or her cultural community
3. A good child is ready for school
4. A good child does indeed succeed in school

Just as all of the participants in this work—researchers and cultural community participants—could agree readily that ECE is made up of warm, caring, sensitive, and responsive adult teachers intending to and actually enhancing children's social and academic competence, all participants could agree that the goal of the early childhood programs was to produce good or competent children.

As with quality, good children and child competence have contested definitions. Is competence consistent with the ideas of "good" child behavior in the eyes of the adults in the community? Is competence being "ready for school"? Or is competence defined by the theoretical and empirical literature of developmental psychology? Again, parallel to the notion of quality, what makes up children's competence often is assumed rather than defined. When the community advocates first nominated the early childhood programs for this project, they made the assumption that only programs that, in their words, provided children with "positive" outcomes would be included (advisory board minutes, October 1996).

The advisory boards did not find it necessary to further define "positive" outcomes, perhaps assuming that this was a universal understanding. When linked to early childhood, positive outcomes often mean to the general public and to policymakers that the children will do well when they go to "real" school, meaning formal school or kindergarten—in other words, that they are "ready for school."

Consistent with the notion of multiple angles of vision that informed this project, we assume that evaluations of children's competence vary among participants and within cultural communities (Lamb, 1999). For example, if maternal employment is valued, mothers may particularly enjoy watching their girls engage in complex pretend sequences involving mothers' work routines. If traditional gender role definitions are valued and boys pretend to be baby-tenders, the content of the pretend play may preclude adults from seeing the complexity of pretend play as competent. In another example, the mother of a child in a program that taught math concepts by having children sort piles of junk (e.g., buttons, washers) into categories, but did not drill them on numbers, said, "It is hard to brag that my child is really good at math patterns when my neighbor tells me that her 4-year-old can count to 100."

Consistent with this assumption that different cultural communities construct their own definitions of children's competence, we fostered discussions among program directors around what they understood as children being "ready for school." The following excerpts are from a program directors' focus group when we asked the directors to respond to the question: "What do you do to make your children ready for school?" All of the program directors ascribed to a general notion that they were preparing children for "real" school. But they varied in their interpretations of what to do to prepare them. Two of the directors argued that it is a disservice to children to have them spend their preschool years focusing on narrow school skills. Instead, they reasoned that if they emphasized underlying concepts during the preschool years, children would be able to map on specific skills when they got to school. The director at Down the Hill stated:

> There is a difference between a center that is going to drill your child in math and letters and a center that's going to teach your child how to think. In my way of thinking, I would rather send my child into kindergarten with good problem-solving skills, creativity, imagination, believing in themselves, having an ability to work through problems on their own, to understand how you get from A to B to C. I would rather send my child into some school with those skills than knowing all their letters, being able to recognize words, being able to count and add numbers.

The Coast director said:

> I want early childhood education students who are working in the program to understand the development of children, what is appropriate, and I want them talking to children, listening to children, asking children questions, letting their minds problem-solve, playing word games and mind games with children. I want them to know how to provide a classroom experience for them that is going to be wonderful and exciting. And I wish that these experiences could last, you know, the preschool life that we have. To me, that's what education should be. I don't know why the public schools haven't figured it out.

In contrast to the directors who believed that school readiness involved teaching children to think, some of the program directors interpreted being ready for school as being able to do the routines that adults (and children playing teacher) often associate with "real" school. This position suggests that if children are good at following directions, they will be ready for school. For example, one of the teachers at Pierce described getting children ready for the routines of school:

> All the children take their seats, after a month or 3 weeks, just as though they'd been doing it all along. The teacher has them in class for an hour and a half inside. For one hour they listen to a story, go over what they're going to be doing. When circle is over each child stands up when they hear the first letter of their name. The children line up at the door. No one leaves until they're all in line.

Another group of program directors defined "ready for school" in terms of specific skills. The children "know their ABCs," "know what letter is the start of their name," "know how to count," and "know their colors."

These categories generated by the program directors—"knowing how to think," "knowing how to follow directions," and "knowing basic skills"—are the same dimensions found in the research literature on school readiness (Graue, 1992; La Paro & Pianta, 2000; Meisels, 1999). So were the children ready for school? To answer this question from the researchers' point of view, we assessed children's school success when they entered school. We discuss these findings in the next section of this chapter.

CHILDREN PARTICIPATING IN THE LONGITUDINAL STUDY

Seventy-three (48% girls) children participated in at least one of the data collection phases of the longitudinal study. These 73 participants accounted for approximately

25% of the children in the classrooms sampled when the children were in their early childhood programs. The number of children from each program participating in the follow-up study ranged from 4 in the smallest program to 11 in the largest programs. In total 67 children participated as kindergartners, 49 as first graders, and 37 as second graders. Thirty children were seen at all three time points—in kindergarten, in first grade, and again in second grade.[6]

Thirty-four (45%) of the total participating children were Latino/a, 18 (25%) were African American, 13 (18%) were White, and 8 (11%) were Asian American. The children ranged in age from 27 to 80 months when we observed them in their early childhood program. At that time 7% of the children were under 3 years old, 24% were 3 to 4 years old, 54% were 4 to 5 years old, and the remainder had had their fifth birthday. Fourteen children (19%) had been living in difficult life circumstances during their preschool years.

The Children as Preschoolers: School Readiness

We examined attachment to teacher, complex play with peers, and complex play with objects as indicators of children's school readiness while they were enrolled in the programs (see Figure 3.1). For definitions of these measures, see Appendix B.[7] Just over half (52%) of the children constructed a secure attachment to their primary caregiver. Fifty-seven percent of the fortunate children not living in difficult life circumstances and 28% of children from difficult life circumstances were categorized as securely attached to their teacher. The children we studied were about twice as likely to be securely attached to their teachers as children in a more representative sample (Howes & Ritchie, 1999).

Almost all of the children engaged in complex play as preschoolers (see Figure 3.1). On average, children spent about one fifth of their time in complex play with peers, and about one third of their time in complex play with objects. For both peer and object play, the percent of the play that we rated as complex is comparable to other studies of children in similar age groups (Howes & Matheson, 1992; Kontos, Hsu, & Dunn, 1994). Ninety-four percent of the children not living in difficult circumstances and 88% of children living in difficult circumstances engaged in some age-appropriate complex peer play. All of the children not living in difficult circumstances and 83% of children living in difficult circumstances engaged in some competent object play.

Measuring School Success

We defined school success as including both achievement in reading and math, and social competence with teachers and other children (Ladd, Birch, & Buhs, 1999). We individually assessed children's content knowledge using two standardized measures, assessing vocabulary and math skills. We observed children

Figure 3.1. Children as preschoolers.

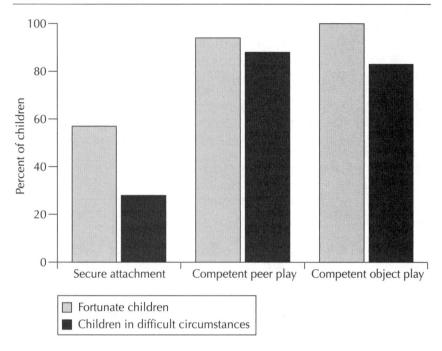

in their school classrooms and rated their social competence with peers and teachers. We asked their teachers to rate their perceptions of their relationships with the children.

Standardized Testing. We used two standardized tests, the Woodcock–Johnson Applied Math Problems Test 25 (Woodcock, McGrew, & Mather, 2001) and Form L of the Peabody Picture Vocabulary Test (PPVT) (Dunn & Dunn, 1997). Calculated standardized scores on the PPVT were used to assess children's vocabulary skills relative to similarly aged children in the nation. Although an achievement test, the PPVT is not a test of general intelligence but of vocabulary for Standard American English. More specifically, it measures listening comprehension for spoken English and receptive vocabulary.[8] A Spanish version of the PPVT, the TVIP (Dunn, Padilla, Lugo, & Dunn, 1986), normed with Hispanic children in the United States, Mexico, and Puerto Rico, was also available and was used to test children whose proficiency in English was limited.[9] We administered one subtest in the Woodcock–Johnson Psycho-Educational Battery to assess the children's kindergarten applied mathematical skills. Nationally standardized with over 6,000 individuals between the ages of 24 months and 95 years, this test provides age and grade comparisons of general cognitive abilities, scholastic aptitudes, and achievement.[10] A Spanish version of the Woodcock-Johnson applied math problems test, from the Woodcock–Muñoz battery (Woodcock & Muñoz-Sandoval, 1996), was used to test children whose proficiency in English was limited.

In kindergarten the average child was doing very well in terms of standardized test scores (see Figure 3.2). At this point, approximately 10 months after the children left their early childhood programs, the average standardized test scores were slightly below the normed average scores of 100 for these tests in the case of vocabulary[11] and slightly above the normed average scores of 100 for these tests in terms of math.[12]

By first grade, and again at second grade with relatively more Spanish speakers in the sample, the children's average standardized vocabulary score had declined.[13] However, their average standardized math scores held steadily above the normed average.[14]

Observed and Teacher Ratings of Social Competence. Children's teachers completed the Student–Teacher Relationship scale (STR) about their relation-

Figure 3.2. Academic school skills.

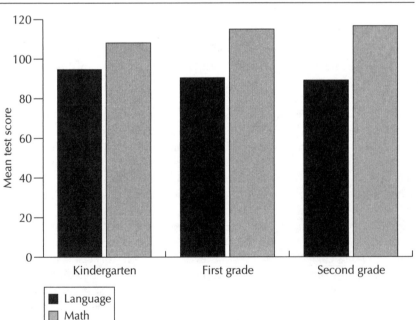

ship with the children (Pianta & Steinberg, 1992).[15] We used the Closeness and Conflict subscales. Conflict and Closeness predict a range of outcomes for children concurrently and in later grades, beyond prediction by child demographics and ability assessments (Hamre & Pianta, 2001). One observer per child spent one morning in the elementary classroom of each participating child. We used the Children's Behavior Ratings (CBR) (Ladd et al., 1999) to rate children's behavior with peers (prosocial, aggressive, anxious). In previous research these observer ratings predicted children's kindergarten school adjustment (Ladd et al., 1999).[16]

Kindergarten children were doing well in their social adjustment to school (see Figure 3.3). Their teachers rated them as very high in closeness and low in conflict.[17] Observers recorded high prosocial with peers and low aggression and anxiety[18] (see Figure 3.4). In first and second grades, the children in our sample continued to be well liked by their teachers.[19] Average scores on peer aggression and anxiety remained very low and scores on peer prosocial were high.

The programs and the advisory boards may not have been able to come to consensus on the proper way to prepare children for school because there may not be a proper way; again, many patterns of practices led toward school success. We suspect that the very high quality of the programs and the very positive nature of the child–teacher relationships we found are the underlying foundation for the children's success. This is consistent with the many research studies that find that high quality in child care is associated with children's future success in school

Figure 3.3. Teacher–child relationship.

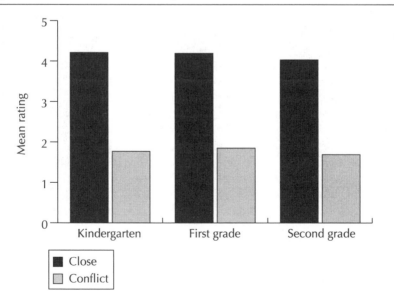

Figure 3.4. Peer relations.

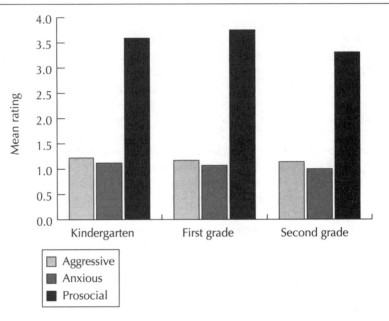

(Peisner-Feinberg et al., 2001). The children from these programs went to school with prior experiences of learning from rich and stimulating environments; they may indeed have known how to learn. They also went to school with prior experiences of using a teacher to organize their learning; they may indeed have known how to get help in organizing their learning. And they went to school with social skills; they may indeed have known how to behave in school. In the words of the advisory boards, the programs were doing a good job with these children and indeed getting them ready for school.

In summary, although at first it appeared that community advocates and program directors were evaluating programs through a different lens than the research team in terms of quality and school readiness, there was agreement. In subsequent chapters we discuss how, when observed through the lens of activities, practices, and interpersonal interactions, there were differences attributable to participation in different cultural communities.

How They Did Things: Practices, Activities, and Activities Embedded in Practices

CHILDREN'S ACTIVITIES, and teachers' and children's interactions around activities, are what a visitor to an ECE program sees. Children are sitting at small tables building, coloring, or practicing writing. They are climbing and sliding. Teachers are talking, reading, helping to tie a shoe, or asking children to change their behavior. Our attachment theoretical framework suggests that teacher–child interactions are used by children and teachers to construct relationships. Our theory of relationship formation within cultural communities suggests that teachers' and program directors' practices shape the activities and teacher behaviors. In this chapter I begin by describing the practices as articulated by adult program participants. In the following sections I describe children's and teachers' activities as coded in the naturalistic observations. In concluding this chapter I describe how activities and teacher engagement with children are embedded within practices.

Practices are what program directors, teachers, and children do as they participate in the cultural community of their early childhood program. Practices also are ingrained habits of doing things, and practices are what were the most similar for programs within a larger cultural community and the most different for programs in different cultural communities. Thus the description of practices forms the heart of this book. In describing practices, it is important to retain the images of foreground and background. When we describe practices, we do so against the background of the larger cultural communities and against the uniformly high scores on program quality and children's school success (see Chapter 3).

According to our theoretical framework, we assume that there will be consistency in the ways that participants from a cultural community describe and enact their practices, and that participants in different cultural communities will describe and enact different practices. These internal consistencies and differences across cultural communities reflect each program's unique historical and social situation. Also, participants within a program are expected to differ in their articulation of practices. These differences will be accounted for partially by different roles in the program, for example, director versus teacher, and by different understandings of the program's history and goals. Because participants in programs are participating in more than one cultural community simultaneously, we also expect different perspectives from these experiences. For example, the experience of migration from a high-status position of teacher in El Salvador to a low-status teacher's aide position in Los Angeles would provide a different perspective on practice than would being born in and attending high school in Los Angeles before becoming a teacher's aide (Hondagneu-Sotelo, 2001).

In Chapter 2 on the theoretical framework, we saw that by their function, early childhood programs must have practices in six areas. The first 3 areas of practices—teaching and learning of pre-academic material; social competence; culture, race, and language—directly influence children's experiences in classrooms. The other three areas of practices—considering children with special needs; how to engage with families; and how to supervise teachers—have more indirect influences because they reflect program organization rather than ways of being with children. In this chapter I describe the range of practices articulated by the participating directors and teachers. These descriptions form the foreground in the kaleidoscope image.

In order to describe cultural shaping of early childhood practices, it is helpful to start with a definition of what is to be changed or shaped. Practices or ways of doing things in early childhood education are shaped by societal and professional expectations of what is "good for children" and "good" for certain groups of children. Although there were prescriptions for "good" early childhood practices in the late 1990s, there was little agreement on what was good education and care for poor children and children of color. Until recently, researchers paid relatively little attention to practices in ECE, although an emerging literature on ECE pedagogy suggests that may be changing (Genishi & Goodwin, 2008; Genishi, Ryan, Ochsner, & Yarnall, 2000; Isenberg & Jalongo, 2003; Yelland, 2005). What ECE did have in terms of practices was NAEYC's developmentally appropriate practice (DAP).

DAP might be considered a prescription for "best practices." The first version of DAP was discussed and published in the late 1980s (Bredekamp, 1987). When we encountered the programs in our study, DAP had been implemented for about a decade. All of the programs were familiar with DAP, although, as we will see, not all agreed with it. This first version of DAP was criticized for failing to understand how social stratification, racism, and discrimination influence child development (Johnson et al., 2003; Kessler & Swadener, 1992; Lubeck, 1998). Some critiques interpreted DAP as prescribing that children should play in order to learn and argued that poor children and children of color deserved more structured learning (Delpit, 1988; Stipek et al., 1998; Stipek, Feiler, Daniels, & Milburn, 1995). A revised version of DAP was published in 1997 (Bredekamp & Copple, 1997), after our program observations were complete. In 2009 yet another revision was completed (Copple & Bredekamp, 2009).

The research team generated descriptions of the practices covered in this chapter by analyzing field notes, transcripts of research team meetings, and the case histories of the programs. Subsequently, these practices were validated with the research partner of the program. We refer to practices generated by this methodology in the text and in Table 4.1 as program practices. We generated other practices from the words of individual teacher participants recorded in the transcripts of focus groups and interviews. We refer to the practices generated by this methodology in the text and in the table as teacher-articulated practices.

In the following sections, I use many quotes from transcripts of interviews, focus groups, research team analysis meetings, and our case studies of each program to illustrate the practices. I have selected the clearest and most representative quotes as examples. Figures 4.1–4.6 show the practices and their prevalence in the programs.[1]

PRACTICES DIRECTLY INFLUENCING CHILDREN'S EXPERIENCES IN CLASSROOMS

Teaching and Learning of Pre-Academic Material

All of the programs intended to have the children ready for school, despite a contested definition of readiness. In order to get the children ready, all the programs intended to help the children learn the concepts and/or skills that the program staff believed would make the children most successful when they left the program and entered kindergarten. As we discussed, this emphasis on pre-academic learning, and, by extension, teaching of pre-academic material, reflects a renewed interest in the value of early experiences for children's school success (Bowman et al., 2000; Shonkoff & Phillips, 2000). Not surprisingly, given the debates within the early childhood field about practices to help children learn, particularly practices appropriate for children of color (Kessler & Swadener, 1992), participants articulated very different practices. We begin this section by discussing program practices and continue with teacher-articulated practices.

Program Practices. We organized different program practices around this central issue in the early childhood field: How much should programs emphasize pre-academic skills, for example, letters and numbers, versus learning to learn? We created one category directly related to this debate, *focus on academic preparation.* The second program practice, *relation to developmentally appropriate practice*, indirectly addressed the debate over academics and in our data may reflect more of a misunderstanding of NAEYC's first edition of the DAP statement (Bredekamp, 1987) than an implementation (or not) of DAP. Both of these program practices are defined in Table 4.1.

Academic Preparation. All of the programs grappled with getting children ready for school. Some programs made academic preparation the center of their work. As the head teacher at Ready to Learn explained,

Table 4.1. Definition of practices.

Content	Articulated by Program or by Teachers	Practice	Categories	Definition
Teaching and learning	Program	Academic preparation Relation to DAP	Implement Oppose Individualize	Focus on direct instruction of basic academic skills Bases program on DAP Believes DAP is not suitable Modifies DAP to fit the program
	Teacher	How children learn	Didactic Child initiated Scaffold	Teach children basic skills Expose children to a wide variety of experiences and activities Create activities and monitor children's behavior; intervene at teachable moments
Social	Program	School adjustment Relationship building		Focus on children learning to maintain internalized control and classroom behaviors Focus on establishing secure and trusting teacher-child relationships
	Teacher	Social skill development	Behavior in school Relationships	Follow directions, sit quietly Resolve conflicts, friendships
Culture, race, and home language	Program	Anti-Bias Curriculum Language of classroom		Focus on delivering a curriculum that counters societal bias English, mix of English and Spanish, Spanish only
	Teacher	Culture and race	Home culture American culture Multiculturalism	Children maintain and respect home language and racial traditions Teach English and American traditions Expose children to all cultures
Special needs	Program	Policy on inclusion		Serve only special needs children Treat all children as typical Include special needs children Include with specialized staff Exclude special needs children
Teacher development	Program	Early mentoring Supervision		Special attention to beginning teachers Intentionally reflective, including observation in the classroom and case conferences
Work with families	Program	Educate Become a partner No involvement		Work to change parenting practices Work with families to solve problems Do not include working with families as part of mission
Hours of care	Program	Full or part day		Intent to care for children of working parents
Family service	Program	Services to families		Intent to provide a range of services to families beyond care of children

"We are more academic. We tell the parents the children are ready for their letters and they are going to get it like this."

Other programs were more interested in children learning to learn, and in their having a positive experience at school, than in basic academic skills. The following quote from a teacher at Down the Hill is representative of this point of view:

I think this center is interested in play and the dynamic of play and I think that they are very interested in language development because I think that they feel that the children really need that language in order to be able to communicate with one another and their teachers when they move on.

Most children were enrolled in classrooms of programs that fell at the midpoint on academic preparation. See Figure 4.1. Less than one quarter of the children experienced classrooms that made academic preparation the center of their practices around teaching and learning.

Relation to DAP. The dichotomy of placing learning in opposition to playing is an old one in the early childhood field (Bredekamp, 1987). This is not consistent with more recent developmental theory on how children learn. DAP argued instead that children learn through dialogue with teachers rather than either playing or drilling of skills. These adult and child dialogues around academic content do not have to be serious and can be embedded in play (Hart & Risley, 1992). In part, NAEYC's DAP was intended to move early childhood education from the play–learn dichotomy toward a more nuanced and articulated set of best practices for teaching and learning (Bredekamp, 1987; Hart, Burts, & Charlesworth, 1996).

In their interviews and in focus groups, program directors in this research project tended to define their own teaching and learning practices in relation to DAP, particularly during the exercise of writing program mission statements. From the transcripts, we identified three mutually exclusive articulated program practices of teaching and learning defined in relation to DAP. See Table 4.1. Following are examples of program directors, first at Down the Hill and next at Coast, who were in agreement with DAP and intended to implement it:

I want teachers and children involved in problem solving, discovery, experimentation, the scientific method, learning through things that you do rather than the things that you are told. Children who are playing in a dramatic play area and planning, thinking, and getting involved with themes and talking with one another and taking that theme to new places, or children who are in the block corner building and planning, experimenting with spatial concepts, is the most wonderful thing. To have those

Figure 4.1. Teaching and learning of pre-academic material.

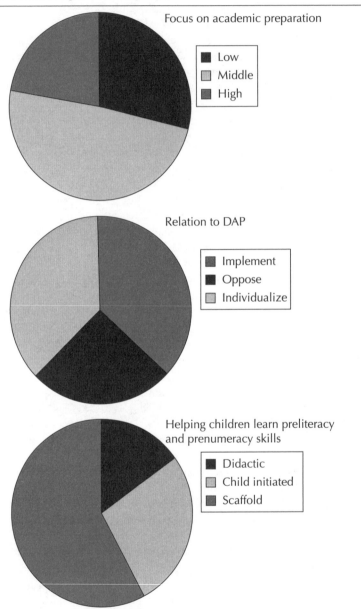

things happening in your classroom is better than anything else that you can do in that classroom.

I want students [in early childhood education classes] to understand the development of children, what is appropriate. I want students to understand individual differences. I want our students to understand respecting children more than anything. Something I love to do and having looked at the brain research recently, talking to children, listening to children, asking children questions, letting their mind problem-solve, playing word games and mind games with children. That's one thing I really like. Helping children be independent. I want our students to, in addition to understanding children's development, know how to provide a classroom experience for them that is going to be wonderful and exciting.

Two of the program directors articulated teaching and learning practices in opposition to DAP. The program director at Love and Learn endorsed didactic teacher-directed learning, but noted that she did not renounce play.

I think it [didactic teaching of basic skills] makes it better for them [children] because they are being offered something right now that academic-wise they are not offered at a lot of schools. . . . As I tell the teachers all the time, make it fun. Whatever you do for them, you have to make it fun and make it a game for them.

Another reason participants appeared to oppose DAP had to do with home language. For example, the director at Ready to Learn articulated that the monolingual Spanish-speaking children served by the program needed particular skills development before they would be ready for kindergarten.

I think one of the most important things is that the children never have a chance to really get off task. If a teacher is going to read a book, she needs to know what underlying skill is being used.

A third group of program directors neither opposed DAP nor wanted to implement it. Instead they argued that it was one of their tools as they individualized the teaching and learning experiences of the children, at times using a DAP approach, and at times modifying it. Two directors, the first at Nickerson and the second at Moms, articulated different aspects of this position.

I think to make it as much like home as possible, not like a school, and then within that home I want to expose children to lots of things in the kind of a way that they don't realize they are exposed to, for example, like the music, you can have the music playing, different types of music, like classical music, some popular music that has positive things, folk music. I put those on a lot of times softly in the background so the child is exposed without actually having to sit down and listen to it.

Communication of love, and I think that that can happen in so many different ways, but I think that that should be happening in day care centers. "I noticed you, hi, how are you. Let's sing. Let's play. Let's be silly with our food maybe one time. Let's look at something beautiful."

Almost half of children (40%) were enrolled in programs that wanted to individualize their use of DAP. See Figure 4.1. Another 22% of the children were enrolled in programs that opposed DAP. This level of dissatisfaction with DAP surprised us. The relatively high level of dissatisfaction may have been because DAP itself was in transition. The program participants were aware that a new version of DAP was soon to be released and they had participated in the revision process. The older DAP was widely believed to be less sensitive to issues of race and home language than the revised version; the dissatisfaction with the first version of DAP in these programs is consistent with these perceptions.

Teacher Practices. Within their interviews and in the focus groups, teachers articulated three mutually exclusive practices around *helping children learn preliteracy and prenumeracy skills*. These were: *didactic teaching*; *child-initiated learning through exposure to a wide variety of experiences and activities*; and *teacher scaffolding*. See Table 4.1.

Didactic. We coded one group of teachers as articulating didactic teaching. Only 15% of the children had primary teachers with this point of view. See Figure 4.1. Adherents to didactic teaching appear to believe that it is the responsibility of the teacher to directly teach children basic skills. The teachers articulating this practice had a predetermined set of academic skills that they expected the children would learn under their direction. They appeared to believe that the role of the teacher was to deliver this information to the children and to make sure that they learned it. These participants, such as a teacher at Love and Learn, articulated a belief that knowledge was in the hands (heads) of the teachers and, in order to succeed at school, children must acquire it from them.

This is basically an academic school . . . and everything in our curriculum is teacher-directed. We relate everything to academics.

Child-Initiated. A second group of teachers (27%) articulated that children learn through exposure to a wide variety of experiences and activities. Therefore, the role of the teacher was to expose children to such experiences and activities; this exposure and the children's actions with the experience would construct a foundation of basic understandings. Participants understood teaching to mean, "Let the children play and they will learn." There was no articulation of the role of the teacher in shaping and extending understandings.

As she described a cooking activity, a teacher at El Peace said, "And they learn not just how to cook, but to count to ten."

A teacher at Pierce beautifully stated the principle of maturation when she said, "Our work seems to me like growing trees."

And still another, at Mountain, said, "We provide experiences that help children grow their ideas and we are always careful to help them understand that they just did something wonderful."

Scaffold. The final, mutually exclusive teacher-articulated practice around teaching and learning of pre-academic material was that the role of the teacher was to create hands-on activities for children, monitor their behavior, and then intervene at "teachable moments" to extend their knowledge. These teachers were the primary teachers of the largest group of children. See Figure 4.1. These participants understood the role of the teacher as active in structuring and extending children's understandings of their activities and experiences. They told us of their work in planning activities, monitoring children as they engaged in the activities, and being involved with the children as they learned. In the words of a teacher at Down the Hill:

> We used to take them down to watch a work site and talk about it and then we would go back to the center and we would take PVC piping and shovels and trucks and we would go work in the yard and put the water through the pipes doing what we saw them doing outside.

Social Competence

Interestingly, practices articulated by program participants around social competence did not share the same dichotomy between skills and underlying constructs that we have been discussing around pre-academic learning. All of the programs endorsed attending to children's social and emotional development, although Love and Learn participants explained that such playful activity happened outside, *not* within the classroom. This focus on social and emotional development is consistent with early childhood programs' historical emphasis on socialization. There were some differences among participants in the articulation of social competence practices that reflected disagreements about whether the primary purpose of programs was to get children ready for school or to have a positive experience during this period of development. There were relatively large differences in how much program practices centered on teaching children how to behave in school. There were also differences in the emphasis on conflict resolution, perhaps reflecting differences in perceptions of the neighborhoods surrounding the programs as dangerous places for the children and families to live. See Figure 4.2 for a graphic representation of the differences in proportion of children experiencing these practices.

Program Practices. We identified two program practices concerning social competence: *school adjustment* and *relationship building*. See Table 4.1.

School adjustment. School adjustment was defined as a focus on children learning to maintain internal control and social behavior appropriate for the classroom. All children experienced a high- or mid-level endorsement of this practice. As a teacher at Nickerson explained,

> Children have to be good listeners, and I can't help anyone if I haven't heard what they have to say because everyone is talking and no one is listening.

A second teacher, at El Peace, articulated school adjustment as the distinguishing feature between an early childhood program and a custodial program.

> Teachers can't just watch children like babysitters. They need to watch the children's development and ensure that the child fits in with children his own age, is adjusting to social aspects of being in a children's center.

Relationship Building. Relationship building was described as a focus on establishing secure and trusting relationships with the children, often perceived by program participants as necessary to counter negative home and community influences. However, unlike school adjustment, there was less consensus among programs on the importance of relationship building. See Figure 4.2. Unlike school adjustment, which had a future focus, relationship building practices were articulated as necessary for the present time. Implied in relationship building is that it is a first step in beginning to work with children. As a participant from Moms explained,

> Mainly, teachers need to get down and put themselves at the child's level, look at them face-to-face, and to see each child's needs, because each child is different. Teachers need to work to understand them, listen to them, help them, support them, give them affection, share with them.

Teacher-Articulated Practices. In their interviews and in the focus groups, teachers articulated two types of practices around children's social competence,

Figure 4.2. Social competence.

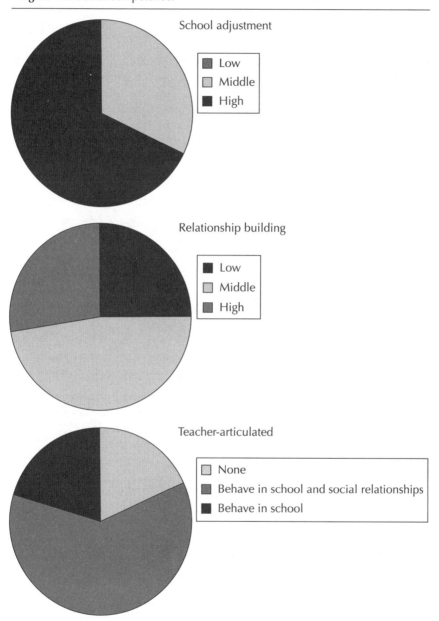

behavior in school and *social relationships*. See Table 4.1. These practices were conceptually similar to the two program practices around social competence.

Behavior in School. One practice, behavior in school, was described as having less to do with motivation to learn and to explore, and more to do with being "good" and, like school adjustment, had a future focus. Some participants appeared to believe that if children knew what was expected of them and rehearsed a school script, then the transition to kindergarten would be easier. For example, as these two participants, the first from Down the Hill and the second from Nickerson, explained, it was the practice of teachers to explicitly teach the school script.

> We teach them how to behave in the classroom, how to clean up, and when we go outside, how to cross the street.

> We walk them to school and we tell them, "This is going to be your teacher."

Other teacher participants, such as a teacher at Love and Learn, appeared to believe that if children had manners, then they would be better received in "real" school.

> I like to teach them the "thank yous" and the "may I please." I think that is very important for children.

Social Relationships. Another set of teacher-articulated practices focused more on working on social relationships than on preparing children to enact school scripts. Many of the Los Angeles programs were located within neighborhoods characterized by high levels of verbal and physical violence. Participants were concerned about preventive intervention, in the form of teaching nonviolent conflict resolution skills. For example, a participant from Moms explained,

> We work toward a place where they can start problem solving together . . . they learn how to work things out between them, come up with ideas.

Other teachers were concerned with children forming friendships and playing with peers. Some teachers, such as one at Mission Hope, talked about the practice of encouraging dramatic play so that children would develop peer relationships.

> Well, children need to be children, and in order to be that, I like to see them play. I like to see them use their imagination.

Some of the teacher participants discussed practices that help children build friendships and feel part of a group. These participants believed that part of their role as teachers was to help children learn to work and play together, and to become socially competent. Teachers such as the following, the first at Therapeutic Preschool, and the second at Down the Hill, defined being part of the peer group as important:

> When they first come I want them to feel safe and cared for. I want them to feel that this is their classroom, that they are a valued member of this classroom, that they have a voice, that other people have ideas and they are part of this group.

> I think the most important thing above all is for them to learn with others, to get along with others, the social skills that are learned here, hopefully learned here, is the foundation of anything else that they are going to do when they get out of here. If you can't get along with your peers, you can't learn to work together with a variety of different people. They need to learn some tolerances.

In their interviews, all teachers mentioned at least one practice around teaching and learning of pre-academic material. This was not true of practices around social competence. Despite direct questions and probes, a number of teachers could not tell us about their socialization practices. Other teachers talked about both school behavior and relationships. To reflect this complexity, we coded teacher articulation of children's social competence into four mutually exclusive categories: (1) no mention of socialization or social competence; (2) teach children how to behave in school only; (3) teach children to behave in school and work on social relationships (teaching, nonviolent conflict resolution skills, talking about dramatic play as an important social activity for children to develop peer relationships, and/ or helping children learn to work and play together and to become socially competent); and (4) work only on social relationships. Most teachers endorsed both *behavior in school* and *work on social relationships*. See Figure 4.2.

Culture, Race, and Home Language

All but three of the programs, Love and Learn, Mission Hope, and Mountain, served groups of children diverse in race, and most had at least one child with a home language other than English or Spanish. Even when the program intended to serve only one group of families—e.g., Mission Hope (Latino/a immigrants); Mountain (Appalachian families)—the programs were located in geographic areas that included people diverse in race and home language. All of the program participants shared an assumption that one of the responsibilities of an early childhood program was to teach children about culture or multiculturalism. Yet despite these commonalities, there was considerable heterogeneity in practices around culture, race, and home language. Teasing out and understanding the nuances was particularly challenging. Initially we attempted to use some classroom rating measures, but abandoned this attempt and moved to asking Carol Cole, who led the teacher focus groups, to lead a special focus group with the research team to help us articulate practices in this area. From the transcript of the focus group, we summarized the position of each program. See Figure 4.3 for the distribution of children around each practice.

Program Practices. We identified two program practices, *implementing the Anti-Bias Curriculum* and *language used in the classroom.*

Anti-Bias Curriculum. Similar to NAEYC's developmentally appropriate practices, NAEYC's Anti-Bias Curriculum (Derman-Sparks, 1989; Derman-Sparks & Olsen, 2010) is a well-known standard that we used to categorize programs as either embracing or placing themselves in opposition to. Although only 12% of the children were in programs fully implementing the ABC, most programs were using it or a similar curriculum in the classroom. See Figure 4.3. Below are excerpts from the summaries of three programs' practices around the ABC. The first two excerpts are from programs implementing the ABC, Moms and Down the Hill.

> Of all the programs looked at in this study, this is the one program that consciously tries to achieve the ABC in their center. Observers find that they have almost all of the material associated with the ABC and that they pointedly raise issues of diversity with the children and parents. They have little baby dolls in wheelchairs, and they have little baby dolls with eye patches, and they talk about every kind of everything at any given moment. They talk about race, they talk about class, gender, sexuality. It is an overt part of the curriculum. It's evident in every part of the day.

> Down the Hill has perhaps the most ethnically diverse group of children—"one of everything," in the words of an observer. They have some materials that reflect diversity, but it does not seem that they use these in particular to start conversations around issues of diversity. Several observers noted, however, that when issues of diversity arise among the children, these are addressed with openness and candidness. So although the center does not seem to raise these issues in particular, they are comfortable discussing them with the children. Furthermore, because of the mix of children, not necessarily because of the materials, such issues seem to arise.

Figure 4.3. Culture, race, and home language.

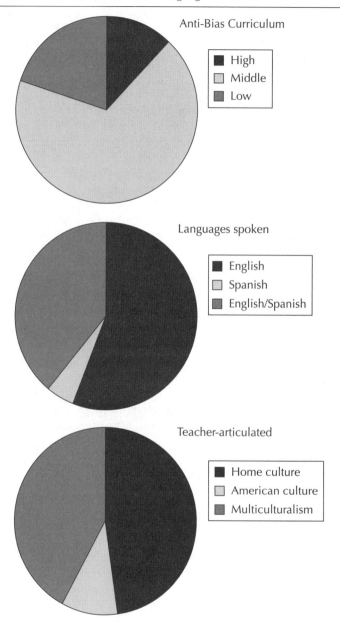

The following excerpt is from a program not implementing the ABC:

> Love and Learn was seen as a very traditional school in many ways.
> Despite the staff as well as its students being all African American, the
> school seems to follow a traditional curriculum that includes celebration
> of traditional holidays. For example, the school celebrates Thanksgiving,
> Valentine's Day, and Easter. The center celebrates Black History Month,
> but this too may now be considered merely traditional curriculum.
> Furthermore, they do not seem to address it from the perspective in
> particular of an all-African American school. Gender roles are also
> extremely traditional. Boys are not allowed to take ballet, and girls and
> boys are referred to as ladies and gentlemen, with specific behavior
> expected along with these labels.

Language Used. A second program practice was the language used in the
classroom. Classroom languages were English-only, a mix of English and Spanish, or Spanish-only. See Figure 4.3.

Teacher-Articulated Practices. We identified three teacher-articulated practices, from the interviews and focus groups, that were designed to enhance children's development in light of issues of culture, race, and language. These were
emphasis on *home culture*, *American culture*, and *multiculturalism*. They were
mutually exclusive; no teacher was found to have more than one of these practices. See Table 4.1 and Figure 4.3.

Home Culture. One group of teacher participants discussed the importance
of children maintaining and respecting their home language, culture, and racial/
ethnic traditions. While these participants sometimes added, as a secondary aim,
the need for children to speak English when they went to school, the idea was not
to assimilate children into American culture, but to preserve their home culture.
Below are quotes from teachers, first at Mission Hope and then at Nickerson, representing this practice.

> We don't want them to come here and be totally Americanized. . . . Most
> of us speak to the children in Spanish because it is the language the child
> is growing up in. When we explain things to the children, they share it
> with their parents. How would they tell their parents if we explained it
> only in English?

> I told him about George Washington Carver and although he couldn't say
> George Washington Carver, he drew a picture of him with glasses and
> mustache and he put some cotton in the picture.

American Culture. Another group of teacher participants told us that it was important to teach children to be Americans so that they would be ready for school. These participants believed that since children would have to speak English and behave properly in school, it was important to give them these skills in a warm and positive atmosphere while they were young, so that the adjustment when they arrived at school would be less traumatic. These participants, first from Ready to Learn and then from Pierce, argued as follows:

A lot of them aren't getting English in the homes, which is okay because we give it to them.

We are preparing kids to live in this country, in this century, in this city. We have to say to the parents, "Do you know what your 3-year-old is going to be expected to do? To pick up their cup of milk and drink it by themselves and we are going to be working on that."

Multiculturalism. A third group of teacher participants subscribed to a belief that all children should be exposed to all cultures while attending their program. These participants described practices, particularly around holidays and food, that would expose children to those who were different from themselves. They believed that this positively toned exposure would make the children more receptive to differences. As a teacher at El Peace explained,

And I guess with pictures and setting up the environment in the dollhouse we try to do things the multicultural way like maybe Chinese dishes and when it comes to the multiculture we stick in the different cultures.

PRACTICES INDIRECTLY INFLUENCING CHILDREN'S EXPERIENCES IN THE CLASSROOM

Disability and Special Needs

By design, we selected programs that served children with disabilities and special needs in different ways. One program, TPS, served only special needs children, and one program, Love and Learn, excluded special needs children. The other programs ranged between these extremes. Some programs treated all children as typical and did not identify or treat special needs children differently. Others made an effort to serve children whose behaviors led them to be asked to leave other programs, but served them without special personnel. A final category was inclusion programs, which had teaching personnel whose main responsibility was to serve special needs children. See Table 4.1.

Teacher Development

In focus groups, program directors identified two practices that they considered important for programs to provide in order to assist teachers in their development: *early mentoring* and *reflective supervision.*

Early Mentoring. Teachers were mentored if they talked about a specific person in their program who encouraged and helped them become a better teacher early in their career. For example, a teacher at Mission Hope said:

> I worked with a teacher, Ms. T, and she helped instill in me that I had the know-how and helped me build my confidence that I could do it and be a teacher.

Seventy-two percent of the children had primary caregivers who had been mentored. As the director at Nickerson explains below, mentoring in these programs was not happenstance but planned.

> I have Ms. P. who is the epitome of what I would call the elder. And one thing when I came to this center, everyone was the same age. I had a staff whose ages ranged from 25 to 35. And most of the time it was their first experience in working—their first working experience. So I needed to get some seasoning in my staff. Ms. P. is seasoned, has a lot of positive experience in the community. And in the African American community, we have some real historical foundation on our elders in our community because those are the ones we look to for direction. They are the ones we look to for guidance. They are the ones that give us permission. And I respect that because it has worked for me and it has worked here at Nickerson.

Also, because every program had at least one person on the teaching staff who had been at the program since it began, and because turnover was very low (over half of the programs had no turnover, and the highest turnover was 15% annually), the mentors as well as the mentees tended to still be in the programs. Teaching staff also had long tenure in the programs, ranging from 6 to 30 years.

Reflective Supervision. Reflective supervision was intentionally reflective and took a variety of forms. In programs engaging in reflective supervision, each teaching staff person was provided with a mentor and/or a supervisor. In every case the mentor had at least a BA degree. Teachers were observed by their supervisor and/or mentor. Teachers and supervisors met regularly to reflect on teaching. Teachers took part in staff meetings and/or case conferences that included discussions of children and teaching strategies. Primary caregivers who engaged in reflective supervision cared for 76% of the children.

Parents

Using field notes, interviews, and ratings by research partners, we identified three program practices having to do with parents: *working with parents, providing child care,* and *providing family services.* See Table 4.1. Participants articulated one of three patterns of working with parents: *parent education, parent partnerships*, and *no involvement.*

Parent Education. Programs that articulated that they engaged in parent education intended to help the parents be better parents. The program defined what made a better parent, for example, less likely to spank. A teacher at Ready to Learn, which scored high on parent education, said:

> We work with parents to help them be better parents. They come in and they do projects and they help out and in this way we teach them to do things that will help their child in school.

Parent Partnerships. Programs that scored high in parent partnerships did not intend to change the parents but articulated that children's development was enhanced when parents and the program worked together. A teacher at Down the Hill stated:

> There is communication both ways, so that there will be a match between home and school values. We want to have children behave in this program in the ways that their parents respect and appreciate.

No Involvement. The remaining programs did not become involved with parents. As a teacher at Mission Hope said,

> We provide a safe, clean, warm place for children so that parents don't worry when they work.

However, not involving parents did not mean disregarding parents. Instead, the programs with high scores on not involving parents believed that it was more useful to take good care of the children and support parents' working than it was to ask them to do more. A teacher at Mountain explained:

> They don't have a lot of time because they are working and going to school, but we always have time to have a brief conversation when they are coming in or picking them up. And I make a point when they pick them up especially to give them a little rundown on the activities and this is something that they have done. Keep it positive for the day. And we might say just simply, they learned to tie their shoe and we can share that.

They put 16 pieces of a puzzle together by themselves. But they always have a few minutes to talk and we schedule home visits and conferences, but they don't have a lot of time to volunteer in the classrooms, but at parents meetings, 100% attend.

Hours of Child Care.   There was a considerable range in the number of hours of child care provided by the different programs. For example, Mission Hope began as a program to provide care for the children of working mothers and provided full-day child care. In contrast, South Central did not intend to provide full-day child care and required parent participation during the daytime hours. One of its teachers said:

> We have generational families coming, parents that were teenagers that used the program that watch and want their children here; we have parents who have had teenage children that were in the program before and purposely bring their children here. They are comfortable and they feel they are getting a good start, getting prepared to be in school is very important. They understand that importance and they understand the commitment of parents participating.

Providing Family Services.   Family service was defined as the practice of intending to serve the parents in terms of occupational training or other services not specifically directed at children. Programs that rated high on parent services functioned as family service centers, providing child care as only one of a number of family services. For example, Mountain was part of a larger Family Service Center and viewed the program as only one of the many services offered to families.

We have described many practices in this chapter. These descriptions illustrate the rich variability in the ways that program participants served children and families. This variability informs the debate over the enactment of ECE quality in different ethnic communities. Our findings are consistent with the literature that suggestions that adults from different racial and ethnic backgrounds differ in their beliefs and behaviors (practices) around taking care of children (Fisher, Jackson, & Villarruel, 1998; Miller-Jones, 1988; Slaughter-Defoe, 1995).

CHILDREN AND TEACHERS INVOLVED
IN ACTIVITIES AND INTERACTION

In thinking about the homogeneous descriptions of program quality and the heterogeneous practices, it is notable that there was a narrow band of high ECE quality represented in these programs. All of the practices that children experienced occurred in the context of a rich and stimulating learning environment, with teachers who were sensitive rather than harsh or detached in their interactions with children, and who were responsively involved with children, whether they were facilitating peer play, including special needs children, or intending to help children learn school skills. Therefore, to be precise, we have succeeded only in describing a heterogeneous group of practices enacted within ECE programs of exemplary quality. That these practices are heterogeneous is very important in this context; there is clearly more than one pathway to enacting quality.

Who Are the Children and Teachers in the Classrooms of the Program?

The categories of participants of the 12 programs were the directors, the teachers, and the children in the programs. The children's families and the larger cultural communities were part of the background for these analyses. We did not interview or observe the children's families, but we knew of the families' participation in the various cultural communities, the programs, and other cultural communities through the advisory boards, our own participation in the Los Angeles and North Carolina child advocate communities, and the case histories and field notes generated for this project. For example, at Moms we knew that all of the mothers were young and enrolled in a continuation school. We knew something of their lives because one of the members of our Los Angeles advisory board also participated in the committee that provided adult mentors for these young women. We knew even more about their lives because our field notes for this program were especially focused on the young mothers, as the director at Moms was particularly vocal in discussing her involvement with their lives and brought one of them to several advisory board meetings. For another example, I knew something about the families that moved Down the Hill to a low-income neighborhood because I belonged to another cultural community in Los Angeles that included some of those mothers. As a result, long before a Los Angeles advisory board nominated the program, I had heard of the idea to move the program "down the hill."

When we focused on children's experiences in their classrooms, we were including 170 children, half girls and half boys. The children ranged in age from 15 months to almost 6 years old, with the majority 3- and 4-year-olds. Almost 40% of the children were Latino/a. One third of the children were African American. The remaining children were White, Asian, and biracial. Sixty-four percent of the children had primary teachers who shared their ethnic identity.

Thirty-four different teachers served as primary teachers for the 170 children.[2] Ten of these teachers served as a primary teacher for only one child, eleven for between 2 and 5 children, seven for between 6 and 10 children, and six for between 11 and 15 children. The number of different teacher–child pairs from each program ranged from 8 to 22, with programs enrolling larger numbers of children having more teacher–child pairs included.

Activities

We recorded children's activities and experiences across the duration of a program day, using naturalistic observation procedures (as discussed in Appendix A). By program day we meant that we observed in the programs from the time the children arrived until they left, taking time out for naps in full-day programs. We used our activity codes to form a picture of how children spent their days. See Figure 4.4. On average, children in all the programs spent the most time during the day—close to one third of their time—simply "hanging out" with peers and adults. Initially, children spending so much of their time hanging out surprised us. In full-day programs, children were spending an hour to more than 2 hours of their days hanging out. In half-day programs, the amount of time was, of course, smaller, but still relatively large. On reflection, we believe this is an indicator of how ECE programs mirror the everyday life of the children and adults who "live" there. Hanging out is an important form of social behavior. Hanging out is not primarily making or learning something. During these times, adults in the programs were available for a chat, or teachers spent time sorting out children's interpersonal issues. Also, hanging out included simply playing with other children. By hanging out, adults and children were engaging in an activity setting that fostered styles of social interaction and provided children with the type of experiences that lead to relationships with others.

Almost one quarter of the time, on average, children were engaged in creative activities. These activities are what we often imagine when we think of children in ECE programs: playing with blocks, painting, and playing pretend. And almost one quarter of the time, on average, children were engaged in language arts activities, including both prenumeracy and preliteracy activities. Creative activities and lan-

Figure 4.4. Activities.

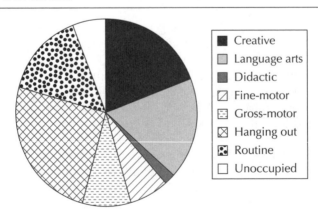

guage arts activities, as we defined them in our coding scheme, often are considered to be the basis for future academic learning and achievement (Bowman et al., 2000).

Relatively small amounts of the children's days were spent in gross-motor, fine-motor, or didactic activities, or being unoccupied. This relative distribution of activities provides another source of support for the high quality of care provided in these programs. In work using these same categories of activities, but a more representative sample of quality in child care, children in higher quality programs were found to spend more time in creative and language arts activities and less time in gross-motor and fine-motor activities (Tonyan & Howes, 2003).

Most of the time, the children were engaged with objects: playing with toys and learning materials. This is what many in the early childhood education field in 1995 might have defined as the essence of an early childhood program. About one third of the children's time was spent in dramatic activities, with and without toys, and with and without peers.

Children's Participation, Teacher Engagement and Involvement

Children were very sociable in these programs; they were almost never alone. Children were within 3 feet of an adult somewhat less than half of the observation period, and about half of that time the adult that they were close to was their primary caregiver. Children were engaged with peers about three quarters of their time and played alone only about 5% of the time.

When teachers were engaged with children, they were most likely to be talking. Conversations and language play accounted for the largest proportion of teacher–child engagement. See Figure 4.5. Classroom management, either positive or negative, and facilitating peer interaction took up a relatively small proportion

Figure 4.5. Teacher engagement with children.

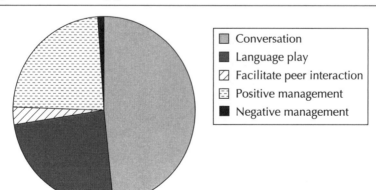

Conversation
Language play
Facilitate peer interaction
Positive management
Negative management

of the children's engagement with teachers. This is quite different from many other early childhood programs, where much of the children's experience consists of waiting for the class to be cohesive enough for an activity (Hamre, 2007; Howes & Ritchie 2002; Pianta et al., 2005).

There were no gender differences in children's participation in the life of the program. The lack of gender differences is surprising given the development of gender segregation in this age period (Maccoby & Jacklin, 1987). Our participant observers reported that while some programs, such as Ready to Learn, actively made gender distinctions, for example, that only boys can do some things—"Which one of you boys is going to be the troll when we act out Billy-Goat Gruff?"— others stressed the importance of letting all children experience all gender activities. For example, El Peace had an amazing variety of gender-specific work apparatus, such as aprons, hard hats, firefighter boots, and a baby carriage, that were all available to both girls and boys in the fantasy play activity center.

Teacher Involvement with Children

Finally, our naturalistic coding scheme allowed us to describe the responsiveness of teachers to children's actions. Recall from Chapter 3 that teacher responsiveness was coded only when children were close to a teacher. As can be seen in Figure 4.6, the teachers in these ECE programs were very responsive to children, and were most likely to elaborate the children's behavior, for example, asking the child to describe the picture being painted. The summary score for responsive involvement suggests that the teachers were responsively involved with the children more than half of the time we observed. This is remarkably high compared with representative child care programs (Howes et al., 2003).

Figure 4.6. Teachers' responsive involvement with children.

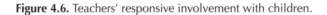

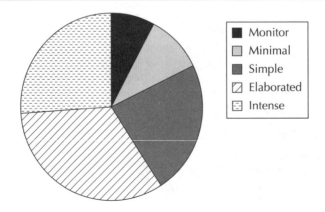

TEACHER ENGAGEMENT WITH CHILDREN
AND ACTIVITIES EMBEDDED WITHIN PRACTICES

In this section of this chapter I discuss how practices, activities, and teacher engagement work together to fully describe the daily life of the programs. In general, program and teacher articulation of practices was consistent with our observations of children's activities and teachers' engagement. Children whose programs and teachers articulated teaching and learning practices that emphasized pre-academic learning engaged, as was expected, in more didactic activities. See Table 4.2. We

Table 4.2. Academic practices, classroom activities, and teacher engagement.

Teaching and Learning Practices	Activity	Teacher Engagement
Academic preparation		
Higher scores	More didactic and less fine-motor[a]	More positive and negative management and less conversation[b]
Relation to developmentally appropriate practice[c]		
Oppose	More didactic and less fine-motor[d]	More positive and negative management[e]
Individualize		More language play and conversation[f]
Teacher: How children learn[g]		
Didactic	More didactic[h]	More positive and negative management and less conversation[i]

[a] Didactic: $r(157) = .44$, $p = .001$; fine-motor: $r(157) = -.21$, $p = .001$.

[b] Positive: $r(157) = .39$, $p = .001$; negative: $r(157) = -.26$, $p = .01$; conversation: $r(157) = -.22$, $p = .001$.

[c] Activity: multivariate $F(8, 364) = 5.45$, $p = .03$, $\eta^2 = .21$; engagement: multivariate $F(10, 328) = 6.41$, $p = .03$, $\eta^2 = .16$.

[d] Didactic: $F(2, 157) = 32.89$, $p = .001$, $\eta^2 = .28$; fine-motor: $F(2, 157) = 3.91$, $p = .05$, $\eta^2 = .05$.

[e] Positive: $F(2, 157) = 16.04$, $p = .001$, $\eta^2 = .51$; negative: $F(2, 157) = 8.31$, $p = .001$, $\eta^2 = .11$.

[f] Language play: $F(2, 157) = 4.6$, $p = .001$, $\eta^2 = .51$; conversation: $F(2, 157) = 17.79$, $p = .001$, $\eta^2 = .18$.

[g] Activities: $F(2, 157) = 2.40$, $p = .02$, $\eta^2 = .11$; engagement: multivariate $F(10, 328) = 7.21$, $p = .001$, $\eta^2 = .18$.

[h] Didactic: $F(2, 157) = 4.02$, $p = .02$, $\eta^2 = .05$.

[i] Positive: $F(2, 157) = 14.89$, $p = .001$, $\eta^2 = .15$; negative: $F(2, 157) = 24.64$, $p = .001$, $\eta^2 = .23$; conversation: $F(2, 157) = 16.78$, $p = .001$, $\eta^2 = .17$.

were surprised that academically minded teachers and programs provided fewer fine-motor activities. In the minds of these participants, shape matching or puzzle games did not appear to be important to children's learning of pre-academic skills. Children in programs where academic learning was more important to adults also received more management of their activities, both positive and negative. Children in programs that de-emphasized pre-academics were engaged in conversations with teachers more often and, when the teachers articulated individualizing DAP, were engaged in more language play with teachers.

Similarly, when programs articulated practices around helping children learn to behave well in school, children experienced more didactic activities, facilitation of peer interaction, and negative management. See Table 4.3. Children in programs that emphasized school behavior were less likely to engage in conversations with teachers. In contrast, when program participants emphasized relationship building, children spent more time simply hanging out and in conversations with teachers. These children also spent more time in language arts, engaged in more language play, and had fewer didactic activities. Not surprisingly, when programs emphasized relationship building, teachers were more likely to engage with children to facilitate peer relations.

Table 4.3. Social practices, classroom activities, and teacher engagement.

Social practices	*Activity*	*Teacher engagement*
School adjustment		
Higher scores	More didactic[a]	More peer facilitation, negative management, less conversation[b]
Relationship building		
Higher scores	More language arts and hanging out, less didactic[c]	More peer facilitation, conversation, and language play[d]
Teacher relationship		
Higher scores	Less didactic[e]	More conversation[f]

[a] Didactic: $r(157) = .19$, $p = .01$.

[b] Peer facilitation: $r(157) = .21$, $p = .01$; negative: $r(157) = .15$, $p = .05$; conversation: $r(157) = -.25$, $p = .001$.

[c] Language arts: $r(157) = .31$, $p = .001$; hanging out: $r(157) = .20$, $p = .01$; didactic: $r(157) = -.19$, $p = .05$.

[d] Peer facilitation: $r(157) = .31$, $p = .001$; conversation: $r(157) = .25$, $p = .001$; language play: $r(157) = .22$, $p = .04$.

[e] Didactic: $r(157) = -.15$, $p = .05$.

[f] Conversation: $r(157) = .25$, $p = .001$.

Table 4.4. Culture, race, home language practices, classroom activities, and teacher engagement.

Culture, Race, Home Language Practices	Activity	Teacher Engagement
Anti-Bias Curriculum		
Higher scores	No differences	More conversation; less positive and negative management[a]
Teacher culture, race, home language	No differences	No differences

[a] Conversation: $r(157) = .329$, $p = .001$; positive management: $r(157) = -.44$, $p = .001$; negative management: $r(157) = -.31$, $p = .001$.

Differences in program participants' articulated practices around culture, race, and home language were the least likely practices directly related to children's experiences to be associated with particular activities or teacher engagement. See Table 4.4. Children in programs most intent on implementing NAEYC's Anti-Bias Curriculum experienced more conversations with and less management by teachers.

As expected, there were no associations between practices only indirectly related to children's experiences, and children's activities and teacher engagement. There also were no associations between teachers' responsive involvement with children and their activities or types of teacher engagement. This suggests that practices, activities, and forms of teacher engagement can be strikingly different in content and almost identical in sensitive responsiveness to children (Howes & James, 2002).

ECE Programs Nested Within Larger Cultural Communities

PROGRAM DESCRIPTIONS FOCUS, like a kaleidoscope, on each dimension of the early childhood programs, always considering the other dimensions as background. Thus, in this chapter I am describing ECE programs where teachers are sensitive and responsive, children trust teachers to take care of them and are learning school readiness skills, and the classrooms are well organized with plenty of materials for learning. We also have seen that within these programs there is a diverse array of practices, activities, and teachers' engagement with children.

CULTURAL COMMUNITY, RACE, AND ETHNICITY

In this chapter I begin the process of examining the role of the participants' home cultural communities in influencing practices within the cultural community of the ECE program. In three of the larger cultural communities, racial identity and socialization of children around race were central. In Los Angeles, four programs—Love and Learn, Nickerson, South Central, and Ready to Learn—were part of an African American larger cultural community, and three programs—Pierce, El Peace, and Mission Hope—were part of a Latino/a larger cultural community. The other programs in Los Angeles—TPS, Moms, and Down the Hill—were part of a larger cultural community that was committed to fighting racism and providing good child care programming for multicultural and economically mixed families; I refer to this group as Diverse Families. In North Carolina the two programs—Mountain and Coast—were similarly part of rural larger cultural communities.

Focus on the Larger Cultural Community: Race and Ethnicity

Race or ethnic categorization is the most important underlying issue in the work of describing patterns of practices for each larger cultural community. Patterns of practices in early childhood programs take on meaning against the backdrop of the United States as a country where race/ethnicity underlies discrimination and stigma. The missions of early childhood programs that are rooted within larger cultural communities defined by racial identity and by resisting bias and discrimination are to provide caring environments where children can develop adaptive competence and do well in a world perceived as hostile to them. The programs within each of the larger cultural communities defined this mission with different nuances. The participants within the African American cultural community defined their mission as helping all children in their community become strong in their own racial identity as African Americans and skilled at adapting to the demands of the dominant culture. These participants have the longest history of constructing an adaptive culture: 400 years of discrimination, the civil rights movement, and active involvement in constructing a larger cultural community focused on educating their young through participation in Head Start and the public school system. Serving Latino/a children rather than their own children leads to some discordance in practices of the African American community (Sanders, Deihl, & Kyler, 2007). As we will see, these participants struggled with this challenge, sometimes viewing the Latino/a children and families they served as stigmatized, as they themselves were, and therefore being fiercely protective of them, and sometimes viewing them as others.

The participants in the Latino/a larger cultural community also saw their mission as protecting their own from discrimination. Compared with the participants in the African American larger cultural community, perhaps they defined their mission as more to protect families than children. The issues of discrimination and adaptive culture are more complicated in Latino/a than in African American racially defined communities. Latino/as, unlike African Americans, are not a self-defined group but a category (Hispanic) made up by the United States Census Bureau. As I will describe, participants classified as Latino/a are perhaps as diverse within their cultural community as they are from other communities in terms of education, immigration experiences, and socialization beliefs. Unity within the cultural community comes from a common language—Spanish—that is not the dominant language of the United States and from discrimination. The participants in the Latino/a larger cultural community came to the United States voluntarily to make a better life for their children. Stigmatization and discrimination may have caught some members of the community by surprise. The Latino/a-heritage members of our research team, who were highly successful in the world in terms of education, described mixed messages from their own parents: If you do not succeed it is your own fault, and If you do not succeed it is because of discrimination. For all of these reasons, at the time of our project the participants in the Latino/a larger cultural community were best described as in the process of constructing a fully articulated and integrated pattern of practices for early childhood programs that promoted adaptive competence. A prime example of the "in process" nature of this articulation is that each of the early childhood programs within this larger cultural community had very different practices for using Spanish. Another example is the uneven integration of early childhood knowledge into teacher practices. At times our observations suggested that teachers were caught between didactic and child-centered behaviors with children, perhaps as a result of conflict between heritage practices and perceptions of best practices in the United States (Halgunseth, Ispa, & Rudy, 2006). It is important not to confuse inarticulated or nonintegrated patterning of practices with poor care. The child participants in the Latino/a larger cultural community were by all standards—advisory board, research team, and their later success in school—cared for well and doing well.

In contrast, the participants in the North Carolina larger cultural community were most likely of all the participants to articulate and implement practices suggested by NAEYC's developmentally appropriate practices, 1987 version, and NAEYC's Anti-Bias Curriculum. The participants in the North Carolina larger cultural community were loud in their determination to serve well the children and families in their geographic area, and more silent in their overt discussions of race. From this perspective it is probably most accurate to consider the two North Carolina programs as belonging to two different larger cultural communities, because only one of the two programs actually enrolled other-than-White children.

The all-White and poor participants at Mountain belonged to a larger cultural community that celebrated regional mountain culture. These participants wanted to preserve a cultural heritage for their own children and the children they served. In this way their mission was not unlike that of many of the participants in the African American larger cultural community. But as in the African American cultural community, the demographics of the geographic area were changing. Unlike in the Los Angeles area, these changes were barely discernible in terms of children and families served and had not yet influenced practices. For example, although census data identified Latino/a immigrants, there were no monolingual Spanish-speaking children in the programs. However, there were perceived encroachments on regional mountain culture from both affluent people building vacation homes and undocumented Latino/a families.

In contrast, the second North Carolina program, Coast, was located within a geographic area that was historically racially mixed and served a diversity of children—White, African American, and a few Latino/a. We know that these participants lived through the civil rights struggle, and by their wholehearted adoption of the ABC we can infer that the participants' intentions were to be equitable in their service to White and non-White families. Participants talked about respecting individual differences rather than directly addressing race.

The mission of the Diverse Families cultural community was straightforward. In the largest sense, these participants intended to change the world. In a more manageable sense, their mission was to construct patterns of practices for early childhood programs based on anti-bias for their own communities and as models for others. Similar to the participants in the African American cultural community, the participants in this community had historical roots in movements to change the dominant culture: the civil rights movement, the feminist movement, and the social justice movement that led to Head Start, Legal Aid, and other antipoverty programs. They were not silent on race, but reflective and self-conscious in their pathway toward antiracist practices. They were also similar to the participants in the Latino/a cultural community in not being very well integrated in their practices. For example, anti-bias practices around atypical and typical children in this larger cultural community were very diverse. And more than in any other larger cultural community, there were struggles with the parents of the children served over what were appropriate practices. But once again, lack of integration of practices is not the same as poor care. The children in these programs were doing well in the programs and beyond. And unlike the participants in the other cultural communities that served children who were and were not like the teachers in racial/ethnic background, there were no differences in positive teacher–child relationships between racially matched and not matched teacher–child dyads.

In the remainder of this chapter I analyze differences and similarities in practices and activities and interaction across the larger cultural communities of the programs. As discussed in Chapter 3, there were no differences in rated program quality or in children's behaviors in preschool and in early elementary school by ethnic, racial, or language group.

Making Comparisons

In making comparisons, I used 168 children and their teachers. There were 41 teacher–child pairs from the three programs within the Los Angeles Latino/a larger cultural community. The teachers in these pairs were all Latino/a. There were 32 teacher–child pairs from the three programs in the Los Angeles Diverse Families cultural community. All of these pairs included a Latino/a teacher. There were 24 White teacher–child pairs and 11 White teacher–African American child pairs from the two programs in the rural North Carolina larger community. In total there were 60 teacher–child pairs from the four programs within the Los Angeles African American larger cultural community. I divided these into two groups, 43 African American teacher–African American child pairs, and 17 African American teacher–Latino/a child pairs.

I compared five groups of teacher–child pairs: teacher–child pairs from the Latino/a, Diverse Families, and North Carolina cultural communities, African American teachers of African American children, and African American teachers of Latino/a children.[1] There were five comparison groups rather than four because preliminary analyses suggested that within the larger African American cultural community, teachers of African American children systematically differed from teachers of Latino/a children.

FOCUS ON PRACTICES

As discussed in Chapters 2 and 4, we identified six areas of practices within our theoretical framework: teaching and learning of pre-academic material; social competence or socialization; culture, race, and language; disability and special needs; teacher development; and parents. We consider the first three of these areas of practices to directly influence children's experiences in classrooms; we consider the teacher development and parents areas to reflect program organization rather than ways of being with children. As discussed in Chapter 4, we created descriptions of practices for each of these areas by triangulating material from field notes, interviews, and focus groups. As you read this chapter and those in Part II, refer to Table 4.1 for descriptions of practices.

Practices and Formal Education

Program participants with different levels of education are likely to describe different practices. Early childhood education has an uneasy relationship with formal education. There is a body of evidence based primarily on research from developmental psychology that informs the content of formal education for teachers of young children (Daniels & Shumov, 2003). And, not surprisingly, teacher beliefs about working with children are influenced by their exposure to formal education (Bryant, Clifford, & Peisner, 1991). Also, teachers with more education simply may have the verbal fluency to articulate more complex practices.

There is also a body of research evidence that examines how formal education in child development or early childhood education influences classroom quality ratings and children's pre-academic knowledge (Early et al., 2007; Howes et al., 2003). This literature, as discussed earlier, is contradictory and simply may suggest that formal education is not sufficient to produce effective teaching.

Even though these programs were held in high esteem by the advocates, and teacher compensation in the programs was higher than average, teachers were only relatively well paid and the education level of participants in this project was heterogeneous (Howes et al., 2003). Therefore, before analyzing differences in practices within and across programs, I examine differences in practices by participants' education levels.

The teachers who served as primary teachers, across all the programs, had more formal education than is often the case for early childhood teachers. Over half (51%) of the teacher participants had BA degrees. Somewhat over one quarter had AA degrees. Only 6% of the teachers had no college education. The rest of the teachers (16%) had college-level early childhood education units but no degree.

However, teacher credentialing in early childhood education was not distributed randomly. Teachers in the African American larger community were more highly educated than teachers in the rural North Carolina larger community, who were in turn more highly educated than teachers in the other two larger cultural communities (Latino/a and Diverse Families).[2]

We made comparisons between teachers with different levels of formal education while controlling for membership in larger cultural community.[3] There were large and meaningful differences in teachers' articulation of practices between teachers with different levels of formal education. Level of formal education appeared to be most important in the articulation of teaching and learning practices.[4] Teachers with BA degrees were more likely than all others to articulate scaffolding as a teaching and learning practice, while teachers with no college courses were more likely than all others to articulate didactic teaching and learning practices. Teachers with ECE units or AA degrees were more likely than the others to articulate child-initiated teaching and learning practices. Scaffolding is a more nuanced teaching practice than the other two. It requires attending to both what the child is doing and what the adult perceives to be the next step in the child's understanding. Being able to articulate this practice may require the same kinds of cognitive activity as completing formal education. Alternatively, instructors in lower level child development courses may consider scaffolding too complex a construct to articulate to their students.

In terms of socialization practices, the only difference was between teachers with no college and all others.[5] Teachers with no college were less likely than others to articulate a socialization practice at all. Teachers with ECE units, AA degrees, and BA degrees were equally likely to articulate behavior in school and social relationship practices. Unlike the teaching and learning practices, there were no differences in complexity between these two socialization practices.

There were also large education-level differences in articulation of practices around culture, race, and home language. Teachers with AA degrees were the most likely to articulate multicultural rather than home or American cultural practices.[6] This was the only significant difference in this area of practice between teachers with different levels of formal education. This difference suggests that as teachers progress toward an interim degree in child development, they are introduced to an interpretation of the ABC that they understand and articulate as multiculturalism. Because the majority of the teachers were in cultural communities in which race and home language were very salient, beliefs about how to teach children about these issues were salient as well. Within these communities, home and American cultural practices were core and contested beliefs. Therefore, it is not surprising that teachers with more and less formal education would have well-articulated notions of these practices.

Comparisons of Practices Across Larger Cultural Communities

To test the theoretical assumptions that practices are associated with the activities of a cultural community and that participants in a cultural community tend to be similar in their practices, we compared the patterning of practices across the five comparison groups:

1. Latino/a cultural community
2. Diverse families cultural community

3. North Carolina cultural community
4. African American teachers of African American children
5. African American teachers of Latino/a children

We made these comparisons separately for program practices and teacher-articulated practices.[7] Here I will briefly report the differences found in this analysis but defer the interpretive analysis to the chapters specifically associated with each larger cultural community.

The five groups described very different program practices.[8] It is important to note that the meaningfulness measure, effect size, for these differences between the five larger cultural communities is more than three times that for differences in formal education. This means that cultural community participation is a more important determinant of practices at the program level than is formal education. All of the program practices, except for supervision and mentoring, were different across the cultural communities.

There were also meaningful difference between the five groups in teacher-articulated practices.[9] In this case the meaningfulness measure, effect size, for cultural community was somewhat smaller than the effect size for formal education. This suggests that individual teachers, as opposed to program practices, were more influenced by formal education (and relatively less influenced by cultural community). Nevertheless, for all kinds of practices, participation in a cultural community was associated with meaningful differences.

Teaching and Learning. African American teachers of Latino/a children, followed by African American teachers of African American children, were most likely to endorse academic preparation. See Figure 5.1. Participants in the Diverse Families and North Carolina cultural communities were least likely to report academic preparation practices.[10] Participants from the North Carolina and Latino/a larger cultural communities were most likely to endorse implementing developmentally appropriate practice, while African American teachers of both African American and Latino/a children were most likely to oppose it.[11] Participants from the Diverse Families cultural community were most likely to endorse individualizing DAP.[12]

Teacher beliefs about learning followed a similar pattern. African American teachers of both African American and Latino/a children were more likely than all others to endorse didactic teaching and learning strategies rather than child-initiated strategies.[13]

Social Competence. The North Carolina and African American participants were more likely to articulate school adjustment—children learning internalized control and classroom behaviors—as a program practice.[14] See Figure 5.2. Participants from the North Carolina larger cultural community were most likely to

Figure 5.1. Comparisons of teaching and learning practices.

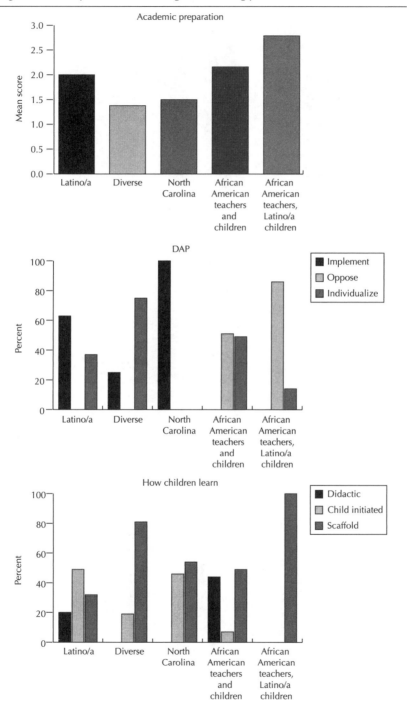

Figure 5.2. Comparisons of social competence practices.

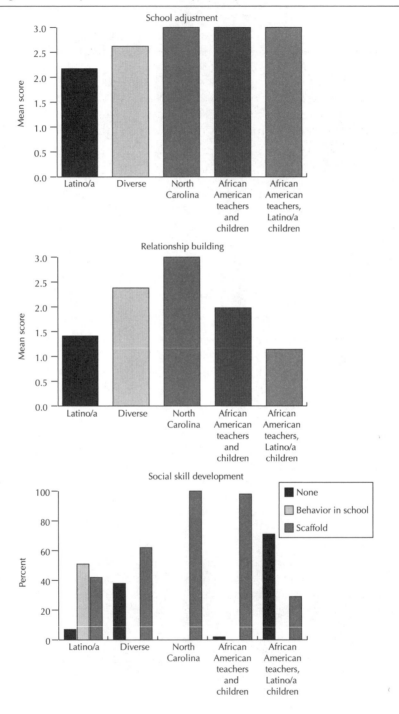

endorse relationship building as a program practice.[15] Teachers in the Latino/a larger cultural community and African American teachers of Latino/a children were most likely to articulate behaving in school as a practice.[16]

Culture, Race, and Home Language. Participants in the Diverse Families larger cultural community were most likely to endorse the Anti-Bias Curriculum as a program practice and African American teachers of African American children the least likely.[17] See Figure 5.3. Programs in North Carolina and African American teachers of African American children used only English in their classrooms. The other classrooms used a mix of English and Spanish in the classroom.[18] Twenty percent of the children in the Latino larger cultural community spoke only Spanish in their classroom. Teachers in the North Carolina larger cultural community were most likely to articulate multiculturalism practice. African American teachers of Latino/a children and Latino/a cultural community participants were most likely to articulate American culture practice. African American teachers of African American children and participants in the Diverse Families larger cultural community were most likely to articulate home culture practice.[19]

Special Needs. Program participants from the Diverse Families and North Carolina larger cultural communities were most likely to include special needs children. Participants from the Latino/a larger cultural community and African American teachers of both African American and Latino/a children were most likely to articulate practices of excluding special needs children or treating them as typical.[20]

Families. Participants in the North Carolina larger cultural community and African American teachers of Latino/a children were more likely to articulate educating families practices. Participants in the Diverse Families cultural community were most likely to articulate that they were partners with families.[21] Programs with African American teachers teaching African American children and in the Latino/a and North Carolina larger cultural communities provided more hours of child care than programs in the Diverse Families cultural community, which provided more hours than programs with African American teachers teaching Latino/a children.[22] Programs with African American teachers of Latino/a children and programs from the larger Latino/a cultural community had more of a focus on family service practices than did programs within the Diverse Families cultural community or programs with African American teachers of African American children.[23]

In summary, in all areas of practice and in almost all individual practices there were differences among teachers' and programs' articulation of practices, or ways of doing things, in their ECE programs. Overall, these differences were larger and more

Figure 5.3. Comparisons of culture, race, and home language practices.

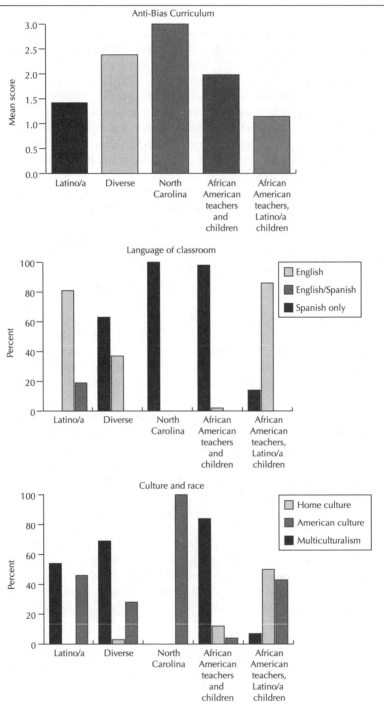

meaningful than differences due to educational backgrounds of the teachers. This pattern of findings suggests that teachers work together within their ECE programs to construct practices. Teachers similar in ethnic identity or consensus around the meaning of race and home language (as in the Diverse Families community), or similar in teaching children from a home cultural community different from their own (African American teachers of Latino/a children), create distinct sets of practices in their ECE programs. These findings are consistent with the theoretical premise of this book that within the cultural community of an ECE program participants work together to construct practices that work for them in caring for children.

ACTIVITIES AND INTERACTION

As described in Chapter 4, activities and interactions are embedded within practices. Because we found such large differences in practices between the participants from different cultural communities, we also expected to find differences in children's activities and teachers' engagement with children.

Activities

There were differences among children from different larger cultural communities in activities (how they spent their days).[24] See Figure 5.4. Children in the Latino/a and Diverse Families cultural communities spent more time hanging out than did children (both African American and Latino/a) in the African American cultural community, who in turn spent more time hanging out than did children in the North Carolina cultural community.[25] Children in the North Carolina cultural community spent more time in creative activities[26] and in fine-motor activities[27] than did children in other cultural communities. Children in the African American cultural community (both African American and Latino/a children) spent more time in didactic activity than did children in other larger cultural communities.[28]

Interactive Partners

There were differences among the participants in larger cultural communities in the proportion of the observation period during which children were engaged with peers or adults, and played alone.[29] Children were most likely to be engaged with peers if they participated in the African American cultural community and had an African American teacher, and least likely if they participated in the North Carolina cultural community.[30] Children who participated in the African American larger cultural community and had an African American teacher were most likely to be engaged with their primary caregiver,[31] and least likely to be engaged with other caregivers[32] or alone.[33]

Figure 5.4. Comparisons of children's activities across cultural communities.

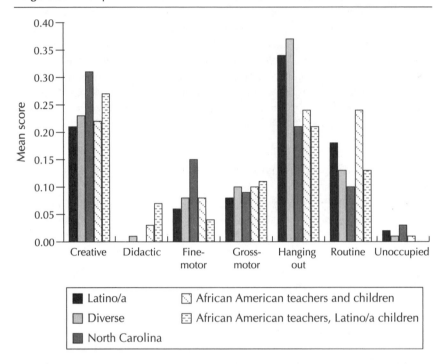

With these differences in interactive partners, it is not surprising that children in different cultural communities played differently with peers in the ECE program.[34] Children who participated in the North Carolina cultural community were more likely than other children to engage in dramatic play.[35]

Teacher Engagement and Responsive Involvement

Despite large differences in articulated practices and observed activities, teachers engaged with children in similar ways across all cultural communities. Teachers across all cultural communities were responsive to children, actively engaging them in play and learning.

In the next chapters, I will address each of the larger cultural communities in turn, describing first the social and historical context of the community, and then interpreting the differences between cultural communities in practices, activities, and teacher–child interactions. I then will go on to discuss differences within cultural communities.

ECE Programs Within Cultural Communities

Los Angeles Early Childhood Programs Within the African American Community

THE MISSION OF THE ADULT participants in the African American larger cultural community was to other-mother their children. That is, they were to implement their responsibility to raise the children in the cultural community in ways that resulted in children having positive self-identities and adaptive competence as they moved closer to the "real" world of school and racism (Collins, 1990). We will examine the pattern of providing early childhood education in the programs in this larger cultural community by focusing in turn on their social and historical context, their practices in implementing the ECE programs, and interactions among program participants.

FOCUS ON THE LARGER CULTURAL COMMUNITY

African Americans have long been the leaders within the early childhood advocates of Los Angeles, despite the decreasing numbers of African American children in the city. At the time of our work, there were many very experienced African American program directors and teachers and excellent early childhood programs serving low-income children. These historically good programs tended to be identified with a larger cultural community defined primarily by racial identity as African American. That is, the programs were developed by people who themselves identified as African American and who funded the programs (usually with public money) in order to serve well African American families and children.

One reason why African Americans have been so central to child advocacy in Los Angeles is that within the city and the rest of the United States there is a long tradition in African American families of involvement in providing excellent education for their children (Slaughter, 1988; Slaughter-Defoe, 1995; Washington, 1988). Teaching in early childhood programs and elementary and high school has long been a respected career pathway for African American women (Collins, 1990; Ladson-Billings, 1999). Furthermore, many African American educators have been instrumental in Head Start programs (Brice-Heath, 1988; Heath, 1983; Lubeck, 1985). Not surprisingly then, African Americans have been leaders within the Los Angeles community advocating for and implementing programs for young children. There were several representatives from this community on our advisory board, and we received many nominations of outstanding programs based within the African American community.

In the end we selected four programs, intentionally introducing some variety reflective of the programs for young children within the African American larger community. Two of the programs were intended to serve a historically very low-income, very race-segregated African American neighborhood, Watts. These programs were South Central and Nickerson. A third program, Love and Learn, was located in a more racially mixed and marginally more affluent neighborhood than Watts and intended to provide an alternative Afro-centric educational program for Black children rather than to serve a geographic neighborhood that was historically African American.

The fourth program was representative of an increasing demographic trend. As the proportion of Latino/a children increased and the proportion of African American children declined within the geographic area, programs that once served African American children now served Latino/as. This was the case at Ready to Learn. The program was staffed by highly educated African American women, tenured within the public school system and experienced in providing early childhood services to African American children. They became bilingual when they took on a school site composed entirely of new immigrant, primarily Mexican, monolingual Spanish-speaking families. We placed Ready to Learn within the African American larger cultural community because conversations with these teachers led us to believe that they had strong personal identification with African American education and because doing so allowed us to highlight issues around home–school bridges and racial identification.

As our theoretical framework suggested, the programs that were within African American larger cultural communities had commonalities and differences. Two programs were linked by geography and a common commitment to serving African American families in Watts. Both of these programs were conducted entirely in English. The South Central program began as part of the reconstruction of the neighborhood after the 1965 Watts riots. For more than 30 years Kaiser Hospitals Foundation had supported a multipurpose service center that included the early childhood center. The early childhood program served primarily low-income, disadvantaged families who lived in a 6-mile radius of the Watts-based center. We focused on the half-day morning ECE program intended to teach parenting skills as well as provide early education. The program was staffed almost entirely with African American women who had worked there since its inception. The one Japanese American teacher also had been in the program since it began, reflecting the fact that at one time in its history Watts was a neighborhood of African American and Japanese American families. When we studied the program, children were all African American except for one Latina child, although there are far more Latino/a children than this in the neighborhood. Over the past

2 decades, the community has shifted from predominantly African American to one equally divided between African American and Latino/a families, with more Latino/a children than African American.

South Central's early childhood program was small; 24 children attended when they were 3- and 4-years-old. The focus of the program was as much on parent development as it was on child development. The program was half-day, and there were many expectations placed on parents that required them to be present during daytime working hours, although the parents had to be in school, working, or in job training for the children to attend. Many of the families had been involved with the community center for many years. They often had already had one or more of their children in the program and/or had been in the program themselves as children.

Almost within walking distance from South Central was Nickerson, our second program in Watts. Nickerson was physically located within Nickerson Gardens, a very large public housing project. In the mid-1980s Congresswoman Maxine Waters had had a vision to build a child care center in the project. She organized the Black Women's Forum to implement this vision. The Nickerson Gardens residents embraced the idea and worked closely with Project Build, Black Women's Forum, and Crystal Stairs, the local child care resource and referral agency, to make the dream a reality.

The result of that work was a landscaped, fenced area with five bungalows and two playgrounds, which served up to 112 children ages 5 to 12, 243 days a year. Although the kindergartners we studied went to the local elementary school for their 2-½-hour school day, they spent most of the day at Nickerson. The program opened at 7:00 a.m. with a full classroom of children. Morning and afternoon kindergarten groups were delivered to school and brought back. At 2:00 in the afternoon the two kindergarten groups joined together at Nickerson and stayed until 5:00 or 6:00 in evening. All of the children and many of the teaching staff lived in the housing project.

The program participants at Nickerson believed that meeting the needs of a low-income community required a program that welcomed parents, allowed them to work and at the same time feel that their children were safe, eating wholesome food, completing homework, and playing. Children were viewed as capable and resilient, but also as vulnerable, needing care and guidance. The program staff, particularly the charismatic director, made clear that their high expectations for both parents and children included first enacting strong cultural, community, and family values. The director and an equally charismatic kindergarten head teacher actively taught children to change their stereotypes around issues such as culture, gender orientation, shade of skin, and intellectual ability.

Like South Central, Nickerson was a program deeply rooted in African American racial identity. Nickerson also had only one Latino/a child. Both the child and her parents were fluent in English. During a feedback session we conducted at

Nickerson, the director articulated that her intention was to serve well African American children rather than use the NAEYC Anti-Bias Curriculum, which she considered too multicultural in its approach. We did not know then of the one Latino/a child so missed our opportunity to ask about serving others in the community. That same day we did a feedback session at South Central, where the director asked us to talk about what other programs did in their anti-bias work and wondered how the program might change if they served Latino/a children.

Ready to Learn, in contrast, was an early childhood program within the African American cultural community that was in the process of having its African American children completely replaced by Latino/a children. By the late 1990s, school readiness language development programs had been sponsored by the Los Angeles Unified School District for over 2 decades. They were dedicated to helping children acquire the language and literacy skills that the teachers believed best prepared them for kindergarten. They were an exceptionally well-funded Title 1 set of programs located within elementary schools. Unlike the Children's Centers (El Peace) and State Preschool Programs (Pierce) to be discussed in Chapter 7, Ready to Learn did not have to worry about funding. It was structurally part of the elementary school and was not licensed as a child care program, and thus could have more children per teacher than a Children's Center program. Furthermore, its teaching staff had to have elementary school rather than child care credentialing. For the two African American teachers at Ready to Learn who had BAs as well as California teaching credentials, and who had been teaching in the same classrooms for several decades, having all monolingual Spanish-speaking children in their classrooms meant getting a bilingual teaching credential and a salary increase.

Ready to Learn, like South Central, was a half-day program that served parents as well as children. Forty-five children came in the morning, and 45 in the afternoon, 4 days a week, for an elementary school academic year. On Friday the parents came to school and the teachers did home visits. The 3-½- to 5-year-old children were there because their parents lined up early in the morning, months before school started, to enroll them. Parents and their children stayed in the program provided that the parents completed lots of paperwork, showed up at the times required by the program, and completed ten sessions of parent education and weekly volunteer hours. All of these parental responsibilities were justified by the teachers as important to giving their children the opportunity to get ready for school.

And the children did get ready for school. The program was designed to immerse children in a language-rich environment. The days and weeks were highly structured around activities that involved the children in speaking, prereading and prewriting. The program was conducted in both Spanish and English. Children had homework, organized by parents into homework packets. Large baggies filled with all necessary supplies and bilingual instructions for creative and interesting science experiments, art projects, reading activities, and math games went home with the children. Children were expected to take very good care of these packets, complete them with parents at home, and bring them back on time.

Love and Learn, our final program in the African American larger community, also took schoolwork very seriously. It was an African American academic academy that offered full-day care for 60 children ages 2 through 14. Children arrived as early as 6:45 a.m. and remained for up to 9 hours. They ate hot meals and healthy snacks prepared for them at the site. For full-day child care, as well as meals and schooling, the weekly cost was just over $100 in 1996 dollars. For some of the families who brought their children there, this was a significant cost, which meant that they chose to make the education of their children a strong economic priority. For others, the cost did not challenge the family budget, but the parents chose the education and underlying philosophy of this school, even though they had the economic ability to make other choices. Scholarships were available to a small number of families, and other poor families came to the school through a state-funded child care voucher program.

The primary costs of the program, including the beautiful physical plant, were a gift from the director's family. The director, a faculty member at a local community college and a leader in the Los Angeles child advocacy community, had a strong, well-articulated philosophy that young children are capable of learning far more academic content than most early childhood educators advocate. She passionately believed that African American children deserved a highly structured, content-rich approach to learning. In common with the children at Nickerson, children at Love and Learn were to obey and respect adults. Manners were important, but even more so, children were valued and loved by the adult program participants. The families served at Love and Learn were all African American, as were almost all of the teachers. As was true at Nickerson and South Central, children were taught to value African American cultural activities rather than a multicultural approach.

The four participating programs within the African American cultural community served an average of 72 children; all of the programs were relatively large. The children were mostly 4- and 5-year-olds, except for the 2-year-olds at Love and Learn and the kindergartners at Nickerson. All but one of the African American teachers who participated in our research taught at one of these four programs. Seventy-seven percent of the children were African American children taught by African American teachers. The other 23% were the Latino/a children taught by African American teachers at Ready to Learn.

FOCUS ON PRACTICES

In this next section of the chapter I focus on practices that were distinctive within the African American cultural community. As discussed in Chapter 5, I analyzed as two separate groups the African American teachers with Latino/a children at Ready to Learn and African American teachers who taught African American children at the other three programs.

Teaching and Learning of Pre-Academic Material

The participants in the African American cultural community were the most likely of all participants to endorse an academic approach to teaching and learning, and the African American teachers of Latino/a children were the strongest in their endorsement of these academic practices. They had the highest academic preparation scores in the sample. In the words of the director of Ready to Learn:

> So I think the Ready to Learn program or working in the program really gives them a head start on social skills, particularly oral language skills, before they go to kindergarten. And many of the kindergarten teachers have told us [that] it makes a difference [for both] the ones who have been in school and the ones who are just coming for the first time.

Delpit (1988) argues that African American teachers are likely to endorse and enact teacher-directed learning as part of an adaptive cultural response to African American children struggling with elementary school classrooms constructed around a White middle-class style of learning. Our findings of higher academic preparation scores for participants in the African American cultural community are consistent with these sentiments. Our discussions with the participants from Ready to Learn suggest that, like the teachers described by Delpit (1988) and Ladson-Billings (1999), these teachers believed that their job required equipping children with practical tools to help them survive in an unreceptive school environment.

Teacher beliefs about teaching and learning are consistent with the programs' strong focus on academic preparation. Participants in the African American larger cultural community who taught African American children tended to articulate didactic or teacher-directed teaching, while participants in the African American larger cultural community teaching Latino/a children tended to endorse scaffolding. Recall that the African American teachers of Latino/a children had the most formal education of teachers in the sample. As a result, articulating scaffolding as a teaching and learning belief may have been easier for them. This construct and the words to articulate it tend to be associated with more advanced education (Early & Winton, 2001).

Participants in the African American larger community were most likely of all participants to oppose implementing DAP, again, particularly the African American teachers of Latino children. The director at Love and Learn made this position very clear:

I think an African American program would need to be more academic and more structured than the developmentally appropriate curriculum. I would look at that as a White curriculum.

There is, of course, a difference between talking about a practice, intending to implement it, and actually implementing it. Our participant observations suggest that academic preparation and didactic, teacher-directed practices around teaching and learning were strong in only three of the four programs in the African American larger community. South Central shared with Mission Hope in the Latino/a larger cultural community a history of involvement with early childhood training professionals who entered the community as outsiders to teach what the experts believed about child development. In the case of South Central this contact occurred when the program began, in the late 1960s. Quite remarkably, the director and teachers who were trained during that period are still working in the program.[1] The South Central director, approaching retirement age at the end of the time of our project, was enthusiastic about any reports that our research team provided to her. Perhaps because of this history, South Central participants firmly believe both that children should play—that young children's learning is based on play—and that they should be academically prepared. Thus, practices within a larger cultural community are shared and contested, in part due to the social histories and experiences of the participants.

Social Competence

Participants in the African American larger cultural community were more likely than other participants to articulate social competence practices around school adjustment. Wanting children to have a script for school was consistent with endorsing academic preparation practices.

Again, there were differences within the African American cultural community between the teachers of African American and Latino/a children. The teachers of African American children were more likely to articulate social relationship practices than were the teachers of Latino/a children. These findings highlight an emphasis on social as well as academic competence in African American teachers of African American children. It appears that two theories of social development—relationship building and social skills training—co-existed in the practices of African American teachers of African American children. This illustrates both the complex and well-integrated cultural transformation of traditional early childhood educational practices within the programs of the African American larger community and the challenges to this pattern of practices when adult participants in the community taught other than African American children.

The emphasis that African American teachers of African American children placed on relationship-based social competence is consistent with other literature that finds dramatic play and storytelling to be part of cultural socialization between African American caregivers and children (Haight, 1999; Reilly, 1992). In one of our interviews, an African American teacher of African American children at Love and Learn explained that she interpreted her role as helping children to elaborate their dramatic play.

> Someone should monitor how far they go with dramatic play. I had one kid walk up to me saying, "Ms. G., guess what?" I said, "What?" She said, "Jennifer is going to have a baby right now." "Wait a minute," I said. "We have to wait until we get to a hospital."

Culture, Race, and Home Language

English was the classroom language of the programs for African American children in the African American cultural community. And within this community, stressing home culture, including language, was very important—so much so that, as mentioned previously, two of the programs had serious reservations about the NAEYC Anti-Bias Curriculum. We interpret the reservations of one of the programs (Love and Learn) to be part of a general distancing from NAEYC and, in its eyes, all "progressive education." As its director said, "I would look at that as a White curriculum." The other program (Nickerson) had an appreciation of the anti-bias aspects of the ABC, but believed that its main responsibility was to teach children about the African American experience rather than to give them an appreciation of other cultures.

As part of their determination to have "their children" succeed in school, the Spanish–English bilingual African American teachers at Ready to Learn used only enough Spanish to help the children to adjust to the program at the beginning of the year. They introduced English as rapidly as possible to prepare the children to learn in the English-only kindergarten classrooms that awaited them the next year.

These same teachers had the strongest articulation of the cultural belief practices we called American culture. American cultural beliefs are that children need to change to become like the dominant culture in order to be ready for school. The teachers passionately articulated their perception that the elementary school was not willing to adjust to "their" children, and recounted their multiple failed efforts over many, many years to make the school's approach to children more like early childhood education. They also told stories of how their children "failed" in kindergarten and how they worked to make sure that this did not happen. The practice of American culture is certainly consistent with their approach to classroom language. They expected their children to be ready to speak English in kindergarten because they knew that Spanish would be forbidden and they wanted their children to succeed.

The Ready to Learn teachers, unlike the other participants in the African American larger cultural community, implemented the Anti-Bias Curriculum. We attribute this practice to their educational background. The African American teachers of Latino/a children were extremely well versed in traditional early childhood educational practices, including the ABC. Just as they worked passionately to change their children to meet the perceived standards of the school district, they monitored and implemented traditional best practices for early childhood education in their classrooms. We also interpret this endorsement and use of the ABC as a strategy that is readily available to teachers who both value equity and teach children whom they perceive as different from themselves.

Children with Special Needs

There were large inconsistencies among participants in the African American larger cultural community in practices around children with special needs. Love and Learn excluded these children, while the other programs made no distinctions between special needs and typical children. Ready to Learn participants had the services of the school system available for special needs children, and perhaps some of the children's language issues could have classified them into the system. Given that services were available, we found it interesting that these teachers did not discuss their children as special needs children. Rather, they treated all of the children at Ready to Learn as not being ready for school primarily because of language and family background. In essence, they did not treat them differently from typical children in a good early childhood intervention program. As we will see in the next section, these teachers identified more closely with intervention than child care; this may be the key to their approach to special needs children.

Families

The participants in the African American larger community who taught African American children provided more hours of child care than any other participants. Indeed, these children averaged 9.1 hours per day in child care, an average of 2 hours more per day than other children. This is remarkable, given that one of the programs included in this average cared for children while they were not in kindergarten and another had a half-day program.

This practice of providing full-day child care is consistent with an African American community practice whereby nonbiological mothers share the responsibility for the upbringing of children (Collins, 1990). Cultural community participants who define themselves as other-mothers believe that by taking on the responsibility for other people's children, they are helping children survive and fight racial oppression and discrimination. Embedded in this belief system is the belief that the community, not the child bearer, decides how the child will mature into a member of the society.

The people here take very good care of their children and their sisters'
children, their neighbors' children, and anybody else's children around
here. So that is one thing that has really helped me here at Nickerson
because I know I'm in here without any real blood ties, but I also take care
of the children.

Interestingly, African American teachers of Latino/a children were the least
likely to endorse full-day child care. Ready to Learn was open for the shortest
number of hours per day—3.6 hours, the same as kindergarten—and available for
children only 4 days a week. The short program and short week were not perceived as a problem within this program, and we doubt that these teachers would
have ever defined their program as a child care program. They were physically
housed in a school and, as described above, articulated practices around getting
children ready for school as a priority. And as we will see, the program expected
mothers or other family members to be available during the workday hours. This
suggests that they did not extend the notion of other-mothering to children not
matched to them in ethnicity, despite their loving and fierce determination to get
them ready for school.

There were also consistent differences between participants in the African
American cultural community who taught African American children and those
who taught Latino/a children in practices relating to the families of the children.
African American teachers of African American children endorsed the practice
of becoming partners with families twice as often as they endorsed educating family
practices. In contrast, African American teachers of Latino/a children unanimously
endorsed educating parents. The notion of educating as opposed to partnering with
families carries with it an idea that the parents as well as the children need to change
to accommodate to some external standard if the children are to be ready for school.
In the words of one of the Ready to Learn participants, the parents are not quite as
they should be in order for the children to succeed:

The interviewer asks: Do you think what you do here is different some-
how from what happens at home?
    The head teacher replies: Yes, I definitely think it is. Mainly because
so many of our parents are so—I don't know—not that they are not good
parents. I think all of them genuinely love their child. They just don't
know how to talk to children or what kinds of things to expect, what to do.
And by the end of the year, we can see a big, big change in what happens
at home. So I think even little things like teaching the children to be
independent and teaching them to make choices, just being able to hang
up their coats and open their lunch boxes and button their coats, whatever.
At home the mom thinks that they are her babies and they treat them like
babies. A lot of us who have children at home, we know about homework
and we know that they need to have a well-lighted place and a comfort-

able place to do their homework and they should do it every day, and we know to review the homework, and we know to talk about what they did in school today. But I know a lot of these parents were not successful in school, did not enjoy school, maybe dropped out of school, and had children very, very young. So they don't know how to build up schooling and to make school a positive place in their children's lives. So, yes, I think it's a lot different than what happens at home, but hopefully by the end of the year school and home are getting a little close.

We read these words of the African American teachers of Latino/a children as a rejection of other-mothering of these children who are unlike themselves in race and ethnicity. The teachers at Ready to Learn see their roles less as being available to care for the children, and more as making sure that the children will succeed in school by changing them and their families.

These same African American teachers of Latino/a children had the highest level of endorsement of parent education of any participants. It appears that the participating African American teachers of Latino/a children recognized the need to bridge between school and home, but envisioned the bridge as moving in one direction—from school to home. Education and services should flow to the home in order to change it in ways that make home and school a seamless set of influences on children's learning.

This is a big contrast from the approach of the African American teachers of African American children toward families. One teacher from Love and Learn told us:

I just feel that parents obviously want their children to be at the school. We talk to them about their children if they want to talk, but primarily we provide a safe and good place for their children to be while they are at work.

And as the director at Nickerson put it, "Our job is to be part of this community of caring for children."

African American teachers of African American children could draw on an old and well-articulated set of practices around other-mothering of the children in their community. They both felt responsible for the children of the community and saw the children's parents as simply having a different set of responsibilities within a partnership designed to instill adaptive competence.

FOCUS ON THE INTERPERSONAL

We now shift the kaleidoscope to focus on the interpersonal,[2] against the background of high quality and the particular practices just described. We begin with a description of how children spent their days in the programs, based on our field notes and case histories, and continue with descriptions of patterns of interaction based on naturalistic observations.

How Children Spent Their Days in the Programs

The daily activities within the programs varied within this larger cultural community. At Love and Learn, children were in very large rooms, and there were group sizes of 20 or so children. But although the numbers of children were impressive to our observer, what was more salient was how the children and the teachers were busy and engaged. Children sat in small chairs at tables with one teacher directing their activities: practicing long and short vowel sounds, reading words and small books, filling in pages with neat cursive writing, doing math problems, and reciting in unison. On the outside playground the children were just as intensely involved in playing as they had been inside in academic learning. There was a whirl of bikes, balls, and baskets; sandbox digging; and pretend play in a castle structure. Outside the children did a lot of talking and pretending. Inside they were quieter, talking only in response to a teacher.

Inside South Central, children worked, often alone or in small groups, at activity centers. They had a computer lab and a science center as well as the tables of fine-motor manipulatives, cozy corner with books, and dress-up and kitchen areas more commonly seen in early childhood programs. Teachers rotated among these areas, at times watching, at times participating with the children, but never leaving play unmonitored. Every day teachers and children formed small groups to listen to "Big Book" stories (written so children can easily focus on print) and engage in open-ended and teacher-guided discussions about the story.

The kindergarten children at Nickerson were brought to the program early, in time to eat breakfast before being taken to school. When they came back from school they had a healthy home-cooked meal waiting for them, and no child left at the end of the day hungry. Ms. P., the kindergarten head teacher, was a retired kindergarten teacher. She was ready and available to help with homework right after school or later in the afternoon, but children had the choice of just playing when they got back to the center. Teachers in the program focused their attention on conversations about how things were going rather than on making sure homework was done. There was a dynamic feeling in the room. There was always a lot to play with. Afro-centric music played at all times. Most children spent some of their time in the computer lab and at the art tables. There was also plenty of time and space for curling up in a chair to read or to take a nap, and plenty of outdoor room for running, sliding, and swinging.

At Ready to Learn teachers, not children, were in charge of the schedule, the activities, and the pace of the day. For the teachers, language development was key to future school success and therefore they organized multiple opportunities for children to express themselves through songs, stories, writing, art, puppets, and play. For part of the day, children could choose to be in a learning center. But the learning centers were organized and set up by the teachers in line with their goals that the children use language and gain emergent literacy skills. There was no down time in this short program. Children could not choose not to participate in the activities of the day. Teachers also spent much of their time working with parents in the classroom with the children and in parenting education classes. They taught the parents activities to do with their children at home and made home visits to see how the home activities were progressing.

Observations of Teacher–Child Pairs

What They Were Doing: Activity Settings. Although the participants in the African American larger community—both with African American and with Latino/a children—particularly articulated the importance of language arts, they were no different from the other participants in observed time spent in language arts. They were, however, the only participants in the study whom we observed engaged in didactic activities. The amount of time spent in didactic activities was very small, only on average 3% of the time, but they were the only set of participants to engage in this practice with any frequency at all. This finding is consistent with the previous discussion of the articulation of academic practices and the general emphasis on formal education within this larger cultural community.

With Whom: The Participants in Interaction. There were striking differences in interaction partners between the child participants in the African American larger cultural community and the other child participants. The African American participants were more likely to be involved with peers and with their primary caregivers, were less likely to be with the other teachers, and were rarely alone. These findings highlight the importance of being part of a social group within these programs. They also may reflect early socialization toward the pleasures and responsibilities associated with other-mothering.

Some African American scholars have criticized attachment theory as irrelevant in contexts where significant numbers of children are cared for by people who are not their mothers (Jackson, 1993). In our interpretation of attachment theory, other-than-mothers as well as mothers are considered attachment figures. In this context we find it particularly noteworthy that the African American child participants taught by African American teachers spent far more time with their primary caregivers than they did with other teachers in the programs, maintaining proximity to the primary caregivers rather than to adults at random. As we will see below, these teacher–child pairs were also the most likely to be securely attached (although not significantly more so than ethnically matched teacher–child pairs from other cultural communities) of any of the pairs in the sample.

How They Were Interacting

Children. On average, child participants in the African American larger cultural community spent almost all of their time engaged with objects. Even when the stated intentions of the program were academic learning and when children were not expected to learn by play, they still played with objects. The following excerpt comes from field notes at Love and Learn:

> Unlike in most preschools where children can choose from shelves full of toys, at Love and Learn children are not to get their own materials from the shelves. That is the responsibility of a teacher. Today a group of children was offered a crate full of Legos. The teacher gave a small pile of Lego pieces to each child, not really enough to do much with. The children then spent most of their time in the activity trading pieces. Eventually all of the children had the pieces they needed and the structures produced were quite creative.

Child participants in the African American cultural community were similar to child participants in other cultural communities in spending about one quarter of their time in dramatic activities, with and without toys, and with and without peers. This is quite remarkable, given that their teachers were noteworthy for articulating practices around academic activities. This amount of time in pretend play illustrates our contention that in these programs, early childhood education includes preparing for school and for social relationships.

Teachers. African American teachers participating in the African American cultural community were extremely responsively involved with the children in the teacher–child pairs, remarkably so compared with representative child care programs (Howes et al., 2003). African American teachers of African American children were highly likely to facilitate peer interaction. This is consistent with the teachers' endorsement of practices around constructing positive relationships and socializing children to be part of a social group responsible for one another.

FOCUS ON THE CHILDREN

Child participants in the African American larger cultural community were competent, according to our research criteria. Three quarters of the children constructed secure child–teacher relationships and almost all of the children were rated as competent in peer and object play.

A story told in a focus group by one of the African American teachers provides a context for these very high scores for child competence. The focus group was discussing practices around separation from parents at the beginning of the year. One teacher discussed the rule in her program (Love and Learn) that no child, and particularly not the young and just beginning 2-year-olds taught by this teacher, could bring into the program any toys or other objects from home. This policy was consistent with the mission of the program to emphasize academic learning. Part of preparing children for school included children's learning how to be at school: wearing uniforms, not talking with one another inside, forming lines, and having homework. The teacher argued that having children carrying around things from home distracted from the main goal of academic preparation.

The other teacher members of the focus group expressed a fair amount of concern with this policy, arguing that the emotional distress of the separation was eased when children could come to the program with their "lovies." With a great deal of surprise at these concerns, the Love and Learn teacher responded that it was no problem at all and not the point of this discussion. The other teachers pressed on: Didn't she understand that these children were practically babies, that they needed sensitive and warm responses, that they needed loving as well as learning? Oh, responded the teacher, that is of course true, and she (of course) simply let the children bring their "lovies" to her and she attached them to her chest and became a walking transitional object. She stood up and demonstrated how she looked with all those blankets and stuffed toys pinned onto her. She explained that she had no intention of ever letting a child in her group feel unloved or unlovable.

African American teacher–child pairs were more likely to construct a secure attachment relationship than African American teacher–Latino/a child pairs. Seventy percent of the African American teacher–child pairs and 55% of the African American–Latino/a child pairs were rated as secure. Fifty-five percent is a larger percentage than found in more representative child care programs (Howes & Ritchie, 1999), yet the teachers in the Ready to Learn program were concerned that it was too low. In response, they reorganized their program days so that children were assigned to work with a primary caregiver more often. At their request, we returned to the program 6 months later to assess the differences following this change and found no change in security scores. This finding, that the children in the Ready to Learn program were not as trusting of their African American teachers as were the African American children taught by teachers like themselves, brings us back to the issues of home–school bridging and adaptive competence. It also illustrates that it is not one practice (assignment to caregivers or not) but the pattern of practices that influences child development.

SUMMARY

The African American participants who worked entirely within the African American cultural community (taught African American children and worked with

African American parents) articulated and implemented early childhood educational practices designed to enhance cognitive and social development as well as adaptive competence in their children. These participants gave their children a structured academic preparation for kindergarten as they prepared them for the social responsibility of being part of a larger social community in which elders are respected and mothers are expected to take responsibility for all the children of their community. Children were taught to count and to sound out letters and words as they played and pretended.

The African American teachers of African American children worked within the tradition of other-mothering. If their cultural community was to survive, then they had to care for all the children of the community. Recall that the director at Nickerson said that the parents were doing the best they could in extremely difficult circumstances. If that meant that the child got most of her mothering—her meals as well as her hugs—in the program, then the program had to take on this responsibility and let the parent be as she was.

The Latino/a children and families were a challenge within the African American larger cultural community. We are all too aware that we worked with only one program that faced this challenge.[3] However, in our eyes, the participants in this program demonstrated a fierceness similar to the other teacher participants in wanting the children succeed in a hostile world. However, their stance was not as other-mothers, but more as responsible professionals. Their practice was extremely well articulated, and their intentions honorable, but we found that their relative difficulties in forming a secure bridge from home to school created difficulties for enhancing children's ability to use their secure and trusting relationships with teachers to organize their learning in school.

Early Childhood Programs Within the Latino/a Larger Cultural Community

THIS CHAPTER DESCRIBES the patterns of practices of the Latino/a larger cultural community. Latino/a children are the largest proportion of the child participants in this sample, reflective of the increasing number of Latino/a children in Los Angeles. The early childhood programs in this larger cultural community were all in Los Angeles.

FOCUS ON THE LARGER CULTURAL COMMUNITY

At the time of our work 62% of the births in Los Angeles County were to Latina mothers (Ball Cuthbertson, Burr, Fuller, & Hirshberg, 2000). In the late 1990s Latino/as had the highest labor force participation rate in Los Angeles (69%), so large numbers of Latino/a children needed child care while their parents worked. Also, 43% of Latino/a children in Los Angeles were living in poverty, the county's highest poverty rate (Ball Cuthbertson et al., 2000). Thus the overwhelming majority of children, particularly poor children, in the age range for early childhood education programs in Los Angeles were Latino/a.

These demographic figures are reflected within our selected Los Angeles programs. All but one of the programs (Love and Learn was the exception) enrolled Latino/a children. These demographic trends suggested that most of the children in our Los Angeles programs would be part of a larger cultural community based on Latino/a heritage. Yet this was not the case, and a historical explanation is necessary to understand why. At the time of our work, there were, relative to the proportion of Latino/a children in Los Angeles, few child advocates whose primary ethnic identity was Latino/a, and few center-based programs that identified themselves as representing the Latino/a community. However, in seeming contradiction, the teaching staff within early childhood programs across the city was increasingly Latino/a. Latino/as may be moving into teaching in early childhood because position openings at the assistant or aide level require little formal education or English-language ability. This increase in Latino/a teachers also may be fueled by widely held perceptions that Latino/as make good caregivers (Hondagneu-Sotelo, 2001).

So why are there so few early childhood programs that represent themselves as serving the Latino/a community? The answer may lie in the historical differential in public dollars, in public perceptions of Latino/a child care values, and in the tremendous variation in Latino/as within Los Angeles.

California provides relatively large monetary support for child care. The first wave of funding dating back to the 1940s provided, and continues to provide on a contract basis, relatively well-supported, center-based, full-day programs based in public schools—the Children's Centers. Another wave of funding in the mid-1960s provided, and continues to provide, contracts for half-day prekindergarten programs for 4-year-olds, again in the public schools. Contracts for center-based, full-day child care programs in community agencies were funded at much lower rates in the 1970s, and various welfare reform efforts since then led to a voucher system. The vouchers, called the alternative payments program, are need-based, are administered through state-supported child care referral agencies, and can be used for any form of child care. The dramatic increase in the number of Latino/a children in Los Angeles occurred after the initial funding of center-based programs with contracts with the State Department of Education and when it was almost impossible to get a new contract for these programs. As discussed in Chapter 6, African Americans tended to be the program directors and teachers in the programs both within the school district and in community agencies. New programs had to rely instead on the voucher system, a far less stable and reliable source of public monies.

There is a widely held public perception in Los Angeles and elsewhere that Latina mothers prefer home-based rather than center-based child care. Latina mothers who work full-time are indeed less likely to use center-based care than are African American or White families (Fuller, Holloway, & Liang, 1996). However, using a particular form of child care does not necessarily imply a preference. The usage figures simply may mean that there is an insufficient supply of center-based care in Latino/a neighborhoods, and in Los Angeles there is documentation that this explanation is true (Fuller, Holloway, Bozzi, Burr, Cohen, & Suzuki, 2003; Fuller et al., 1996; Liang, Fuller, & Singer, 2000).

The relative lack of Latino/a programs also may reflect the heterogeneity of the Latino/a community in Los Angeles. This heterogeneity includes diverse migration histories; extremely variable educational backgrounds prior to migration; extent of geographic isolation after migration, as there are parts of Los Angeles where Spanish is the dominant language; and contested beliefs about using Spanish. Not all Latino/as in Los Angeles are immigrants; some of the children born to Latina mothers are the fourth or fifth generation of their family in Los Angeles. Migration history alone influences beliefs about child care. For example, in Los Angeles Latina mothers born outside the United States were more likely to express a preference for licensed child care centers than were either U.S.-born Latina or Anglo mothers (Buriel & Hurtado-Ortiz, 2000).

Latino/as come from many different countries, and the country of origin often is tied to their reason for migration. In particular, Latino/a immigrants from Central America are more likely than immigrants from Mexico to have come to the United States for political asylum rather than economic reasons. El Salvadoran immigrants are likely to enter the United States with relatively high levels of formal education and often professional training, whereas Mexican immigrants, particularly from rural areas, are likely to enter the United States with almost no formal education. Across the United States, Latino/a country of origin and formal education differences influence family values around child care (Cauce & Domenech-Rodriquez, 2002; Chavez, 1989; Roosa, Morgan-Lopez, Cree, & Specter, 2002).

While *educado*—a socialization goal for children to be attuned to social relationships and respectfully attentive to the teaching, directions, and advice of elders—is important for many Latino/as, it may have different meanings for immigrants with different heritages and different levels of formal education. For a mother or a teacher's aide with only a rural elementary school education, *educado* may imply, "I can only help my children develop good social relationships; academic instruction is to be left to the teachers" (Galimore, Goldenberg, & Weisner, 1993). For a teacher who was trained to be a teacher in El Salvador, it may mean instilling social relationships as she teaches pre-academic skills.

Not all Latino/as in Los Angeles speak Spanish at home. Latino/as in Los Angeles who speak English at home are more likely to enroll their children in center care than are Latino/as with Spanish as their home language (Liang et al., 2000). And whether or not to speak Spanish at home may be contested across generations at home (Orellana, Reynolds, Dorner, & Meza, 2003). Sometimes only the elders of the family speak Spanish, and sometimes the elders in the family forbid children to speak English. And, as we will see, whether to teach very young children in English or Spanish is contested by program participants within early childhood programs (Winsler, Diaz, Espinoza, & Rodriguez, 1999).

Our selection of programs for young Latino/a children reflected these variations in Los Angeles Latino/as, most of whom are Mexican in origin. However, Mexican-heritage families in Los Angeles reflect far more than one distinct group. One Mexican-heritage cultural community is represented in this study by the El Peace program and includes mostly families who have lived in this geographic neighborhood for several generations. Many of the parents of the children at El Peace had gone to El Peace as children themselves and graduated from high school in Los Angeles. The parents tended to be Spanish–English bilingual, but until recently this particular community was primarily Spanish speaking at home and in the neighborhood. Both Spanish and English were used at school. Passage of a state law that requires English to be the language of schools was changing this, but as we conducted our research, the Mexican-heritage children enrolled in El Peace all spoke Spanish at home and were learning English in school.

A second, more recent immigration from Mexico is reflected in the Pierce program. Although the program director was third generation in a long established and relatively tiny Mexican-heritage neighborhood on the westside of Los Angeles, the children served at Pierce were part of a new wave of immigrants, primarily from rural areas of Mexico. These children were also monolingual Spanish speaking both at home and at school, but unlike the children at El Peace, their parents had little experience with schooling past elementary school, in the United States or in Mexico.

The final program from the larger Latino cultural community of Los Angeles, Mission Hope, was established to serve another group of new immigrants, primarily Central American. These children were also monolingual Spanish speakers, but their parents were more likely to have had high school and in many cases college experiences prior to migration. And because this program was new, it was, paradoxically, less isolated from the larger ECE advocacy community than the other two programs, which were within school districts. For example, during the very beginnings of this program, a graduate student of mine worked for several years as a volunteer, not in the program with the children, but helping to sort through the paperwork and permits necessary to establish the center.

Beyond serving different segments of the Los Angeles Latino community, the three programs had distinct social histories. Not only did El Peace represent the most established Latino/a families, but as a Children's Center within the Los Angeles Unified School District (LAUSD) it had long-term public financing. To elaborate on the brief history offered above, California's Children's Centers were established as full-day child care centers during World War II. They are funded through the State Department of Education's Child Development Division (CDD) through subcontracts. In Los Angeles, all of the Children's Centers are contracted through LAUSD. El Peace, more than other LAUSD Children's Centers, was very successful in supplementing its basic operating budget by adding other publicly funded programs—a half-day State Preschool Program and an after-school program, also funded through the CDD, as well as a Special Education Inclusion Program, a bilingual program, and a school–community improvement program, funded through LAUSD. El Peace was physically located on the same campus as an LAUSD elementary school and had a good relationship with the school. The program was the largest one included in our sample. It served 200 children, with no more than 114 present at one time.

The early childhood program at El Peace had a long shared history with the geographically proximal long-time Latino/a community. Most (74%) of the 11 teaching staff were Latino/a and, unusual for a Children's Center, the program director was Latino/a. All of these participants, including the director, had been at the program for over a decade (in some cases more than 2 decades). Many of the teaching staff began working at the center as untrained women from the neighborhood and had, over the years, taken classes and obtained their early childhood education units, promotions, and job security at the center. These women often talked knowledgeably about earlier neighborhood children and about the children of those first children that they had taught over the years.

In addition to the Latino/a teaching staff, there was a White male teacher (the only male teacher who participated in the project); a special education teacher, whose position was funded by LAUSD Special Education money and who worked with the other teachers on inclusion; and a Chinese-immigrant teacher. Although the program was located in a Latino/a neighborhood, it was adjacent to Los Angeles's Chinatown. So many new Cantonese-speaking immigrant families wanted the Children's Center services for their children that, with the help of bilingual program money, one classroom served Cantonese-speaking children while the others served neighborhood Spanish-speaking children.

Pierce shared with El Peace its roots in a long-established Latino/a neighborhood and its funding through the public schools. The director at Pierce had a personal story shared by many teachers at El Peace; she too was a Latina neighborhood woman who started working in the kitchen of her neighborhood elementary school, gravitated to the children's program at that school, earned her early childhood credentials, and became both a highly respected member of the child advocacy community on the westside of Los Angeles and a beloved spiritual grandmother to the generations of teachers she had trained at her program. Pierce was funded as a part-day State Preschool Program through the Santa Monica Public School System. It too was located on the grounds of an elementary school. As at El Peace, Spanish often was used in teacher–child and child–child interaction, and English was taught to the children as well. But the similarities with El Peace ended there.

Pierce was tiny. It enrolled 32 children, 16 in the morning and 16 in the afternoon. Physically it was a small bungalow, surrounded by a garden and play yard, and separated from the elementary school by a fence. The fence was more than physical; relationships with the school were at times problematic, and the program was seen as an outsider to the school more often than at El Peace. The older Mexican-immigrant neighborhood in which Pierce's director grew up and raised her children was disappearing. Now the surrounding neighborhood was filled with expensive, single-family houses owned by very affluent White and Asian American families whose children made up most of the elementary school population. In fact, if Pierce could not find enough poor children to fill its program, more affluent families could purchase a "slot," and each year some did.

The Latino/a children at Pierce lived in a small neighborhood that was surrounded by a freeway and connector roads. This neighborhood was geographically isolated from the rest of the residential section of town and barely within walking distance of Pierce. Immigrant Mexican families lived there because it was the only housing they could afford due to rent control and public housing in this section of the city.

Mission Hope, the third program within the larger Los Angeles Latino/a cultural community, was, like El Peace, located on the eastside of Los Angeles, within a neighborhood historically home to generations of primarily Mexican immigrants. But, unlike the other two programs within the Latino/a cultural community, Mission Hope was relatively young (10 years old) and had begun as a project of the Society of Jesuits, under the leadership of an activist priest and El Salvadoran immigrants. In the mid-1980s when the project began, El Salvadoran immigrants were coming to Los Angeles for political as well as economic reasons.

The program for young children emerged from a women's collective within the larger project. The women, many of whom had been professionals in El Salvador and less often in Mexico, were struggling with how to survive in this new country where they did not have the language, the credentials, and often the legal documentation to support their children. Many were single mothers, often due to the war in their country of origin. They decided to work out a system of caring for one another's children around their work schedules. In the words of one of the early participants in this effort,

> We were living in the projects and the people who lived in the projects were involved in the church. Father G. had just come to this parish in 1986 and established the "comunidades de base." These were groups of people who got together to read the Bible. They sat down to read the Bible and to see what was happening—I think we were hoping God would come and solve our problems. The Bible study groups changed. They still got together to read the Bible, but they began to relate it to the reality of what was happening in the area.
>
> In '88 the Amnesty Program started, where many people could qualify for citizenship. One of the conditions to qualify was that you couldn't be on welfare. The mothers had to think: "Either I stay on welfare and I don't qualify, or I stop receiving it so I can qualify." But if they stopped receiving the assistance, how were they going to support their families? And they had to find work, because they had to prove that they were self-supporting. "Who's going to watch my children when I work?" One day Father G. said, "I'm going to start a program to help people get amnesty, and I want to see if you can help me coordinate child care while the mothers legalize their status."

Mission Hope had a beautiful physical space within the Los Angeles Mission. Thirty-two children arrived at dawn and stayed until sundown. Private foundations helped pay for many of the program's operating expenses. The local community college offered a Child Development class on Saturdays at the school. The college used the school's materials and provided neighborhood women a chance to obtain their early childhood education units. Mission Hope's teaching staff included interns from this program. Families were asked to pay a minimum of $30 per week, a significant expense for the working poor. The program helped parents get assistance from GAIN NET, APP, and Cal Learn (all projects that helped support mothers when they were in school, in job training, or at work). This money paid for materials and supplies, while teaching staff salaries came from foundation grants.

Mission Hope, in different ways than others in the Latino larger cultural community, struggled as it balanced the needs of the local women, the philosophy of the program, and the constraints of licensing and of foundation and public monies. The director, the teachers, and all of the children were Latino/a, primarily El Salvadoran, with some Guatemalan and Mexican new immigrants. Mission Hope was at its heart an extended family, a safe home for the children of the women in the collective. It was a place where only Spanish was spoken, where the teachers were very reluctant and somewhat frightened to leave the neighborhood to attend the research project's focus groups, and where the children were taught pride in their own cultures of origin before appreciating multiculturalism. It was not a place that wanted to worry about whether the teachers were properly credentialed, whether the adult–child ratio was legal, and whether the bathrooms were child-sized, but if it was to accept public money and survive, it had to.

While on average the programs within the Latino/a larger community served 46 children, an average is a misleading number, with El Peace serving 200 children while Pierce and Mission Hope each served 32 children. There was a smaller range of ages than in the other larger cultural communities—2 to 5 years old in all programs, with the median child a 4-year-old. All but two of the teachers in these programs (the White man and Chinese-immigrant woman, both from El Peace) were Latino/a. Therefore, most children were taught by teachers who shared their ethnic heritage; 66% of the children were Latino/a children taught by Latino/a teachers. At El Peace, White and Asian teachers taught Latino/a children, and Latino/a teachers taught Asian children.

FOCUS ON PRACTICES

Against this background of the larger cultural community, all the program participants had practices, or "ways of doing," to implement the early childhood programs. In the next section of the chapter we focus on practices that were distinctive within the Latino/a larger community.

Teaching and Learning of Pre-Academic Material

Participants in the Latino/a larger cultural community fell at the midpoint in each of the three teaching and learning practices. These participants' scores indicate that practices around teaching and learning were only moderately academic in focus. Participants believed that they prepared children for school by either engaging them in direct instruction or letting them set the pace in child-initiated play. Program participants were more likely to want to implement developmentally appropriate practice than to intentionally oppose it.

The midpoint scores on these practices around teaching and learning mask important differences among the programs within the Latino/a communities in their approach to teaching and learning and are illustrative of lack of integration into a single pattern of practices within this cultural community. El Peace was a leader within LAUSD in training teachers and implementing Creative Curriculum (Dodge, 1988), which is based on the same theoretical position as DAP. As they implemented this curriculum, teachers and the director at El Peace set up ingenious and complex activity centers for children. One day the entire playground was turned into a water system with pipes and hoses. The intention of this articulated practice was to monitor children rather than to either actively engage in teaching them how to use the materials or have them simply explore on their own. This observed practice of activity settings was consistent with the program staff's articulated beliefs that children learn by teachers scaffolding their learning.

Teachers and the director at Pierce defined themselves as helping children to learn through play, and they were particularly proud of the hands-on gardening activities they provided for the children. However, the interviews with the teachers, as opposed to the interview with the director, suggested that although teachers had many opportunities and were encouraged by their director to engage with children in this small, intimate program, they tended to articulate practices around teaching and learning from a didactic point of view. The teachers at Pierce who participated in the project were classified by the Santa Monica school district as teacher's aides. No educational background was required for these positions, and the only ECE classes that the teachers received were at the urging and insistence of their director. Yet we observed these teachers engaging with children in ways that maximized teachable moments that captured and expanded children's learning. Thus, this may be a case where articulation of practice does not match the implementation of practice. Teachers articulated didactic practices and implemented scaffolding.

Mission Hope participants also had a disjuncture between practice articulation and implementation, but in the opposite direction. The college classes required and provided for teachers at Mission Hope explicitly taught NAEYC developmentally appropriate practices, and teachers tended to articulate that they agreed with this pattern of practices. Unfortunately, the teachers of these DAP classes were not fluent in Spanish and the teachers generally spoke only Spanish. Translation during the class was done by people with no child development background. These translators appear to have translated words, but not necessarily meaning. We think that, as a result, the teachers often got the vocabulary of DAP without the meaning or the knowledge to implement it. One of our observations included 30 minutes of children grouped around a teacher who very explicitly taught them how to play pretend with a doll. She corrected their holding of the doll, instructed them to pick up a replica bottle, and praised them for feeding the doll. The observer noted that this could have been a class for new parents rather than a group of 3-year-olds.

We believe that because the teachers in the Latino/a larger community had the least amount of formal education, the articulation of practices was very difficult for them. The teachers at El Peace were an exception to this generalization in that they could, with reference to the Creative Curriculum, talk coherently about their practices. In general, the research team felt that it learned more about teaching and learning practices in these programs from participant observation than from the interviews. We also suspect that because Latino/as have been more recent arrivals to the debates within the early childhood community around teaching and learning practices, the programs' positions on practices were less sharply defined and contentious than those in the other cultural communities.

Social Competence

Teacher participants from the Latino/a community were distinctive from participants in other cultural communities in their articulation of school adjustment as social competence. As opposed to teaching and learning practices, there was considerable homogeneity within the programs in the articulation of practice around social competence.

The participants in these programs did not endorse relationship development as a program goal. Teachers endorsed having good school behavior as more important than social relations. This articulation of social competence as school adjustment is consistent with the concept of *educado* (Azmitia, Cooper, Garcia, & Dunbar, 1996; Farver & Howes, 1993). However, it would be incorrect to say that the programs within the Latino/a community disregarded positive relationships. Certainly the history of the programs, particularly Mission Hope, and the emphasis put on intergenerational relationship knowledge at both El Peace and Pierce, speak to valuing social relationships and connectedness.

According to *educado*, teachers are respected as elders who can impart knowledge to children. In this framework, it is the role of the mother to help children learn respectful behavior rather than to instill or impart school-like knowledge (Richman, Miller, & Levine, 1992; Uribe, LeVine, & LeVine, 1994). Program teachers, especially when the program begins as a mothers' cooperative (Mission Hope), or when staff are hired as aides not teachers (El Peace and Pierce), may self-identify in this dichotomy as mothers rather than teachers. If one is a mother, then one helps children learn to behave in school.

Culture, Race, and Home Language

Although all of the Latino/a children who attended the programs in the Latino/a larger cultural community spoke Spanish at home, the early childhood programs we studied did not agree on what language was appropriate to use in the class-room and on how programs should relate to culture. This was in part an artifact of the selection process, as we deliberately included a range of practices around home language.

At Mission Hope, only Spanish was spoken in the classroom. Due perhaps to the influence of their college teachers, the teachers at Mission Hope articulated that the Anti-Bias Curriculum should be part of children's experiences. Our observations suggest that at Mission Hope the Anti-Bias Curriculum was implemented more as a "celebrate holidays and heroes" part of circle time than as a curriculum that penetrated all of the children's experiences. This discordance between articulated belief and observed practice was consistent with the strongly articulated practices that children need to be deeply comfortable with their home culture before other cultural practices are introduced. For the Mission Hope program, monolingual Spanish in the program was based in practices that strengthened the links between home and the program, creating a program that was home-like for the children. Despite the emphasis on preparing children to behave in a respectful manner at school, discussed above, the teachers at Mission Hope did not articulate any responsibility for having the children English speaking as part of school readiness. This was not true of the other programs.

At Pierce and El Peace, Spanish and English were both used throughout the day. Both programs expected that children would be fluent in English when they left for kindergarten. Because El Peace was larger and multiaged, and the youngest children were usually younger siblings of older children in the same classroom, Spanish tended to be the language of intimacy. Spanish was spoken when a younger child needed comfort, or when an aide helped a child through toileting, napping, or snack. English tended to be used at group time. English between adults and children and among peers gradually replaced Spanish as the children got older and closer to going to kindergarten. Because at Pierce there was only a small group of 4-year-olds, Spanish and English tended to be mixed across the entire program and with all the children.

Both of these programs agreed with the ABC and had sufficient money to buy many of the materials associated with it. Children played with dolls in all colors and shapes, had dress-up clothes for all possible occupations, and read stories that featured children from all over the world and all sorts of families. Because some of the children at El Peace were Chinese, there were some opportunities for cultural crossings on the playground. However, the Spanish-speaking and Chinese children were in different classrooms, had only limited overlapping time on the playground, and tended to play separately.

Special Needs

Children with special needs at Mission Hope and Pierce were treated as typical children and individually incorporated into the programs. El Peace had an inclusion program primarily for children with autism. As discussed earlier, this inclusion program was implemented as part of the director's skillful fund-raising for the program. Although the teachers who had been at El Peace long enough to teach generations of children told us they liked the "new" special education teacher who came with this funding, we rarely observed those teachers engaging with the special needs children. Our impression was that the autistic inclusion program was an add-on rather than an integrated part of early childhood education at El Peace. To our eyes there were children in the regular child care programs who might have been identified as special needs but, due to funding streams and perhaps more consistent with the teachers' point of view, were treated as typical children. Thus, there was some consistency within the larger cultural community in practices around special needs children.

Families

Two of the three programs in the Latino/a larger cultural community, Mission Hope and El Peace, provided full-day child care for working parents. The long waiting lists for these programs underscored the need for full-day child care in geographic areas of Los Angeles with large Latino/a populations. The participants in the programs in the Latino/a cultural community articulated both educating and partnering as ways of working with parents, with no special emphasis on either practice.

In contrast, the Latino/a teachers who participated in these programs articulated a high priority on providing family services, both as partners in children's development and as education for parents. The practice of providing family services within Latino/a cultural communities is consistent with Latino/a immigrant families' traditions of close social networks—that is, systems of family and friendship relationships built upon the principle of consistent mutual help around specific sets of needs (Suarez Orozco & Suarez Orozco, 1995). The Latino/a cultural community participants worked to create programs that acted like extended families of kin and friends to care for children as mothers worked to support their families. Included within this belief system is the value of keeping alive culture and home language while preparing children (and families) for life in this society. They accomplish this by maintaining that families are the core feature of the social networks that sustain children.

> Having the school was a way to help the women. That's how our program at Mission Hope started. If the child is an immigrant, the most important thing for us is to help him adapt his behavior to this country. It wasn't as

important for them to know their ABCs or their numbers; we needed a program implemented specifically on the child and family's needs.

FOCUS ON THE INTERPERSONAL

We now shift the kaleidoscope to focus on the interpersonal. Again, keep in mind that these interpersonal activities occur against the background of high quality and the practices just described. We begin with a description of how children spent their days in the programs, based on our field notes and case histories, and continue with descriptions of the patterns of interaction based on naturalistic observations.

How Children Spent Their Days in the Programs

Pierce, perhaps more than any other program, looked like a traditional nursery school. The children spent most of their time in free choice, and the choices tended to be creative activities rather than academic. Children were building with blocks; dressing up to be mamas, papas, firefighters, and construction workers; painting; using Play-Doh and real clay; and planting or tending their garden. The teachers kept each play area well organized and well stocked. There were dozens of bins filled with every kind of materials imaginable. Children had access to the neatly labeled bins and could use whatever they chose. Teachers tended to stay in the background, to watch or to assist, rather than to direct children's play.

Children's days at El Peace were filled with exploring and playing, much of the time outside on an enormous playground. It was widely believed at El Peace that if children did not go home dirty, then they did not have a good day—they had not had many learning opportunities and had not explored their environment fully. In one of the classrooms, the teachers made circle time a choice because many children were struggling to sit through it and others were very disruptive. After it became a choice, a few children continued to wish to play in other areas, but most of the children chose the circle time and disruptions were far fewer.

There were so many children at El Peace and so much room that at times it was hard to find the teachers. However, when we looked we found that there was always at least one teacher inside the classroom, helping children who needed a quieter place. Outside, teachers often participated in activities with the children. Because children were in mixed-age groups and siblings were kept together in the same group, older children as well as teachers served as experts in solving problems.

Children at Mission Hope spent the hour after breakfast in a whole-school meeting. All of the program participants—younger and older kids and all the teachers—gathered close together to sing songs and tell stories. There was often live guitar and drum music and dancing. After the meeting children were divided into same-age groupings. Children played under the direction of a teacher, with no free choice of learning activities. Meals and naps were important and intimately shared with a teacher and a small group of children. However, the children stayed inside the building for only a relatively small part of the day. This was the only program where children wore uniforms—T-shirts with a picture of a mother cradling a child on the front and the school's phone number on the back. This shirt was in part a safety feature, as every child spent part of the day in the neighborhood, outside of the school grounds. Children went on walks and to the local park with their teachers and neighborhood volunteers. The neighbors watched out for them, often giving them flowers to bring back to the center, and in return the children sang to the neighbors as they went walking along. We could always hear them returning to the center.

Observations of Teacher–Child Pairs[1]

What They Were Doing: Activity Settings. Participants in both the Latino/a and Diverse Families cultural communities were most likely to spend their time hanging out. In visiting some of the programs within the Latino/a communities, we were struck by a similarity between life on the playground and the *paseo* tradition of evenings spent walking and visiting within the town square in villages in Mexico and Central America. On the playground at El Peace, in the park at Mission Hope, and in the garden at Pierce, small groups of children with and without teachers stopped to visit as they moved between activities, gossiping, seeing and being seen, being social. Similar to participants in the other cultural communities, children and their teachers in the Latino/a community were next most likely to spend their time in language arts activities.

With Whom: The Participants in Interaction. Unlike in other programs, children in the Latino/a cultural community were never seen alone. This is not totally surprising, given the amount of time children spent hanging out. Although the Mission Hope and Pierce programs were conducted in small spaces, a child who really wanted to be alone in any of the programs could have found a cubby hole. But this finding suggests that being part of a group played an important role in participating in the programs within the Latino/a cultural community. It is interesting in this context that the children in the Latino/a community were as likely to be in proximity to another teacher as to their primary caregiver. This suggests that the group as a whole was privileged over individual adult–child dyads.

How They Were Interacting

Children. Relative to children in other larger cultural communities, the children in the Latino/a community spent little time pretending with objects or peers.

The relative lack of pretending is problematic for later language development and is unfortunately consistent with other early childhood programs serving primarily Latino/a children (Howes & Wishard, 2004). Our field notes indicate that there was inconsistency within the larger cultural community around pretending. Social pretend play was central to Pierce, and we saw many examples of traditional pretend play—dressing up and acting out scripts. El Peace had the materials for pretend play, but we saw relatively little pretending, perhaps because the activity centers set up on the spacious playground were more compelling than the dress-up corner inside. Given the observation described above of teachers at Mission Hope teaching pretend, it is not surprising that we saw next to no spontaneous pretending as part of play in this program.

Teachers. Teacher participants in the Latino/a larger community were never observed engaging with children in language play, facilitating peer play, or managing children's behavior. Although it is tempting to wonder whether the language play finding was an artifact of home language use, no language play appeared, regardless of whether Spanish was predominantly used in the classroom. There is a paradox here; such relatively low levels of engagement, especially around language, in a program with high scores for teacher sensitivity is not the usual pattern. However, these observations are consistent with the role of mother—sensitive, warm, and responding—rather than the role of instructor or teacher. There is considerable research support for interactive adult–child language exchanges across various cultural communities being associated with children's language development (Hart & Risley, 1992; Hoff-Ginsberg, 1991; Tamis-Le Monda & Bornstein, 2002; Tamis-Le Monda, Bornstein, & Baumwell, 2001). However, the children from all these programs, as we will see, entered kindergarten with receptive vocabulary scores similar to those of more advantaged children. These Latino/a teachers tended to have lower levels of formal education. Other work (Howes et al., 2003) suggests that formal education is linked to teaching behaviors. Thus teacher engagement scores in these programs may be driven by education level as well as participation in the larger cultural community.

FOCUS ON THE CHILDREN

As in the other larger cultural communities, child participants in the Latino/a cultural community were competent in their relationships with teachers and in their play with objects and peers. The proportion of children securely attached to teachers who were matched in ethnicity was 54%. In contrast, 26% of the children with teachers who were not matched in ethnicity were securely attached. The children at Mission Hope were all Latino/a and therefore all children and teachers were ethnically matched. Both El Peace and Pierce had predominantly Latino/a children. In both programs, new immigrant Asian children were the children not ethnically matched with teachers. Teachers in both programs spoke of the other-than-Latino/a children as outsiders. A teacher at Pierce commented:

> We had to teach one of the children to eat on his own. His parents, you know they don't really understand American ways, they need to let their children be independent. We can't be feeding them like babies.

At El Peace, both the Chinese-speaking children and special education programs were imposed on a long-term program whose mission was to provide community-based child care for working parents. While the director was admired by the teachers for her pursuit of special projects to fund the program at a time of diminishing public monies, teacher implementation of these various project was not always smooth or easy.

SUMMARY

The mission of the participants in the Latino/a larger cultural community was to protect families and their children from discrimination, in most cases to allow mothers to work, and always to create a safe place for children to be when they were separated from their families. The participants in these early childhood programs were a heterogeneous group in terms of migration histories, formal education, and isolation from the dominant culture. These participants had a shorter history of constructing patterns of early childhood education practices in caring for children. As a result, the pattern of practices was more contested within the larger cultural community, and less well articulated and less integrated than the pattern of practices within other larger cultural communities. Exceptions to this generalization were practices designed to enhance children's sense of a social community where elders and teachers were respected for their knowledge and the knowledge that could be imparted to the children.

As we saw in Chapter 6, at the core of the early childhood education practices in the African American larger cultural community was a belief that the community was to raise the children—other-mothering. At the core of early childhood education practices in the Latino/a larger cultural community was the belief that the community was to help families; by collective action all could benefit. Both of these enactments of early childhood education practices provided children with adaptive competence within their own larger cultural community when the children shared the racial/ethnic identity of the larger cultural community. In both cultural communities, the children who did not share this identity were less likely to construct secure attachment relationships with their teachers. Adaptive competence usually is considered a positive strategy for children of color, and these findings suggest that for children from the dominant group within the larger cultural community, it was. These findings also suggest that more work in understanding cross-racial and cross-ethnic teacher–child relationships within communities of color is an important endeavor.

Early Childhood Programs in Rural North Carolina

IN THE PREVIOUS two chapters we have focused on early childhood programs within two larger cultural communities identified primarily by race—the Latino/a and African American communities. We now turn to a cultural community self-defined by geography—the rural mountain and coastal plain communities of North Carolina. When we designed this research project we thought of the North Carolina programs as rural comparisons to urban Los Angeles. With my urban White academic eyes it took me a long time to see race in these communities. It was only when I calculated the demographics and realized that all but one of the teachers were White, and three quarters of the children were White, that I began to read the interviews with my eyes on race. When we view the two programs through the lens of race, they are most accurately described as belonging to two overlapping larger cultural communities rather than one. This realization is consistent with Rogoff's (2003) definition of cultural communities. The two North Carolina programs, Mountain and Coast, were part of a larger cultural community defined by membership in rural areas and the mission of providing exemplary child care in a state with historically low-quality child care; simultaneously, the programs belonged to separate larger cultural communities defined by racial or ethnic identity.

Mountain program staff shared racial and ethnic identities with the children and families they served, and talked in terms of preserving their special regional/ethnic Appalachian heritage, as well as preparing children to avoid the problems that historically had plagued their community. Coast teachers adopted a "color-blind" philosophy that never directly mentioned race, but instead taught respect for individual differences in a geographic area where historically both White and African American families had lived. Once more, as we describe these participants and the early childhood programs, keep in mind that we are describing practices, interpersonal interactions, and competent children against the backdrop of programs with very high environmental rating scores and with very warm and sensitive teachers.

In retrospect, the North Carolina programs were interesting also because as we were collecting data, North Carolina was just beginning to use one of the first high-stakes quality rating systems, in which funding levels were tied to ratings. One of the programs in this project went through the process of being rated during the period of the observations. The North Carolina programs also had ties to the Frank Porter Graham Child Development Center, the institutional home of Richard M. Clifford. Many of the participants had completed continuing education with Dick through the Center and were eager to show us what they had learned. Finally, the North Carolina programs were very familiar with the first version of the Early Childhood Environment Rating Scale (Harms & Clifford, 1980), again through their work with the Frank Porter Graham Center. They were the most likely of any of the programs to think of the ECERS as a tool for quality improvement. Unlike in the Los Angeles programs, no one in the North Carolina programs expressed any hesitation about the use of ECERS as a quality rating system. Like NAEYC's developmentally appropriate practice, the ECERS was redesigned in the later 1990s after we used it in data collection. The original version of the ECERS was very closely aligned with the original DAP.

FOCUS ON THE LARGER CULTURAL COMMUNITIES

Both of the programs in North Carolina served relatively large rural geographic areas. Coast was in the eastern part of the state, in the area where Hurricane Floyd and the resulting catastrophic flood created widespread losses of homes, crops and livestock, and businesses in 1999. The county was one third African American and had an increasing immigrant Latino/a population. Mountain was in the west, in the Blue Ridge Mountains area, historically predominantly White, rural, and poor. Mountain was experiencing an influx of Latino immigrants from Mexico and Central America, but at the time of our data collection the population was still 97% White and non-Latino.

Both programs were located within larger institutions—Coast within a community college and Mountain within a Family Service Center—and both programs articulated a responsibility to the families of the region to provide good ECE for their children. In this case ECE was defined as providing child care as well as education. Perhaps because of their allegiance to the Frank Porter Graham Center, the teaching staff participants from the North Carolina programs were particularly enthusiastic adherents of the original version of DAP. They articulated an insistence on providing good care for children, and a certainty that the way to do it was through DAP. In the following section we will describe in more detail each of the selected programs, focusing on the similarities and differences of programs in each of the larger cultural communities identified above.

The two North Carolina programs, located at opposite ends of the state, provided a rural contrast to the urban Los Angeles programs, while sharing a strong concern with doing a good job for children and families. Both of the North Carolina programs were proud of their regional responsibility to provide model ECE. In their eyes, a model ECE would have a high ECERS score and be closely aligned with NAEYC's DAP.

The Mountain early childhood program was located within a Family Service Center, a sparkling modern facility perched on a slope with a fine view of the Blue Ridge Mountains. The county's 517 square miles range in elevation from 1,900 feet to 5,500 feet. Only 11 square miles of this mountainous terrain were devoted to cropland; pasture was more common and vacation homes were an increasingly common "crop." The county's permanent population in 2000 was 29,811, but was estimated to double during the summer (U.S. Census Bureau, 2004). Tourism, mining, the timber industry, and a number of manufacturing plants provided employment. The county recently had acquired several large national retailers that increased the number of low-paying service jobs available to residents.

The Mountain center was designed as a place where families could bring their children for child care and where family members could get job training, various kinds of assistance, and counseling. The center was also a supportive environment in a geographic area marked by poverty and underemployment. It was almost as if staff viewed providing child care as a doorway to providing more comprehensive services and generally improving life for that family. The majority of the staff at the center did not work directly with the children; they worked with families and the community to provide services and information. Their focus on serving families resulted in a commitment to providing a child care environment that parents could feel secure in using, thus removing one barrier to employment.

All of the teachers in this program were White, most with deep generational ties to the mountain region. Most of the 80 children shared this ethnic heritage. The few non-White children who did attend were immigrant Latino/a children whose families increasingly were moving to this isolated rural area to work in low-wage jobs.

The Coast program also was located within a larger institution. As a community college preschool lab, the program served as an observation and internship laboratory for students in the Early Childhood Education Department of the college. Furthermore, a state university known for its early childhood and teacher training programs was located in the same town, and the Coast program served as an internship program for its students as well.

The county in which Coast was located is on North Carolina's coastal plain, midway between the coast and the state capital. It is 646 square miles with a population of some 134,000 (U.S. Census Bureau, 2004). The county is largely agricultural, with some industry and a growing medical establishment. The Coast program was located in the county seat, a city of over 50,000 people. Sixty-two percent of the county's population were White, and 33% were African American. There was a growing Latino/a population of at least 3% (U.S. Census Bureau, 2004).

While both programs' central mission was the education and care of children, each had a prominent additional mission. Mountain's was serving mountain families, and Coast's was serving early childhood professionals in the region.

Coast also considered itself responsible for raising awareness throughout the eastern region of North Carolina about what high-quality child care was and why it was important. The director was energetic in using the media for this purpose; when we selected the program as part of the research project, she sent out a press release about being in the study and got the local evening news to cover it.

North Carolina's new child care quality rating system was instituted during the life of the project. This system awards from one to five stars to centers based on quality, teacher education, and history of compliance with child care licensing requirements. In the first year of the new system, center directors could voluntarily request that their centers be rated. Many in the state chose not to do so and accepted one star by default. The staff at Coast, however, were determined to get five stars. They were the first center in the state to schedule their rating visit. They worked hard on self-assessment, consulted with one another about improving their classrooms, got technical assistance wherever they could, and used private grants to assist the process. Their joy at receiving five stars was tremendous.

The Coast program served 120 children. Their parents worked or went to school at the community college or were residents of the surrounding area. Parents paid fees and/or received child care grants. The center was active in soliciting and receiving grant money. Community college students were regularly in the classrooms doing projects, observing, and being student teachers. One teacher had a MA degree and the others had AA degrees in early childhood education. Three of the four teachers at Coast were White; one was African American. Fifty-four percent of the children were White, 23% were African American, and 23% had more than one ethnicity (White and African American or White and Latino).

Both of the rural North Carolina programs were large compared with the Los Angeles programs, with 80 children at Mountain and 120 at Coast. The children served by both programs were preschoolers, with an average age of just under 4 years old.

FOCUS ON PRACTICES

Against this focus on cultural community, both programs had practices, or "ways of doing," to implement early childhood programs. In the next section we again focus on practices that were distinctive within this larger cultural community. Because there were only two programs, we used the North Carolina rural larger cultural community as the analytic unit.

Teaching and Learning of Pre-Academic Material

In many ways the teaching and learning practices of the early childhood programs in this larger cultural community were the best match of any of the programs with the NAEYC's developmentally appropriate practices at the time. The rural North Carolina participants were less likely than those within the Latino and African American larger cultural communities to have an academic focus and to have teacher-directed beliefs about teaching and learning. The only group of teachers to unanimously endorse implementing DAP were in the rural North Carolina cultural community. This endorsement of NAEYC practice is consistent with Coast's role as a lab school and its emphasis on providing a model for good early childhood education for other programs in the larger cultural community of early childhood programs.

During the period of the project, the state of North Carolina was a national leader in improving child care. As a result, there were opportunities for participants in both Coast and Mountain to engage with others in discussions and workshops about how to improve child care quality using the Early Childhood Environment Rating Scale as a benchmark. Coast's response to a star rating system of centers based on quality rests on basic agreement with the goals of the system. This is in sharp contrast to the way Love and Learn and Nickerson (and, as we will see, Moms) defined high-quality teaching and learning practices in terms of opposition to DAP.

Social Competence

While the participants from North Carolina were no different from the African American teachers of African American or Latino/a children in endorsing school adjustment as a practice, they were significantly more likely than other participants to endorse relationship development as a program goal. Teacher participants' articulated social practices were consistent with this relationship program goal. Participants from the North Carolina community articulated beliefs that were more similar to instilling social relations than having children learn to behave. Field notes from both programs highlighted practices around social competence.

> Teachers at Mountain talked about social interactions as the most important thing they could do to prepare the kids for success (success is implicitly understood as a lack of problems in school, in work, with family, and with the law). Perhaps this focus on families occurred because about half of the teachers were current or past Head Start parents. As Head Start parents, they experienced comprehensive services, extending child development beyond education. As Head Start parents who became teachers, they had personally experienced successful life transformations.

> The teaching staff at Coast prioritized fostering successful social interactions. The children were helped to learn to communicate with others about needs and problems, resolve differences, and control themselves in

appropriate ways. The program was so effective in this area that they have a reputation in their county as the place to send a child who's having trouble meeting expectations for behavior. Children who got "kicked out" of other centers found their way to Coast, and did well.

Culture, Race, and Home Language

Only English was spoken in the North Carolina classrooms. At both programs most of the children spoke only English at home as well. And all of the children would be expected to speak English once they were in kindergarten.

The participants in the North Carolina cultural community, unlike in other larger cultural communities, were unanimous in their endorsement of multiculturalism. They also knew about and intended to implement the Anti-Bias Curriculum. These findings highlight the importance of having the ABC as part of NAEYC's approach to children for early childhood professionals in geographic areas newly experiencing children and families unlike themselves.

Children with Special Needs

The programs in these cultural communities had only slightly different practices around children with special needs. The Coast program included children with special needs as part of the laboratory school activities. While Mountain did not define itself as a program for special needs children, it had a reputation for providing good care for children whom other early childhood programs found difficult.

The North Carolina participants were more willing to identify children as having special needs than were the participants in the African American and Latino/a larger cultural communities. In North Carolina, best practices included early identification and appropriate intervention for children with special needs. The intervention in both programs included classroom strategies for full inclusion of these identified children, and at Mountain the host agency provided a full array of services for both the children and the families. As I will describe later in this chapter, the day-to-day interactions of children and teachers at both Coast and Mountain reflected a balance of attention to the needs of the individual child who was having difficulty with regular classroom activities—especially transitions—and the needs of children who easily negotiated these same activities and transitions.

Families

Both of the programs in the North Carolina rural cultural communities provided full-day care for the children. This is consistent with the goal of the programs, which was to provide a full range of services, including child care, family services, and teacher training, and was in keeping with their articulated feelings of responsibility for entire families, not just the children.

Participants in North Carolina articulated that being responsible for families meant educating and providing services for families rather than partnering with families. The participants in the rural North Carolina cultural communities were highly likely to endorse the practice of educating or teaching families. This is consistent with a dominant cultural model of parental involvement that sees parent education as part of the process of socializing parents to be like White middle-class parents in supporting children's school success (Delpit, 1988; Powell & Stremmel, 1989). And, not surprisingly given this pattern, participants in the North Carolina cultural communities were highly likely to endorse family service practices.

We found the North Carolina participants' views of families, as with much of their practice, to resonate with both Head Start and NAEYC's program standards, which place the responsibility for changing families, as well as children, in the hands of early childhood educators. This contrasts with the position of the African American and Latino/a cultural community participants, who were more likely to view the interests of the children and their parents as at times in conflict, and to not automatically try to change the parents in order to further the interests of the children.

FOCUS ON THE INTERPERSONAL

As we did in the two previous chapters, we now shift the kaleidoscope to focus on the interpersonal, against the background of high quality and the practices just described. We again begin with a description of how children spent their days in the programs, based on our field notes and case histories, and then continue with descriptions of patterns of interaction based on naturalistic observations.

How Children Spent Their Days in the Programs

Both of the North Carolina programs saw themselves and were seen in their geographic area as model programs. Both were in relatively new buildings with state-of-the-art classrooms. Each program had all the materials found in the ECERS, including the workbench, sandbox, and water table. The teachers' use of manipulatives, low shelves, and outdoor play was in some ways right out of the pages of an early childhood education textbook on how to use developmentally appropriate classroom materials. In both programs there were many visitors and trainees inside the classrooms, with teachers modeling how to use the developmentally appropriate materials to extend children's play.

But each of the programs also had an individual flavor that is not often represented in textbooks. At Mountain, the classroom did look like a model early childhood center with activity centers, lots of free-choice time, circle time, naps, and snacks. The teachers actively monitored and engaged with children as they learned by playing. However, the Mountain program was also a comprehensive services program. Teachers defined their goals for the whole child not only as social and cognitive readiness for school, but as preparing the children to overcome difficult life circumstances and to live their lives without serious problems. In other words, the teachers wanted the children to have different lives than their parents. And so the daily flow of children's play and activities was accompanied by attention to remediating problem behaviors. On the way from the classroom to the playground, the activities of all of the children might need to be readjusted in order to help a child who was having a hard day.

The day at Coast was very similar to the day at Mountain. The children had many learning centers to choose from. There was plenty of time in the relaxed day for children to be alone, to be with a teacher one-on-one, and to be with a small or large group of children. Because the program was a teacher training lab school, there were both skilled and novice teachers available to the children. The children tended to gravitate toward the more skilled permanent teachers. These teachers focused on helping children learn to communicate with others about needs and problems, resolve differences, and control themselves in appropriate ways.

The teachers were also particularly skillful in communicating high expectations to a child while also communicating affection, respect, and liking. One of these teachers had a large contingent of rowdy boys in her class. While classroom management was at times difficult for the student teachers, the head teacher worked to establish, for the children as well as the novice teachers, that these were lovable, normal children, not defective children determined to annoy and challenge the trainees. The teacher referred to the children as "my action heroes" and demonstrated how to provide constructive opportunities to use their energy. In addition, she skillfully separated children out of the boys' group at times to allow each child to develop other, quieter talents. Thus, she gave attention to the special needs of the boys without taking anything away from the experiences of the other children in the classroom. Although the teachers at Coast were active in their interactions with children, they tended to monitor rather than direct children's activities in learning centers.

Observations of Teacher–Child Pairs

What They Were Doing: Activity Settings. The patterning of activities in the programs in the North Carolina cultural communities was significantly different from the others. Children in these communities spent more time in creative and manipulative activities and less time hanging out than did children in any of the other programs. This is consistent with these participants' endorsement of DAP and its emphasis on children's hands-on experiences with materials. However, recall that the teacher–child pairs across all cultural communities were similar in emphasizing language arts activities. Children in both programs read books, were read to, practiced their writing, told stories about their artwork, and acted out dramas from books and their imaginations.

With Whom: The Participants in Interaction. Child participants in the rural North Carolina cultural communities were similar to children in the African American larger cultural community in spending much of their time with their primary teacher. The following excerpt from the research partners' field notes at Mountain is illustrative:

> Relationships are very important here. There are a remarkable number of kids in foster care or living with grandparents or other relatives. The staff are the allies of the children's families, not their critics or adversaries. Today I observed a little girl whose behavior was quite difficult to cope with during the day. I was aware that she had been taken into protective custody in the past but had now been returned to the care of her parents. When her mother picked her up and read the daily report from the teacher, the child looked on fearfully. She asked, "Mama, are you angry?" Her mother replied, with words learned from the teacher, "No, I'm not angry, but tomorrow I want you to listen better."

How They Were Interacting

Children. Children participating in the rural North Carolina larger cultural communities were the most likely child participants to be engaged in pretend play with peers during our observations. This is consistent with their high participation in creative activities and with our notion that these programs looked more like traditional early childhood programs than the programs within the other cultural communities. Children had plenty of materials for pretend, a dress-up corner, a kitchen area, and a block area ready to become a town or railroad. Teachers encouraged pretending, seeing it as important for children's development. Teachers suggested a play theme and brought in new materials to stimulate further pretend play.

Teachers. Teacher participants in the rural North Carolina cultural communities were more engaged with children in a number of ways than were teacher participants in other cultural communities. Of all the teachers, those in the North Carolina cultural communities were the most likely to facilitate peer interaction and to positively manage children's behavior. They closely monitored children's social interactions and did not hesitate to enter into the play, make a suggestion, or anticipate and divert a meltdown.

FOCUS ON THE CHILDREN

All of the children in the North Carolina cultural communities were rated as competent in social relationships and in play with objects and peers. It is important to note that in these full-day programs that emphasized free choice and free play, children had more time to play, to negotiate friendships, and to fully develop dramatic play and constructive play with objects than did children in other cultural communities. This program organization is a reflection of the adult participants' deeply held belief in the importance of play in early childhood for later school success.

SUMMARY

In many ways, the participants in the rural North Carolina cultural communities articulated and implemented a pattern of practices that maps extremely well onto notions of best practice within traditional early childhood programs. Our observations of teachers and children's interaction suggest classroom environments that were warm, sensitive, and stimulating, and provided a high level of attentive care for *all* children—White children and children of color. All children were securely attached to their teachers, children of color with White teachers as well as White children with White teachers. The teachers provided all of the children with trusting relationships, and more than in other programs, many of these children came from difficult life circumstances.

However, the bridge that connected home and school in these programs was strongest for the White children. In both programs, the goal was to educate, and at times change, the families rather than to consider them partners in a mission to enhance adaptive child competence and produce strong children who could understand and withstand discrimination. This is different from the mission of developing adaptive competence within the African American and Latino/a cultural communities. At Coast, respecting individual differences was important and laudable, but race was not directly addressed. In contrast, research on adaptive competence suggests that directly addressing race and discrimination is important for developing adaptive competence (Garcia-Coll et al., 1996). The participants at Mountain had a strong regional identity and few experiences with other-than-White children. If the Latino/a presence in the program grows over time, it would be fascinating to watch the transformation (or not) of the program.

Serving Children in a Multicultural Context: The Diverse Families Cultural Community

RACIAL IDENTIFICATION—directly or indirectly—has been a defining issue in the three previously discussed larger cultural communities. In the final cultural community, Diverse Families, race is less an issue of identity and more an issue of bias or, to be precise, of anti-bias. The three Los Angeles early childhood programs in this cultural community had similar historical roots. All of these programs began because a group of White, relatively affluent people who were committed to anti-bias and to children struggled to create programs that provided good developmental services within a multicultural and economically mixed context. All of these programs, Therapeutic Preschool, Moms, and Down the Hill, were begun and directed by dynamic White women. These women had a similar political vision of providing care and education, in a manner that respected race and culture, for children and families facing difficult circumstances.[1] In each of these programs Latino/a teachers who were trained and supervised by these directors provided most of the care and education of children. While each program had a particular focus—TPS served emotionally disturbed children, Moms served teenage mothers, and Down the Hill served a particular mix of affluent and poor children—they shared a common commitment to integrating anti-bias and multiculturalism within a self-conscious and reflective approach to teaching and learning.

These three programs, although established more recently than some of the other programs rooted in race-identified cultural communities, were well known to Los Angeles child advocates as model programs. In part this was because these programs, unlike the other Los Angeles programs, were not self-contained. TPS and Down the Hill, officially, and Moms, unofficially, were the hub of technical assistance to other early childhood programs in their geographic area. Interestingly, none of these programs was funded by ECE funds, and by 2005 two of the programs were closed.

SERVING CHILDREN IN A MULTICULTURAL CONTEXT

The three programs we clustered together as participating in a Diverse Families cultural community also interacted more with one another than other programs in the Los Angeles sample. The Moms and TPS program participants began visiting each other soon after the first directors' focus group, and by the end of the project, one of the teachers trained at Moms had become a teacher at TPS. Moms and Down the Hill became involved in an ongoing school readiness partnership after the end of our research project. In their common commitment to integrating anti-bias and multiculturalism into the programs, there were similarities, indeed many compatibilities, as well as significant differences between these programs. One similarity, which emerged only through this analysis and was not identified directly by the programs, was tension between the programs and the families they served. This is not unexpected, given that in every case the program director was White, the teaching staff was primarily Latino/a, and at least half of the children were Latino/a and/or African American.

TPS's central mission was to provide an alternative model for serving emotionally disturbed children whose social behaviors were so challenging that they were not tolerated in community-based child care settings. The program was located within a mental health facility in a large urban hospital. All of the children had official diagnoses and received mental health department funds. Most of the 16 children at TPS had "failed" at school and been asked to leave by the time they were 4 years old. TPS's teaching staff believed strongly in a theory of attachment to other-than-mothers as a way to help these children become able to participate in regular school. Their success in doing this had been documented before the program became part of our research project (Howes & Ritchie, 1998, 2002).

Two classrooms of 8 children each taught by two teachers participated in a 4-½-hour daily program. On one level, the program looked like a regular preschool. Children began each day in learning centers. They had circle time with books, songs, calendar, and show and tell. Children often cooked their own snacks. There was outside play, free choice, and lunch. Children's problems, however, often were based on their difficulty with relationships and communication, so there were many periods of the day when children, their teachers, and their peers struggled with tantrums, poor communicative skills, and difficulties in being sociable within a group.

As this research project progressed, the staff's struggles around race and home language became more central, both within the program and as the program director and the teachers engaged with the other programs. Half of the children at TPS were African American or Latino/a. At the time of the project the teaching staff included a White woman, who had been with the program from the beginning and served as a mentor to the other teachers; a bilingual Latina, who was not using her Spanish in the classroom; and an African American woman. The interactive social behaviors within the TPS classrooms were constructed by teachers intent on disconfirming past relationship difficulties (see Howes & Ritchie, 2002). These ways of interacting with children were different from the patterns of interaction that were most common in the children's homes. The parents or guardians of the children, particularly the African American grandparents who had custody of the children because the children had tested positive at birth for drug exposure, often found what went on at school disturbing. They worried that the teachers were giving the children "too much leeway." The situation was compounded because the parents often watched the classroom activities through one-way mirrors. The African American teacher talked about her experiences of having parents in the observation booth watching the teachers.

> What they see from the observation room can sometimes be disturbing to parents, especially the African Americans. I wonder if at home Granny gives the child a very strong message that it's not okay to behave that way in school. Granny will say to me while walking down the hallway, "Now, now I want you to tell her to stop screaming like that because you all will have a headache in there and I want you to tell her to cut that screaming out." She says this to me and not to anyone else in the program—it might have to do with the fact that I'm Black.

With the Latino/a children in the program, another discontinuity between school and home had to do with what language was used with the child. The classroom language was English. The Latino/a teacher translated as needed, but the language of the classroom and thus the language heard in the observation booth was English. The Latino/a parents in the observation booth were less likely than the African American parents to speak to the teachers about their discomfort. But the TPS participants worried that they were not reaching these parents, who had the double challenges of Spanish as a first language and discontinuity between practices at home and school.

While the dialogue about race and home language became more central at TPS over time and with interaction between programs in the project, at Moms, which also had a White director, race and home language had been the center point of the program from the beginning. For example, only Spanish was used in the classroom. The director had become fluent in Spanish in order to work with an increasing predominance of Latino/a families in the program. All parent meetings were half in English and half in Spanish, with both languages simultaneously translated. As the Moms director and teachers participated in our research project and interacted with the research team and TPS participants, they changed as well. They began to include building strong relationships in their mission, working from an other-than-mother attachment model more similar to TPS's. They asked the research partners and TPS participants to work with them so that they could understand and change their practices around relationships.

The director at Moms began her work in child care in Los Angeles as part of a collective, the Playgroup project, that organized nonlicensed child care programs in garages in a low-income, mixed Latino/a and White, politically progressive neighborhood. Over the next several decades, the Playgroup project members influenced, among other things, the California legislature, the Los Angeles City Council, the Los Angeles Unified School District Board, the development of UCLA child care services outreach programs, the development of an after-school program at UCLA's lab school, and, most relevant to this account, the NAEYC Anti-Bias Curriculum. The Playgroup centers themselves, after negotiating their status with child care licensing and becoming official, became two centers, one of them Moms.

Located physically and financially within a continuation school of LAUSD, Moms served 32 Latino/a children and their teenage mothers who were returning to school. All of the teaching staff in the program were Latino/as who had been trained over the years by the director. Because of the public face of the program, there were as well a series of very well-educated, almost always White women working in the program directly with the children and mothers as specialists and consultants around mental health issues. When Moms participated in this research project, the director was working almost entirely with the teenage mothers, only supervising the teachers in their day-to-day work with the children but not working directly with the children.

While the children's program was conducted entirely in Spanish, and there was considerable explicit work on the sensitive construction of positive relationships between parents and children and between children and teachers, there was a certain discontinuity between practices at home and in the program, as at TPS. Many of the parents at the program had experienced abuse and domestic violence themselves. The neighborhood around Moms had extremely high levels of violent encounters. In this context it was notable that the parents at Moms were asked to sign a "No spanking pledge" when they began to participate in the program. There was no verbal or physical violence permitted at the program—between adults and children or between children. Toddler-age children were taught to comfort one another and to resolve conflicts in a loving way. Parents met together daily and much of the content of their work was around violence and nonviolence. The parents reflected on how their own experiences of being hurt made them both more likely to hurt their own children and work very hard not to do so.

The program conveyed these messages in a very visual manner. What follows is an excerpt from a field note:

> What is most striking about the classrooms are the signs and pictures that convey the philosophical stance of the program. There are posters talking about the "No Spanking Week" with pledges underneath signed by mothers who are working to break the cycles of violence in their own lives.

Down the Hill shared with Moms a historical origin within a politically progressive organization. In Down the Hill's case, a group of pregnant women who knew one another through their work as Legal Aid lawyers and other forms of social justice political activism formed a nonprofit child care center for their own children. In a deliberate measure to increase the class, racial, and home language diversity of the children, they literally moved the program from the top of the hill to the bottom, from an affluent to a poverty-stricken neighborhood. It took 3,000 volunteer hours from parents, the LA Conservation Corps, LA Works, Chase Manhattan Bank dollars, and 400 free hours from a neighborhood architect to move down the hill. Along the way, the program acquired an experienced director, who instead of retiring, took on the project. Seven years later the program joined our research project.

Forty-five children had full-day care at the program. Sixty percent paid tuition and 40% were supported through public child care vouchers and an ambitious scholarship program undertaken by the center. Sixty-three percent of the children were White, 25% Latino/a, and the remainder Asian. English was the language of the center. Beyond the core center-based program, there were multiple outreach programs with family child care providers, family literacy efforts, and the neighborhood elementary school.

The primarily Latino/a teachers were attracted to the program through their shared philosophy with the director, often taking the classes she taught at a local community college before coming to the program. There was a strong belief in children playing and exploring and in the importance of ongoing teacher–child interaction. Many teachers came from ECE programs where they had been dissatisfied with another approach to working with children and were pleased to find a place to work that felt comfortable. All of the teachers had educational backgrounds in early childhood education, most had their AA degrees, and all of those who did not yet have degrees were in school.

While Down the Hill was organized around a shared belief that children and families benefit from purposeful groupings of people from diverse ethnic and economic backgrounds, there was the same tension surrounding discontinuity between home and school as in TPS and Moms. At Down the Hill this tension was specifically around issues of how and what to teach to get children ready for school. The director was willing to have families of color leave the school rather than change her core belief that young children were to be taught "how to think" rather than basic school skills.

The programs in this larger cultural community averaged 31 children, with TPS's tiny numbers balanced by Down the Hill's larger ones. The children ranged in age from the toddlers at Moms to the older preschoolers at the other two programs. The Diverse Families programs were the only Los Angeles programs with White children. Nevertheless, 44% of the teacher–child pairings were Latino/a teachers and Latino/a children. Another 44% were Latino/a teachers and other-than-Latino/a children.

FOCUS ON PRACTICES

Teaching and Learning of Pre-Academic Material

The participants in the programs in the Diverse Families larger cultural community were, along with those in the North Carolina programs, most likely not to endorse an academic focus. The participating teachers in these programs were also similar to participating teachers in North Carolina in believing that children do best when teachers scaffold rather than direct their learning.

But the similarity with the participants in North Carolina relating to practice around teaching and learning ends at this point. As a whole, the participants in the Diverse Families community were most likely to endorse and practice an individualized version of DAP rather than either implementing DAP, as did the participants in the North Carolina community, or opposing it, as did the participants in the African American cultural community.

DAP was contested within the Diverse Families cultural community. The director at Down the Hill defended DAP most vocally. Indeed, in her struggles with the parents around how to ready children for kindergarten, she frequently invoked NAEYC and DAP as evidence for the correctness of her teaching and learning practices. Also, in one of her several other jobs as an instructor at the prestigious Pacific Oaks College, she taught Child Development and Early Education courses and emphasized that the root of all children's learning was play. At the opposite end of the continuum were the participants in the Moms program. While not articulating as clearly as the director at Love and Learn that DAP was a White middle-class curriculum, and strongly disagreeing with the Love and Learn director about the relation between learning and play, the director of Moms believed that the first imperative for her program was to implement the Anti-Bias Curriculum. She had a basic agreement with DAP, but would modify it as she went along and as she felt necessary to serve her children and families well. The Moms director and the Down the Hill director both had MA degrees in early childhood education and were extremely intellectually sophisticated in their integration of traditional beliefs about children's learning and in programmatic implementation of teaching and learning for nontraditional children. Our research team experienced these two directors as the most eager for written academic materials, and as the most likely to be interested in nuances when we presented feedback to their programs.

The director at TPS was also highly educated and sophisticated in her approach to the program, but, in contrast, her background was in special education and mental health. At TPS, teaching and learning were important, but always secondary to the social and emotional development of the children. Recall that TPS was the only program serving exclusively children identified as having special needs. Within this context, the participants articulated that DAP was individualized for each child. Some children, for example, had more toy choices than others. A child diagnosed with autism and preoccupied with trains had train time and no train time. An electively mute child did not have to take a turn at circle time.

Social Competence

Social competence was the most salient set of practices for participants in the Diverse Families cultural community. These participants endorsed relationship building as a program goal more often than any other participants except for those in the North Carolina cultural community. Also, they had the highest scores on the social relations end of the teacher-articulated social practices scale. After the first feedback session at Moms, the director and teaching staff became particularly interested in constructing positive attachment relationships with children from difficult life circumstances. The result was a series of cross-site visits and discussions between Moms and TPS directors and teachers around relationship building.

Culture, Race, and Home Language

While all three programs within the Diverse Families cultural community were deeply concerned with issues surrounding home language and children feeling comfortable in the program regardless of their racial or ethnic background, there was no consensus on the appropriate language for the classroom. All possible options were present: all Spanish (Moms), just enough Spanish (Down the Hill), and pointedly not using Spanish (TPS).

There was consensus in articulated cultural beliefs; almost all of the teacher participants articulated a belief in home cultural and language practices. We found it interesting that the Latino/a teachers within this cultural community so clearly articulated the practice of stressing home culture and language, and at the same time were divided on the issue of what language to use in the classroom. This articulation is a clear contrast with the Latino/a teachers within the Latino/a larger cultural community, who were divided in their articulation of cultural practices between home language and multiculturalism. These seeming inconsistencies illustrate that participation in a cultural community provides a way to enact racial/ethnic identity, rather than racial or ethnic identity being a proxy for a set of beliefs. It argues against a research tradition that would use race nomenclature as an "address," label, or grouping variable.

While serving children well in a context of racial and ethnic diversity was a central salient issue for the participants in the Diverse Families cultural community, and while they were the strongest endorsers of the ABC, there was disagreement within the community on this issue as well. Within the LA Diverse Families larger cultural community, only participants at Moms endorsed the ABC wholeheartedly. As described earlier, the director of Moms had been a member of the original collective and program (Playgroup project) that had been influential in developing the curriculum and she had implemented it at Moms despite some initial resistance from parents. The Anti-Bias Curriculum, ironically, had not been translated into Spanish at the time of our observations. Although the ABC was implemented by monolingual Spanish-speaking teachers at Moms, the director was able to translate both its literal and underlying meaning into Spanish. Moms thus could be considered a model for implementing the ABC in a monolingual Spanish program.

In contrast, Down the Hill, while committed to the principles of the ABC, often struggled with its implementation. Class was an issue in this program as well as racial identity. The program was faced with balancing the developmental needs of children with very different home environments and access to privilege. Circle time and sharing of things brought from home required a delicate touch as only some children could bring to share at circle time the toys or vacation experiences wished for by all the children.

While all of the programs in this cultural community had more children from difficult life experiences than programs in other cultural communities, only TPS had classrooms that were limited to children who brought troubled social and emotional behaviors to school. It was very important at TPS that every child be valued, but when a child's most salient feature was unremitting tantrums, the staff found it necessary to focus on the behavior and the often concomitant chaotic home life rather than on the child's ethnic heritage. So while the participants at TPS wholeheartedly believed in the ABC, at times it took a back seat to the more acutely pressing problems of the children.

Children with Special Needs

As discussed above, participants in the Diverse Families cultural community had the largest numbers of children with difficult life circumstances. Their practices in serving special needs children also differed from the other larger cultural communities. Children were treated as typical (Moms), were given special emphasis (Down the Hill), and were the only children in the program (TPS). We suspect that the emphasis in the Moms program on implementing a nonviolent and anti-bias curriculum would have made it very difficult to label a child as having special needs. Also, the children at Moms were the youngest ones in the project, and it is more difficult to identify disabilities in younger as compared with older children. Down the Hill had an active inclusion program, with some children accompanied by aides and shadow teachers.

Families

Two of the programs in the Diverse Families larger cultural community were full-day programs and one was not. Moms and Down the Hill considered providing child care for working families an important part of their mission. TPS was only a half-day program, and during the life of our project the director successfully fought a community initiative targeted at making it a full-day program. TPS argued that the children they served demanded such intense care that the teachers needed to be with them only half-days in order to spend the other half of the day in planning and in supervision. The TPS teachers were the only teacher participants who received regular formal supervision from the director of the program. TPS participants felt that their program was a success when one of their children could be in a typical child care setting in the afternoon. Moms and Down the Hill argued that the children they served were too vulnerable to make that kind of transition between programs, and Moms went to great lengths to bend licensing and school district regulations to keep children in the program for as long a day and as many years as possible. After our project ended, Moms closed because changes in the rules and regulations regarding welfare made it impossible to conduct an early childhood program with the kind of continuity the Moms director needed for her program.

The participants in the three programs within the Diverse Families larger cultural community also differed in their practices around working with families. The TPS program participants articulated that their goal was to educate families to work with these special needs children. Moms and Down the Hill participants articulated partnership practices with families. These differences are consistent with the program participants' disagreements around whether or not the programs could be considered child care. For example, the TPS director believed that the children's special needs required that parents adapt their lives to the director's understandings of the children's special needs, and she was unwilling to extend the program hours to provide care for children when their parents were working. Moms and Down the Hill scheduled program hours and parent meetings around parents' work schedules.

Contested family practices among the participants in this larger cultural community did not extend to parent services; these participants were in agreement that they served children rather than families. This may have been a belief rather than an actual practice. TPS had a "sister" unit within the hospital that did provide extensive family services. Moms was a two-generational program, with parents spending almost as much time in the program as children. The parents would leave to go to their school classes (on the same grounds) and quickly come back to be at the program. In many ways Moms provided the kind of stable, responsive, and warm home that was missing in the parents' lives. Down the Hill rented space in a Family Service Center. This meant that a variety of family services were across the lawn from the center.

FOCUS ON THE INTERPERSONAL

As we did in the previous three chapters, we now shift the kaleidoscope to focus on the interpersonal, against the background of high quality and the practices just described. We again begin with a description of how children spent their days in the programs, based on our field notes and case histories, and continue with the descriptions of patterns of interaction based on naturalistic observations.

How Children Spent Their Days in the Programs

Although TPS was an intervention program located within a mental health facility in a large urban hospital, much of what children experienced looked like a typical early childhood program. One critical difference was that the schedule remained the same each day. Also, children in the program had relatively little opportunity to make choices. Children could choose from among the activities provided each day, but could not choose to do something other than what the teachers had provided. Thus, a child obsessed with trains could not go to a shelf and include a train in the block building. The lack of choices was because the program believed that consistency and predictability were essential to the well-being of these special needs children. Circle time was an important part of each morning and included songs, calendar, and sharing. The teacher was the central person in the circle, helping children to take turns, listen to one another, participate as a group, and increase their ability to pay attention. Children who found this difficult, and most did, were helped to stay within the circle by sitting on a teacher's lap rather than being isolated from the group. Only on the outdoor playground were there more choices and the opportunity to stay close to a teacher or not.

Visiting Moms meant finding the program on the parking lot of a huge continuation high school teeming with adolescents, food trucks, and blaring music. At the gate of Moms was a large sign warning that to come inside meant giving up violent language and behavior and junk food. The teenage parents, all but one of them female, and their children arrived early. The whole family qualified for the subsidized food programs, so the parents and children ate breakfast together at the program. The parents and the children socialized together in the program until a short parenting meeting from 9:00 to 9:30. Then the parents went off to their high school classes, returning to be with their children at lunch time. While parents were in school, the children played and played, all free-choice activities. The playground and inside of the center were filled with things to do. Children could come and go at their own pace. Most of the activities encouraged creative play, and there were no academic learning centers. Teachers were attentive to the ups and downs of children getting along with peers, and helped them to provide comfort to one another after the inevitable stumbles and fusses in a very small space filled to capacity with many small bodies. The afternoon began with another group time for parents and children together. Then mothers went to the parenting class or job training and the children took naps. At each of these many transitions for parents and children, the separation of parents and their children was scripted so that both participants came to understand that mothers could be trusted to come back. The teacher would help the parent tell the child, "I will be back after nap."

Down the Hill looked like a model early childhood center in terms of activities and schedule. However, it was very apparent that the climbing structure, the paint job, and the cubbies were the result of volunteer labor rather than a trip to a commercial supplier of early childhood materials. The children were age-grouped by classrooms. Inside and outside spaces were set up ahead of time by teachers who changed them frequently and monitored children as they used the materials in the learning centers. The core of the program was circle time, including children and teachers in each classroom as well as any parents who happened to be present. The circles were planned to give children the feeling of belonging to a group. At morning circle a question was posed about some member of the community, for example, "Who is Judy [the director]?" (Answers: "She is a princess with a kind heart; she is the old lady who works in the office.") The children explained orally, wrote with their own interpretations of letters and spelling, and drew their answers to the morning question. These stories were put up on the wall and shared with parents at the end of the day. Each day ended with a closing circle where the activities of the day were discussed.

Observations of Teacher-Child Pairs[2]

What They Were Doing: Activity Settings. Despite the different approach to practices articulated by the participants in the Diverse Families cultural community, these programs tended to look like the others in terms of activity settings. Children and teachers tended to hang out in a manner similar to the teacher–child pairs in the Latino/a larger community. Children were involved in creative play and language arts, and not observed spending much time in fine- or gross-motor activities and never in didactic activity.

With Whom: The Participants in Interaction. A similar profile emerged among the participants in interactions. Children engaged with peers and teachers and spent some time alone. Child participants in this cultural community were similar to children in the Latino/a cultural community in spending less time with their primary caregiver than did children in other cultural communities. This may be counterintuitive given that the program practices in this cultural community placed greater emphasis on relationship practices. Our observations suggest that in all three programs, children were encouraged to be part of the classroom group as well as constructing positive relationships with individual adults and peers. Recall the descriptions above of circle time not being an optional activity for the children at TPS, and the focus on all children providing comfort and support to one another at Moms.

How They Were Interacting

Children. Child participants in the Diverse Families larger cultural community spent their days playing with objects and with their peers, talking and playing pretend. Again, it is noteworthy how indistinguishable these children were from the children in the other programs in their interactions, given the predominance of difficult life circumstances.

Teachers. Teacher participants in the Diverse Families cultural community were similar to those in the North Carolina cultural community in their high levels of responsive engagement and interactions with children. The teacher participants in the Diverse Families community had less formal education than the North Carolina teachers. We suspect that this level of responsive involvement can be attributed to the supervision and mentoring provided to the teachers by the very sophisticated and committed program directors in the Diverse Families community.

FOCUS ON THE CHILDREN

The children from fortunate life circumstances who participated in the Diverse Families larger cultural community were competent children—competent in relationships, peer play, and object play. While the children from difficult life circumstances were less likely than the children from fortunate circumstances to construct secure attachment relationships with their primary caregivers, children in this community constructed secure attachments with their teachers regardless of ethnic match or nonmatch; children who participated in the Diverse Families community who had ethnically matched primary caregivers were no more likely to construct positive attachments than children who did not. Further research is needed to explore these complicated relations between difficult life circumstances, bridges between home and school, and relationship with other-than-mothers, but this finding suggests that the careful attention both to serving children well and to race, ethnicity, and bias within this cultural community assisted teachers and children in constructing positive attachments across race and home language lines.

SUMMARY

In several senses, the patterns of practices in the Diverse Families cultural community are distinctive. Instead of constructing early childhood practices to enhance the development of cultural adaptation in the children in their care, as did the African American and Latino/a cultural communities, these participants constructed a pattern of practices to enhance children's development of an anti-bias stance. This pattern of practices is especially potent when we consider the kinds of children served in this cultural community. At TPS, children whose troubled behaviors and home lives made trusting relationships and harmonious interactions most difficult were helped to develop secure and positive relationships and to be part of an intimate social and emotional group. At Moms, children who had experienced violence at home and in their neighborhood were helped to develop positive ways of engaging with others and to comfort those who hurt. At Down the Hill, children who were very different from one another were taught to value diversity and to oppose discrimination and hatred within their own group and in the larger world. In the larger cultural communities discussed in earlier chapters, we commented that the NAEYC Anti-Bias Curriculum provided a tool for program staff to use when faced with children who were different from themselves or the population historically served. In this larger cultural community, implementing the ABC meant reconstructing it—extending it and elaborating it to fit the deliberate challenge of anti-bias education within very diverse groups.

The pattern of practices in this cultural community was definitely a work in progress—at times integrated and at times contested within the larger cultural community and between the program participants and the families served. Yet by focusing on race, and by struggling to provide culturally competent care for children who were very different from one another, the participants in this program were able to have teachers and children construct secure relationships, whether or not the children were ethnically matched with their primary caregivers, as well as to sensitively build bridges between very different school and home environments.

Conclusions

CAN CARE FOR CHILDREN simultaneously be culturally adaptive, prepare children for school, and provide them with experiences that make them feel safe, trusting, and eager to learn? The findings of this project suggest that meeting all of these goals is possible but not simple or straightforward. We found that meeting the dual expectations of cultural adaptation and high ECE quality was possible when participants in the ECE programs were willing and able to belong simultaneously to cultural communities defined by race and ethnicity and to cultural communities of advocates for good early childhood education for all children. The program directors and, to varying degrees, the teachers in the programs described in this book were able to do the work of cultural translation between practices embedded in ethnic and racial communities and practices endorsed by professional organizations and research on child care and ECE. The resulting practices were not a mediocre compromise but a transformation. That is, program participants provided individualized, developmentally appropriate care using everyday ways of doing that were rooted within their cultural communities or developed within programs through consensus building between participants from different home cultural communities. Practices originating in ethnic communities, for example, other-mothering, were enacted in ways that reflected the sensitive and individual attention to children and their development advocated by professional groups. Other practices in programs, for example, use of the Anti-Bias Curriculum at Moms, were rooted in discussion among program participants who differed in home cultural communities but were similar in their program goals for children.

CULTURE, CHILD DEVELOPMENT, AND EARLY CHILDHOOD EDUCATION

This project set out to describe ECE programs that community advocates believed provided good care for children and families who did not belong to the dominant culture. Not surprisingly, the programs that community advocates selected were embedded within cultural communities shaped not only by adult participants' race and ethnic identities but also by the participants' beliefs about early childhood practices that would best benefit their children. Because beliefs about caring for children are rooted within cultural communities' ways of doing, the ECE practices of the programs were often but not always consistent with the families' ways of caring for children and therefore provided a bridge between home and program. Thus, the ECE programs were meeting the goal of adapting care to children's families and cultures. Experiences within programs were meaningful, relevant, and respectful to the children and their families. The group of programs not rooted in a particular ethnically defined cultural community—the Diverse Families group—adapted care to children's families and cultures by focusing on family strengths and combating bias against the racial identity of the families.

Perhaps because the community advocates who selected the programs also were involved in conversations across race and ethnic boundaries about the parameters of high-quality ECE and child care, the programs selected met current professional standards of quality. These community advocates also functioned as cultural translators. When the research team asked them to nominate good programs, they needed to translate between their understandings of the researchers' and the ethnic community members' definitions of what constituted good care. In part because the members of the research team were willing to engage with the community advocates in defining quality care, we were able to understand that high-quality care does not prescribe particular early childhood practices. Instead, there are a variety of practices that can be used to enact care for children that is warm, sensitive, and individualized.

The ECE practices within these programs were both specific to particular racial and ethnic groups and universal. The participants in these programs believed in forming positive and respectful relationships with children and families, in engaging children in meaningful developmental activities, and in preparing children for a formal school system that they believed did not respect the strengths of their children. The particular ECE practices used by program participants to enact what might be considered universal principles of care were shaped by beliefs about race, poverty, and bias. Thus, practices looked different from an outsider point of view, and it was fairly easy for observers to focus on what was different. Yet when observers were trained and asked to use standardized rating schemes for child care quality, the programs received similar scores within the sample and higher scores than found in large-scale representative child care samples. These findings support the premise that there is more than one path to ECE quality and that ECE practices are distinctly different from ECE quality. In other words, exemplary early childhood education is both universally good and adaptive to culture.

Are Practices Specific to Cultural Communities?

Can we conclude that there are some "best practices" particular to cultural communities? That, for example, within programs for African American children and their families, the combination of teacher warmth and didactic teaching of basic

skills is a best practice? To do so would not do justice to the complexity and nuances of the practices used by the programs described in this book. It is true that
at least one program, rooted in the African American cultural community, combined warmth and didactic teaching and was successful. In the social-historical
period in which the data were collected, this program stood out for its focus on
academic learning. If we were to replicate this research more than a decade later,
I suspect that every program would include more content instruction in language,
literacy, and mathematics. There is now better empirical support for the predictability of pre-academic learning for school success (Duncan et al., 2007). Professional development efforts have been encouraging teachers to be more directive
in teaching pre-academic content. However, large-scale descriptions of preschool
classrooms suggest that the dynamic and warm teaching of basic concepts found
in the programs from the African American cultural community in this study was
fairly unusual (Howes, Burchinal, et al., 2008; Pianta et al., 2005). Within the
social-historical period of the programs we described, to be dynamic, warm, and
focused on basic concepts reflected a commitment to both other-mothering and
providing a school where children who historically have not succeeded in school,
could excel.

While practices within the African American community could be named, it
was more difficult to identify the practices of the programs in the Latino/a community, in part because they seemed more in transition at the time of the observations. In the intervening years the issue of language use has become even more
salient in these communities. And just as our observations could not make a clear
case for English-only, Spanish-only, or English and Spanish in the classrooms as
a best practice, more current research suggests that while English-language learners
benefit from preschool experiences, there is no best way to organize language in
the classroom (Barnett, Yarosz, Thomas, Jung, & Blanco, 2007). As Latino/a families continue to migrate into Los Angeles, more and more preschools that tradi-
tionally have served African American children are becoming schools for primarily
monolingual Spanish-speaking children. The tensions created by these changes,
and illustrated in our observations, are being replicated in many programs. Providing good care for Latino/a children in these changing schools seems to depend
on the ability of the program directors to make cultural translations of developmentally appropriate practices for all children of color (Sanders et al., 2007).

Bridges Between Home and ECE Program
and Child–Teacher Relationships

We found that, in general, teachers had an easier time constructing positive relationships with children with whom they shared a home cultural community than
with children who were different in home cultural community. However, the re-
verse was not always true. Some teachers who did not share a home cultural com-

munity with the children in their classroom were able to construct positive attachment relationships with them, and others were not as able to do so. The difference between these two groups of teachers was not intentionality; all of the teachers in these programs intended to form positive relationships with all children and were thoughtful in their practices around these goals. What did appear to differ was the curricular tool the teachers selected or had available. The teachers who found the NAEYC Anti-Bias Curriculum useful, particularly the White North Carolina teachers and the Latino/a teachers trained by White directors in the Diverse Families programs, appeared to be able to use this tool to help them form positive cross-ethnic child–teacher relationships.

In our observations, the African American teachers of Latino/a children who were more focused on school readiness were both less likely to adopt a curricular tool associated with NAEYC and less able to form positive relationships across home cultural communities. This issue seemed to be a matter of priorities and of timing. At the time of our observations, NAEYC had not yet published the revision of its developmentally appropriate practice, which included more focus on academic content. In the minds of these teachers, NAEYC and DAP did not mean school readiness. The ABC may have been seen as not essential to the main task of preparing children for school.

Also recall that the study was completed before the No Child Left Behind teacher accountability. In this study, a focus on school readiness was associated with close ties to formal kindergarten and Title 1 funding, with shorter program days, and with meeting standards for pre-academic achievement. With the current greater emphasis on teacher accountability for student achievement, contemporary teachers may be having an even more difficult time forming relationships across cultural communities. In one recent study, teachers who initially perceived children not like them in cultural community as difficult were unlikely to form positive teacher–child relationships over time (Howes & Shivers, 2006). Teachers in large-scale studies of prekindergarten programs, designed to get children academically ready for school, appear pressured to cover academic material (Clifford et al., 2005). Under these conditions it is possible to imagine teachers struggling to form positive relationships with children who are both falling behind and different from themselves in home cultural community.

Dimensions of Programs: Turning the Kaleidoscope Versus Predictions

In an earlier publication, drawn in part from the programs described in this book (Wishard et al., 2003),[1] we found that it was impossible, using a regression model, to predict children's experiences from program quality and practices without also considering the ethnicity of the children and the teacher, and that practices varied by teacher–child ethnic pairing. We concluded that it was essential to consider not only program quality but also the specific combination of practices articulated by the programs in order to understand how community and cultural goals guide both the types of activities that children participate in and the meaning or purpose of the activities.

While a similar conclusion can be drawn from the material presented in this book, using the metaphor of the kaleidoscope to examine dimensions of programs as foreground against the background of the other dimensions permits a more expanded view of the importance of cultural community understandings of the meaning of race, ethnicity, and home language for implementation of high-quality ECE programs. When we assume that all aspects of a program—the children, the interpersonal, the cultural-institutional community, and the larger cultural communities to which the program belongs—work together to form patterns rather than compete for independent predictability, it becomes possible to describe the universal and culturally adaptive aspects of each program. For example, as discussed above, we found teacher–child relationships across cultural communities to be essential in creating care that was both culturally adaptive and sensitive. If we had extracted from this analysis a best practice such as, "It is important to ethnically match teachers and children," we would be doing a disservice. Instead, by using a method of analysis that permits foregrounds and backgrounds, we could clarify practices that enabled teachers to reach across cultural communities and provide adaptive and sensitive care to all children, within and across their own cultural community.

LIMITATIONS

Small Sample

Only 12 programs are described in this book and only two geographic regions. We would not expect to find that the practices or the programs described are generalizable across the vast array of ECE programs available to children in the United States. Because of this limitation of size, it is particularly important for us not to assume that, for example, all African American-led programs serving children in a large urban area would have characteristics similar to the programs described. It is valid to suggest that the issues and challenges faced by programs serving similar ethnic and racial groups in similar communities may be shared and worth considering when examining care for children. The advantage of our methodology and of working small was that we were able to create a more complex and rich description of the participants, classrooms, and programs.

Timing of the Study

It is also important to note that the active data collection of the project took place in a particular social-historical period. In retrospect, it was a transitional period.

Data collection occurred prior to early childhood professional groups' publication of standards for academic content learning, prior to NAEYC's revision of developmentally appropriate practice to include more attention to both cultural diversity and pre-academic learning standards, and prior to teachers and programs being held accountable for student learning. Certainly, if we had evaluated the programs in the subsequent decade, we would have found them to be struggling with these issues and perhaps would have drawn different conclusions about the programs. While the programs struggled with conflicting goals and ideas about what prepared a child for formal school, they did not, with the exception of Love and Learn, formally test the children. As high-stakes standardized assessment has become more widespread, we suspect it would now play a larger and different role in the programs.

At the time of data collection, the two states in question, California and North Carolina, evaluated ECE programs as meeting or not meeting a set of program standards. These program standards were fairly well aligned with the ECERS instrument that we used to measure quality. If we had evaluated the programs according to child outcomes rather than program standards, our entire discussion of what is a "good" child and "school readiness" would have been different. Our recent large-scale work with prekindergarten programs in 11 states suggests that the fit between program standards loosely based on traditional research standards of quality and children's pre-academic gains is not a perfect one (Clifford et al., 2005; Early et al., 2007; Howes, Burchinal, et al., 2008). Enhancing children's learning of academic content requires a different instructional climate than we found in most pre-K classrooms and, we suspect, in the classrooms in this study. To create these instructional climates, teachers need different professional development experiences in teaching literacy and math than those provided in most ECE preparation programs. While I still would argue that providing sensitive care that promotes positive teacher–child relationships makes children's learning from teachers possible, enhancing academic development also appears to require more than teacher sensitivity and warmth (Duncan et al., 2007). Even with a greater recognition of the importance of academic content, the tension over curricular issues—play versus drill and practice—that we observed is still very active in the ECE field.

APPLICATION TO CURRENT ISSUES IN THE ECE FIELD

What Makes an Effective Teacher?

These observations provide rich descriptions of effective teachers. The issue for advocates and educators is how to produce effective teachers. One legacy of the public education program based on the large-scale child care quality studies of the 1990s (NICHD ECCRN, 2002; Phillipsen, Burchinal, Howes, & Cryer, 1997) was state-level program standards for ECE and child care programs. Almost all of these standards and those of professional organizations assumed that if regulations were improved, so would effective teaching, classroom experiences, and children's readiness for school. Unfortunately, this assumption proved to be incorrect (Howes, Burchinal, et al., 2008; Mashburn et al., 2008; Pianta et al., 2005). In part, this assumption was wrong because ECE programs with funding tied to these standards were underfunded and underregulated (Barnett et al., 2007). And in part, this assumption was wrong because the standards set the threshold too low, for example, assumed that slightly larger groups or somewhat fewer teachers could do as well as the group sizes and adult-child ratios specified in the professional standards (Clifford et al., 2005).

The larger issue, and one that the current project informs, is that effective teaching in ECE is imperfectly achieved by requiring a degree, a set of classes, or smaller groups of children (Early et al., 2007). Effective teaching requires teachers who can engage children in warm, sensitive, and meaningful interaction. In order to learn, young children need both warm and sensitive emotional climates, and organized and reflective approaches to content, both academic and social-emotional (Hamre, 2007; LoCassle-Crouch et al., 2007). We conducted the project described in this book within the National Center for Early Development and Learning (NECDL) administered by the then Office of Educational Research and Improvement (now the Institute of Education Sciences) in the U.S. Department of Education. We worked with the Pianta group within the NECDL to establish definitions of effective teaching based in part on the observations we described in this book. Effective teaching is now used as the basis of several professional development programs that are underway and showing potential (Pianta, Mashburn, Downer, Hamre, & Justice, 2008; Raver et al., 2008). In these programs teachers are taught to focus on interactions with children, shown examples of effective teachers engaged with children, and asked to reflect on their own practice as they engage with children.

Prekindergarten

The work of the NECDL and the National Early Childhood Research Center,[2] including the early publications of the project described in this book (Howes, Shivers, & Ritchie, 2004; Ritchie, 2003; Ritchie & Howes, 2003; Ritchie, James-Szanton, & Howes, 2003; Shivers, Howes, Wishard, & Ritchie, 2004; Wishard et al., 2003), and the study of prekindergarten programs (Clifford et al., 2005; Howes, Burchinal, et al., 2008) contributed to the public debate that led to the widespread establishment of prekindergarten programs.

Prekindergarten programs are still a work in progress, a promise rather than a success story (Pianta & Howes, 2009). The descriptions in this book suggest that full-day ECE programs may be better able to convey the promise of ECE programs than part-day programs. Too often the part-day programs described in the large prekindergarten study (Clifford et al., 2005), as well as the Ready to Learn half-day program described in this book, felt rushed—too much expected of teachers and children in too little time. It may take all day for teachers to be warm, responsive, and sensitive to the children who come to ECE programs from home cultural communities very different from the ECE program cultural community, which stresses school readiness and success.

A second insight from the observations in this book concerns children learning English and Spanish at the same time. As we have discussed, the participants in the ECE programs in the Latino/a cultural community were far from unanimous in their practices around these dual-language learners. However, Spanish was still an option for verbal interaction in all programs. Currently, most prekindergarten programs, at least in Los Angeles, are conducted only in English, with an increasing emphasis on a back-to-basics curriculum (Fuligni, Howes, Lara-Cinisomo, & Karoly, 2009). This raises concerns that the children will lose their language bridge between home and ECE program cultural communities.

Quality Rating Systems

Another current issue in ECE, again influenced, for better or worse, by the work of the NECDL and the National Early Childhood Research Center, is that of quality rating systems (QRS). As we discussed earlier, the Coast program was a leader in the North Carolina QRS and found it a positive experience. Quality rating systems have some of the problems of state program standards described above, including setting thresholds for quality lower than what is needed to "produce" desired outcomes (Mashburn et al., 2008). Furthermore, quality rating systems are not necessarily based on observations of classrooms, and when they are, the systems vary greatly in their process for making observations (Howes, Pianta, et al., 2008). The project described in this book illustrates the complexity of making classroom observations, particularly when the observers do not share the same cultural community as the program participants.

WHAT WE HAVE LEARNED

The primary value of this project is that it provides a framework for thinking about ECE programs that serve low-income children and their families with practices that are both culturally adaptive and consistent with professional standards. Essential elements of the study that could be replicated as best practices are the collaborative, respectful relationships between advocates and researchers in defining quality care and our mixed-method approach to collecting data at the individual, interpersonal, institutional, and social-historical level. We were successful at describing ECE practices within a cultural context only when we could think at all of these levels, foregrounding and backgrounding them in order to clarify meaning. The programs described in this book were high quality because the advocates who found them and the program participants who created them were members both of cultural communities defined primarily by race and ethnicity and of cultural communities across race and ethnicity committed to creating early childhood education settings consistent with professional standards of quality.

A Multifaceted Methodology

IF OUR RESEARCH TEAM was to be successful in understanding child development as embedded within cultural participation, we found we had to engage in self-conscious and self-reflective multifaceted methodology. I begin this appendix with a discussion of relationships between the researchers and research participants and within the research team. Relationship construction was essential to our being able to do this work of understanding development and culture. This involved being respectful research partners and at the same time establishing boundaries between researchers and participants in parts of the research process, as well as constructing respectful relationships within the research team and with the research participants around issues of race and ethnicity. While the issue of university–community partnerships was relatively new at the time of our data collection in the late 1990s, such partnerships are increasingly common in this era of educational accountability (Pianta, 2007). These partnerships succeed or fail largely due to the kind of relationships developed within the partnership.

The issue of the articulation of practices by early childhood teachers became central in designing our project. While there is currently a resurgence of interest in ECE curriculum, teachers in the late 1990s were not as exposed to the language of "best practices" and scripted curriculum. This meant that many teachers had no professional vocabulary for discussing their practices. In the last section of this appendix I provide an overview of the various procedures and measures we used to describe the elements of the programs.[1] A detailed description of the procedures and measures can be found in Appendix B.

RESEARCH AND RELATIONSHIPS

Researchers and Participants

Our work was guided by the assumption that this project would be successful only if we were able to construct respectful and positive relationships between the program staff and the researchers. Sharon Ritchie, Los Angeles project director, placed this assumption firmly within attachment theory as follows:

We believed that the quality of our relationships with the program staff would deeply affect the efficacy of our work. In a parallel process with our own assumptions around the need for a trusting relationship between a teacher and a child as the foundation upon which learning and meaningful interaction can take place, we engaged in the very slow process of constructing positive, trusting researcher–participant relationships. We believe that one of the most important consequences of working with the programs has been that researchers and practitioners were able to learn from each other—that we were able to narrow the gap between researchers and what they observe, and the day-to-day practices of teachers working with children. (Internal memo, S. Ritchie, 1996)

The research team had to negotiate two different kinds of relationships with research participants—relationships with programs mediated through the program director, and relationships with individual teachers. In addition, we had to negotiate relationships within the research team. Relationships between the local research project directors and the program directors began to be constructed early in the process. We had to have the permission of the program directors to spend time in the classrooms over the course of several years to interview staff, and eventually for the teaching staff and program directors to spend days or evenings in focus group meetings. No program director would agree to engage in this process without consulting with her staff, so for the most part, after several meetings with the program director, the local project director met with the entire staff of the program. After the program had agreed to participate, a research partner—a graduate student and/or former teacher—began weekly participant observations in the program. The relationships between these research partners and the classroom teachers were essential to our gaining access to the day-to-day practices of the programs.

Relationships with Programs. As we began and continued this work, we engaged in a series of dialogues with the program participants, primarily the program directors but also the teaching staff, about what questions we were trying to answer, the best way to obtain the information, and the roles researchers and program participants would play in the research process. The program directors raised issues of mutuality in this process. They asked what we would be able to give back to the programs. Would they be able to use the data for continuous program improvement, and to report to their funders, boards, and parents? Whom could they tell that they were participants? Could they use the fact that they had been selected as a good program to advertise to children and families? To fund-raise?

We warned them that we would maintain independence as researchers. We would report all findings from the research—both positive and negative—rather than only "wished for" findings. We, the researchers, would retain the responsibility (and the control) when it came to selecting research instruments and designing the procedures, even as we discussed with the participants the best way to get information. We would randomly select participating classrooms, teachers, families, and children rather than having the program select them for us. We would maintain confidentiality of responses. That is, the program director would not get reports on the teaching effectiveness (or ineffectiveness) of particular staff. These discussions provided content for the developing relationships between researchers and participants.

Still, the program directors insisted that we could not simply expect to take from the programs; instead, we needed to provide them with feedback about what we were seeing in a way that was useful to them in a day-to-day fashion. After much discussion of confidentiality and research ethics, we agreed to engage in feedback sessions after each phase of naturalistic observation of children's experiences in the program. We asked whether the programs wanted feedback to their staff, their parents, and/or their boards. Each program invited us to come and provide feedback to at least one of these groups.

At feedback sessions we felt it was very important to engage in dialogue, rather than simply present results. We wanted to present our information in a way that validated the participants' very hard work and real successes, and also to engage with them in a dialogue about how their perceptions interacted with ours. It was essential that their ideas contribute to the accuracy of our data and the interpretation of our results. What we were bringing was a different lens through which they could view their own work. Program staff did not often have the luxury or the means to specifically look at, for example, how the children in their program spent the day, the complexity of play, or their own levels of sensitivity or consistency.

Our challenge here was to make our materials and presentation understandable. We had to be bilingual and we had to take very academic content and make it accessible. We had a bilingual research team member present at all sessions, but in some programs it was one of the teaching staff members who translated our work both from English to Spanish and from academic to useful. We developed materials for the feedback sessions, including a written report that briefly described each measure we were using, and we provided programs with their own scores, grouped in order to protect confidentiality. That is, a program would receive scores on a measure for the entire center, not individual classroom scores.

When looking at the data, it was evident that even in the best of situations there was always room for growth. In light of the relationships that we were forming with the staff, it was impossible not to share these findings. As dedicated, hardworking teachers and directors, they wanted to improve and refine their practice based on new information. As researchers, we were providing opportunities and situations through which the staff could be challenged by increasingly sophisticated ideas. As they learned more from us, and from one another, they became motivated by their desires to make sense of their own work. The following are quotes from project directors as they responded to our query about the value of the feedback sessions in one of our last directors' focus groups:

> I think it became more of an inservice at Moms—we got this information, how do we on a weekly basis go back to it and evaluate? The people that I work with haven't been seen that way before. It was a wonderful gift.

> My staff at Pierce loved the fact that somebody came in and made observations and gave them feedback. Periodically they will say, "Remember this was said at the feedback sessions. Look at what we are doing."

> They came out and they gave the same or very similar presentation to our parents that they had given to the staff at Down the Hill. It was wonderful for the parents to be able to hear and invest in this process.

> We have already made changes at El Peace based on the input that we have gotten and that has been our treat, like our reward for participating. This is what it is all about. If we can't do this, it is like we're dead.

Relationships with Teaching Staff. The research partners became the most proximal bridge between the programs and the research team. The research partners were "matched" in terms of dominant race, ethnicity, and home language of the program. In one sense this matching and other community connections provided the research partners with insider status. For example, the mother and sister of the research partner at Nickerson were both teachers in the adjacent elementary school and she herself had taught at a nearby elementary school prior to graduate school. Yet, by their very status as researchers rather than teaching staff, research partners were outsiders as well. They all had at least MA degrees and most were graduate students. Many of them worked as participant observers under teachers often chronologically older, and certainly more experienced in the classroom, than they were. The research partners had to learn the ways of the classroom. For example, in front of her project director who was visiting that day, one research partner was reminded, "When we hand out the snack, we ask the children to sit quietly before they are served."

When the research partners began, they were prepared to appreciate and to attempt to understand the practices in the programs. They intended to respect participants' capacities and skills in caring for children. But the teachers had to take these intentions on trust, and the research partners' outsider status made this difficult at first. More than 2 years after these partnerships began, the director at Moms explained to us that the teachers believed at the beginning that they would be judged and exposed. They feared that what we would see was that they had little education and did not possess skills that we expected to see. Their fear sparked an internal debate as to whether they would agree to participate at all.

What seemed to be the keys to constructing good relationships—and in the end the research partner–teacher relationships were positive—were consistency and being willing to listen. The teachers came to understand that the research partners would indeed show up week after week and that they were sincerely interested in the teaching staff. This understanding of sincere intent appears to have come as the research partners conducted conversational interviews with individual teaching staff members. It was important, we believe, that teachers were paid for these interviews. It meant that we took them seriously as workers and informants.

Relationships Within the Research Team

We were committed to bringing the same processes of developing respectful, positive relationships to bear within the research team as between the research team and the participants. This process involved considerable attention and care throughout the many years of working on this project. Although we were always well meaning, conflicts inevitably arose. Not only did the members of the research team have different responsibilities, positions in the academic hierarchy, and educational backgrounds and experiences, but we were as diverse in race and home language as our participants. Moreover, our different responsibilities and contacts with the participants meant that we had different points of view and investments in the meaning of the data we collected.

As part of their role as bridges, the research partners also had to be responsive to the insider practices of the research team as well as those of their program. They were low-status members of the research team in terms of research experience. They had to learn and achieve research standards of inter-observer reliability on standardized data forms that sometimes did and at other times did not fit with their own notions of the programs' strengths. They could not collect naturalistic observations, ratings, or child assessments in their "own" program, but had to be present when the "fresh eyes" observers came. And they had to write copious field notes and represent "their" program at research team meetings.

As a research team, we had to construct our own working definitions of race, home language, and ethnic identity. In doing this, we came to understand both that race, ethnicity, and home language mark patterns of beliefs and behaviors that are influenced by and influence racism and discrimination, and that each person has an individual trajectory of development and meaning making around these issues, marked by unique understandings and experiences of his/her own race, ethnicity, and home language. These consensus definitions of race, home language, and ethnic identity came from honest and painful discussions. The particular and personal understandings and experiences of the research team members had to be shared and understood before we could interpret clearly and make meaning out of the data we were gathering. For example, in this transcript of a research group meeting following a program directors' focus group, one participant summed up several hours of discussion as follows:

> It seems that we have a multilevel discussion here. One question is: Do we want to continue to do research in this way? Are we gathering the information that we need? Are we gathering information that we will use? Are we gathering information in a way that it's respectful of our participant?
>
> And then there is another set of questions—how do we bring these uncomfortable discussions about race to inform our big questions about the practices we are describing?
>
> And there is a third set of questions that are more personal and private. I think we need to think about our particular roles in this room, and how we as a group that is different in hierarchy and status, different in class background, different in racial background, different in other sorts of dimensions, work together? This group carries in a way the diversity of the people that we are working with. And so to forget that we represent that diversity is to pretend that we are ostriches and that we are doing research that has no connection to us as people. So I think that we probably need to engage in discussions about our roles and how we are working on this: Are we all okay with the process? Are we all okay with the way we are going? With how our individual voices are being heard in the research process?

THE ARTICULATION OF EARLY CHILDHOOD PRACTICES

Because practices are ingrained habits within cultural institutions—in this case, early childhood programs—teachers and directors who have spent years within the institution may not be able to articulate their practices easily. Practices have become commonsense, natural ways of doing things, particularly within early childhood programs that have institutionalized mentoring. In mentored programs, things are done according to the way that a trusted, more experienced teacher taught them. All of the program participants spoke of mentors, strong leaders who had established the programs and worked in them, often in the earliest years of the program's history, and then passed on their legacy through individual guidance and in some cases formal teacher training programs (Howes et al., 2003). The passing on of the way things are done becomes part of a kind of guided participation between mentors and less experienced teachers. Program participants, the first from Nickerson and the second from Pierce, commented:

She guided me to where I need to go to where I was going to school. I said I thought you gave up on me. Oh, no, honey, don't go there with me, because you got your goals.

I want to do everything I can to make the teacher happy with the work I do for her. At first it was kind of hard to adjust because I didn't know what to do. But later on, I learned. The teacher spends a lot of time with us. She's a good person.

Elementary school teachers are able to articulate practices and the intentions associated with practices (Ladson-Billings, 1999). It was more problematic for the early childhood teachers and directors in the programs to tell us what they did as teachers and how and why they organized the care of children. Early childhood teachers generally have less formal education than elementary school teachers, so have had less experience with verbal explanations and rationales. Moreover, within early childhood education there is a strong emphasis on learning through doing and playing, rather than through verbal exchanges. For example, participants described workshops on math learning that stressed block-playing activities, with no theoretical framework linking children's manipulation of units and shapes to their understanding of numeric relations. Also, there is sometimes confusion in the dominant culture around the roles of mothers and teachers of young children. Mothers, or more accurately mothering, are seen as natural or intuitive, hardly needing formal education. Teachers of young children are to be like mothers in loving children, so why rely on experts for knowledge of how to be with children?

As researchers striving to understand practices in these programs, we found that we had to use multiple techniques to access their meaning for the participants. We asked each director and teaching staff member in each program to talk with us individually about their practices. These conversations were tape-recorded and transcribed. Researcher and teacher expectations about this process were not the same. The researchers were puzzled by the initial reluctance of the staff to be interviewed, because we were paying the participants far more than their hourly wage to be interviewed, and the interviewers by then had spent at least 2 months in the classrooms as participant observers and were feeling comfortable, even welcomed. However, anticipating being asked about themselves and how they thought about their jobs created anxiety for the teachers (personal communication, R. Beaglehole, August 1998). Paradoxically, in the end almost every teacher participated in the interviews, and many of the participants expressed appreciation for being considered experts and being asked for their opinions. The research partners reported a positive change in their relationships with program staff after completing the interviews.

However, the interview material was not as rich a source of information about practices and intentionality as we had hoped. The participants struggled with giving detailed descriptions; for example, following are typical answers to the question, How do you help children learn? "They're 3 years old and up, they're too young"; "They cry and want their parents"; "We've learned how to distract them, telling them something, coloring." These answers led us to more questions—Were children too young because learning meant academic subjects to these participants? Or were the activities of early childhood, for example, coloring, not really learning activities in the minds of the participants?

Similar processes occurred in directors' focus groups. When given paper and pens and asked to delineate the goals of their programs, the directors became, in their own words, "inarticulate and frozen in slogans." In contrast, when asked directly about practices, directors were eager and articulate. Attendance at director focus groups was high; directors were upset when one meeting was canceled, and open discussion sessions were lively.

> And it was very hard to break in to have lunch because people were definitely talking and continued to talk about the morning discussions in different groups through lunch. There were lots of conversations going, and we probably should have taped those. (Research meeting transcript, May 1997)

The directors told the researchers that they appreciated the chance to meet to discuss the ongoing challenges and controversies within early childhood education. With the program directors' collaboration, we modified our original design in Los Angeles, where programs were relatively geographically close, to include 12 monthly focus groups of teachers. This technique, combined with the increasingly complex understanding of practices that developed through sustained participant observation, was the most useful for the articulation of practices.

In order to make up the teacher focus group, each site decided in its own way upon a teacher representative who agreed to attend monthly meetings. A member of the research team, Carol Cole, who was not a research partner, facilitated the meetings; she used the coding categories developed for the interviews to structure group discussion. She asked teachers about what they did, why they did it, whether their own philosophy was in concert with that of their program, and what they thought about the families and children they served. As trust developed between members of the groups, differing and even contradictory practices emerged.

The following segments provide examples of the kinds of discussions that took place in the focus groups. The first dialogue concerns individual testing of children. Marisa is from a program (Pierce) that opposes school readiness testing as inappropriate for young children. Testing is an accepted practice at Lois's program (Love and Learn). In the end the two teachers don't seem to agree about testing, although we have considerable information on how they think about it.

> MARISA: Can I ask you a question on the testing that you do? Can you tell me a little bit about that?
>
> LOIS: The testing is over everything they learned since the beginning of this school year from alphabets, numbers, phonics, dot-to-dot, recognition, in-sequence, eye sequence, writing their names, recognizing first names and last name, recognizing patterns, understanding the sequence story. It's a 10-page test.
>
> MARISA: It's interesting because the things that you mention in this test are things that I have done through the whole year, the sequence, the patterns, the numbers, the math, and the name. I know that our children will be tested in the first few weeks in kindergarten, just to see where they are.
>
> LOIS: We test our children at the preschool level before entering kindergarten to make sure which class they will be in.
>
> MARISA: I met a woman who she said that her son went to your school, and she just spoke so highly, so highly of the program. And I said, "You know, I know someone there."

The second segment from a focus group describes the growing relationships between teachers from different programs. This type of relationship was hinted at in the first segment, where Marisa appears to say, "I may not agree with the practice, but I'm willing to try to understand it from your point of view." In the second segment, Donna refers to an attempt initiated by the program directors, and not entirely greeted with enthusiasm by the teachers, to have mutual visiting of the programs.

> I know that there would be a big difference for me visiting you now than the first time. Why? Because I know you two. . . . We have talked. You have talked about your program. Even though I haven't seen the program carried on, but, if I go and I see certain parts of your program, I know what you're doing. But when I first went I looked at the yard, I looked at the classrooms, and I got a lot of information about what your program was about. And the director took me. Now, if I go back, I don't have to go to the director. I can go to you. And I know that it will be from a different point of view now totally. So I'm willing to go and visit other centers. I know I work 8 hours a day and getting out and visiting other people is difficult, but sometimes we get time off if we want to visit other centers too.

By the end of the focus groups, each of the teachers had visited each program and they decided that each program would host one meeting of the group.

We brought the information we were obtaining from the teachers' focus groups to the directors' focus groups. This served to focus the directors' discussions on practices. The directors were generally pleased with the focus groups but, to the researchers' surprise, they tended to think of them as inservice training, emphasizing that the process of participating in the focus group seemed to make the teacher more reflective and more effective as a teacher. They described the pride that their entire teaching staff took in preparing for the program's turn at hosting the focus group, and the at times overwhelming responsibility the participating teachers felt for fairly representing the program's practices.

ACTIVITIES OF THE RESEARCH TEAM

Overview of What We Did to Describe the ECE Programs

We used research procedures from both ethnographic and developmental psychology research traditions, primarily naturalistic observation and secondarily child assessment, to obtain the information that forms the basis for the analysis in this book. Both research traditions, or what are sometimes called mixed methods, were needed to capture the complexity of the material. Ethnographic methods permit discovery of in-depth material not anticipated by the researchers, while using measures common to studies in developmental psychology permits comparison across other studies of ECE programs.

We felt we needed to strike a balance between the research partners with each program and what we called "fresh eyes." The participant observer research partners became semi-insiders to the practices of the program. This was important for making meaning out of practices. However, this insider status may have blinded them to the uniqueness of the program. Therefore, we used two sets of observations about program activities, the participant observers' field notes and the more systematic naturalistic observations of the researcher who was new to the program. The participant observer completed the interviews as well as making field notes because, as discussed earlier, individual interviews helped to create positive researcher–participant relationships.

A third researcher, who joined in the research team meetings but had not read the field notes or participated in other forms of data gathering, conducted the focus groups. This allowed the focus group leader to form relationships with participants within the focus groups rather than having prior relationships with some but not all members of the group. Still another group of researchers, most of whom had not been involved in the earlier phases of the project, conducted the individual assessments and observations of children once they left the programs.[2]

Ethnographic Perspectives

Ethnographic procedures included participant observation, focus groups, and clinical interviews. Each program had a research partner, a participant observer who worked with the teachers and children in the program for 1 day a week for a year, wrote extensive field notes, and participated in weekly meetings with the rest of the research team. Two focus groups, one of teachers and one of directors of the Los Angeles programs, met frequently. We conducted individual clinical interviews with all the program directors and almost all of the teaching staff of the 12 programs.

We used the electronic files of the field notes and transcripts of the weekly research meetings, the focus groups, and the clinical interviews to create detailed case histories of each program and descriptions of the practices used within programs. More detailed descriptions of these ethnographic procedures and our analysis of this material are presented in Appendix B.

Observations and Ratings of Children's Experiences in the Classrooms

Naturalistic Observations. We collected naturalistic observations of everyday experiences in the ECE programs, once near the beginning of the research partnerships and once toward the end. At each time point we collected 50 time sampling "snapshot"[3] observations for each of four children in each classroom.

Naturalistic observations are different from participant observation with field notes. In naturalistic observations, whom and what are observed and how long the observations last are specified before the researcher begins the work. Naturalistic observations also are different because the procedures are the same across a project. Participant observation and naturalistic observation come from different and, too often, contentious research traditions within child development and early childhood education (Dahlberg & Moss, 2005; Dahlberg et al., 2007; Pianta, 2003). I have created naturalistic observational coding systems since my graduate student days in the 1970s, and this procedure has become my primary research practice; however, while it is second nature to me, it needs further explanation as a research practice.

In the spirit of examining practices, it is important to understand that all naturalistic coding systems for ECE begin with researchers spending hours sitting in many different ECE programs watching and listening to the activities of the program participants. Unlike participant observers, these researchers do not engage as participants in the ongoing activity of the program. In fact, the term *naturalistic* is used to describe a process where the observer makes her/himself as inconspicuous as possible and tries never to interfere with ongoing activity. The notes that these researchers take are examined for common themes, which then are reordered into codes with definitions. The codes then are tried out in still more ECE settings, much as content themes are examined in the coding of transcripts. When the researcher is satisfied that the codes represent meaningful units, the codes are taught to other observers who attempt to see and hear the same material in other programs. Eventually, if the coding scheme is meaningful and can be reliably replicated by other observers and in other programs, it becomes codified, often is given a name, and is used over and over again in programs. If the observers note that material is observed that does not fit the existing codes, the codes are modified, expanded, or dropped. For example, our preliminary observations did not include "hanging out" as an activity. We added it after noting that it was a common activity. The coding scheme and codes also are modified when the researcher is asking a new question. Researchers in this tradition tend to use coding schemes used and published by others, if possible, so that a common language and understanding occur across researchers.

In this project we had several concerns that needed to be addressed in naturalistic coding. We had to make sure that the researchers who collected the data could do so without disrupting the life of the program. And the researchers who observed different programs had to be *reliable*. That is, we had to be certain that the same activity and behaviors would be coded the same way by every observer. We had to have codes that captured the same activities and behaviors across everyday life in the programs. A description of the observers, their training, and how we worked to achieve reliable observations is presented in Appendix B.

Codes for Everyday Life in the Program. In determining what codes to use in our naturalistic observations, we first turned to codes that had been used before in large representative studies of community-based child care. Recall that the starting point for this project was to describe more completely programs that were considered good for children and families. We therefore used the Adult Involvement Scale, the Revised Peer Play Scale, and a measure that describes children's play with objects, all originally designed for naturalistic observations of children's experiences in child care and then used in large representative studies (Howes & Matheson, 1992; Howes & Stewart, 1987; Rubenstein & Howes, 1979). All of these scales include many behaviors that are described in Appendix B and individually coded in the snapshot procedure. Based on our preliminary observations in the programs, we added a number of codes to the snapshot coding scheme. These included ways to describe child and teacher engagement in particular learning activities, and time the child spent with the primary teacher. These also are described in Appendix B.

Global Ratings. Drawing from a developmental psychology research tradition, we included some global ratings at the end of each snapshot naturalistic observation session. We used the Attachment Q-Set (Waters, 1990), the Classroom Interaction Scale (Arnett, 1989), and the Early Childhood Environment Rating Scale (Harms & Clifford, 1980). One Attachment Q-Set was completed for each child, as well as one Classroom Interaction Scale and one Early Child-hood Environment Rating Scale for each classroom. The Attachment Q-Set measures the child–teacher relationship, while the other two ratings have been used in large-scale representative studies of the quality of community-based child care (Peisner-Feinberg et al., 2001). These rating scales are described more fully in Appendix B.

CONCLUSIONS

This appendix serves as an illustration of how the research project was deliberately positioned between extremes of research methodology. We began with a discussion on forming relationships between outsiders and insiders—between the research staff and the program participants, and between research staff who "matched" and did not "match" the ethnic and racial heritage of the programs—and continued with an overview of the procedures and measures. As we discussed in Chapters 1 and 2, we needed approaches from many different research traditions and considered them all essential and salient in order to describe participation in cultural communities and children's development.

Detailed Descriptions of
Procedures and Measures

INCLUDED IN THIS APPENDIX are detailed descriptions of the various procedures and measures used in the project. The procedures, measures, and analytic codes are presented in Table B.1.

ETHNOGRAPHIC PERSPECTIVES

Procedures

Participant Observation. Each ECE program was assigned a partner from the research team who was similar in ethnic background to the modal ethnic group represented by the program teaching staff and children. In all programs that used both Spanish and English in the classroom, the research partner was Spanish–English bilingual. The research partner visited the program weekly. During the visits, the partner engaged in the life of the program, visiting classrooms, working with children under the direction of a teacher, and discussing events with the teachers during naptime and breaks in their work with children. After each visit the research partner wrote a description of daily life in the program and an ongoing interpretive analysis of the meaning of ECE practices in the program. These field notes were shared by members of the research team and preserved in electronic form for further coding and analysis.

Simultaneously, the research team discussed, audiotaped, and transcribed their ongoing understandings of the programs and their practices in weekly meetings. Field notes by the participant observers and transcripts and notes of these research team meetings were used to create a case history of each program. Excerpts from these field notes and research team notes are used in this book to illustrate our understandings of the programs.

Focus Groups.[1] There were 12 focus groups that met monthly in Los Angeles, comprising two teacher representatives from each program. Teachers were paid to attend the focus groups and dinner was provided. In all programs the

Table B.1. How we did this work.

Procedure	Measures	Analytic codes
Ethnographic perspectives		
Participant observation field notes	Transcripts	Practices
Focus groups	Transcripts	Practices[a]
Clinical interviews	Transcripts	Practices
		Teacher
		Demographics
		Professional background
Observations and ratings		
Naturalistic observation	Snapshot	
	Adult involvement	Monitor
		Routine
		Minimal
		Simple
		Elaborated
		Intense
	Summary:	Responsive involvement
	Peer play scale	Solitary
		Parallel
		Parallel aware
		Simple social
		Complementary-reciprocal
		Cooperative pretend
		Complex social pretend
	Summary:	Competent peer play
	Play with materials	Carry/mouth
		Manipulate
		Functional
		Creative
		Dramatic
	Summary:	Complex play
	Teacher engagement	Conversation
		Language play
		Facilitate peer interaction
		Positive management
		Negative management
	Activities	Creative
		Language arts
		Didactic
		Fine-motor
		Gross-motor
		Hanging out
		Routine
		Unoccupied
Child ratings	Attachment security (Q-set)	
Global ratings	Quality	
	Classroom interaction	Sensitivity
		Harshness
		Detached
	Environmental Rating Scale	Average item score

[a] Described in detail in Chapter 5.

teachers themselves, not the program director, decided who was to attend the focus groups. The focus group leader, Carol Cole, structured group discussions around variations in practices. The sessions were audiotaped and transcribed.

Bimonthly focus groups were held with the program directors in Los Angeles. The purpose of the groups was to articulate practices at the program level. Sharon Ritchie, Carollee Howes, and Carol Cole structured and led these groups. Again the sessions were audiotaped and transcribed.

Clinical Interviews. We conducted individual interviews with all program directors and teaching staff who wished to be interviewed. No program directors declined; 95% of teaching staff were interviewed, and the remaining 5% declined an interview due to time conflicts. Interviews were conducted in either English or Spanish depending on the preference of the participant. These interviews both gave staff a chance to articulate their practice and provided a setting and time for a one-on-one conversation between a research team member and a program staff member. The interviews were structured like a conversation, and questions fell under the following general headings: (1) What do you do in the program to help children learn and develop and why? (2) How did you become a teacher? (3) How would you describe the families and children who use the program? At the conclusion of the interview, the interviewer and the participant completed a standardized teacher demographic information sheet that requested personal information, including ethnic identity and home language, as well as information on professional background, education, and training in early childhood. For our analysis, each interview was transcribed and, if applicable, side-by-side English and Spanish versions were prepared.

Case Histories, Categories, and Coding of Ethnographic Material

Coding of Transcripts from the Interviews and Focus Groups. Interview and focus group transcripts were read and discussed repeatedly by the research team. Content codes were derived by repeated reading of the interviews, consensus agreement on codes, and coding at two levels. One set of codes was applied to each meaningful unit within the transcript. Meaningful units were utterances, sentences, or in some rare cases paragraphs.[2] Each meaningful unit then was coded for content category (e.g., teaching and learning practices).[3] All units with the same content category codes then were collapsed within transcripts and a most prevalent and salient content category score (e.g., exposure, direct, or scaffolding) was given to each participant.[4] In most cases, content codes were mutually exclusive; only one response per teacher or program could be coded. In these cases the dominant or most salient response was coded.[5]

Teacher- and director-articulated practices pertaining to teaching and learning of pre-academic material, social competence, language and culture, families, and teachers were coded at both the individual teacher and program director levels.

When a director or teacher participated in a focus group as well as had an interview, we used both sources of information to make the final score for the participant. While participants from the same program could have the same scores, the homogeneity of practices within a program varied with the program and within the type of practice. We use representative quotes throughout this book to illustrate our coding and to let the reader "see" the words of the teacher or director participant.

Case Histories. After all the transcripts had been coded, the current project directors, Sharon Ritchie and Gisele Crawford, wrote detailed case histories of each program using the participant observers' field notes, their own notes and impressions, and transcripts of all research team meetings. Included in the case histories were questions posed by and about the program at the time of its original selection; the history of the program, including why it was started; information on funding, length of day, and classroom organization; descriptions of the parent agency and other services offered; teaching staff education and experience; opportunities for on-site training and supervision; a description of the ethnic composition of the families served; a description of any particular circumstances of families, and how special needs children were served; descriptions of daily life in the programs—priorities in terms of how children spent their time and philosophies around daily decisions; and reflections on changes over the several years of contact between the researchers and program participants. The principal investigators and two graduate students reviewed these case histories. The two graduate students were women of color who had had extensive experiences within the early childhood field and communities of color. The reviewers raised questions about the case histories that led to further clarifications and revisions, and in some cases to returning to the program to ask questions for clarification. These case histories were treated as data in the analyses presented in this book.

OBSERVATIONS AND RATINGS OF CHILDREN'S EXPERIENCES IN THE CLASSROOMS

Naturalistic Observation

Observers and Their Training. A researcher from our research team, but different from the participant observer, was assigned to each program for naturalistic observations. The observers were not necessarily of the same ethnic background as the program participants, but they spoke the same primary language (Spanish, English, or Spanish and English) as the program participants. All of the naturalistic observers also were participant observers in other programs, so they had experience in classrooms and in being respectful of the program participants.

These observers were trained in observing together in programs that were not part of this work but were diverse in ethnicity and home language. The observers met common research standards for reliability, coding the same way what they saw and heard.[6]

Coding Procedures. Over the course of a day (between 5 and 8 hours, depending on the program), 50 time sampling "snapshot"[7] observations were collected for each of four selected children per classroom. To complete a snapshot, the observer located a child and recorded his/her social contacts and activities. The observer used a recording sheet with the codes in the first column. Each code was recorded as present or absent for each child at each snapshot interval. After recording a child's information, the observer moved on to the next child on the list until the contacts and activities of all four children had been recorded. This process of coding all four children was repeated in 5-minute blocks of time. After each 5 minutes, the observer rested and then returned to the snapshot task. Care was taken to space the snapshots across the course of the daily program to capture the children's experiences in the program. Naturalistic observations were collected twice in each program, at 6-month intervals.[8]

Adult Involvement Codes. The Adult Involvement Scale (Howes & Stewart, 1987), a rating measure of the intensity of teacher–child involvement, was included in the snapshot coding. We gave the child a rating on this scale each time the teacher was within 3 feet of the child or when teacher–child interaction occurred over a distance of more than 3 feet. Therefore, a child could have a maximum of 50 ratings (one for each snapshot). Only one scale point could be recorded in each snapshot.

The codes for adult involvement represent increasing complexity and reciprocity in adult–child interaction. The first code is "monitor," which was coded if the teacher was close to the child but did not engage in interaction. "Routine" was coded when the teacher touched the child for changing or other routine caregiving but made no verbal response to the child. "Routine" also was coded during whole-group activities when the adult merely gave instructions, passed out materials, or read a book straight through without making any attempts to interact with the group of children (e.g., adult doesn't ask clarifying or expanding questions, doesn't pause to answer children's questions, etc.). "Minimal" was coded if the teacher touched the child only for necessary discipline, moved one child away from another, answered direct requests for help, or gave verbal directives with no reply encouraged. "Minimal" also was coded during whole-group activities when an adult verbally responded with simple, one-word sentences (e.g., "Okay," "That's right," "Good") or with mere nodding of the head. "Simple" responsive involvement was coded when the teacher used some warm or helpful physical contact (beyond the essential routine care) or verbally answered the child's verbal bids but did not elaborate. During whole-group activities, the adult might have responded to the child/children with short sentences or initiated simple social interaction (e.g., "Yes, you need to glue that piece," or "You're doing such a good job listening!"). In "elaborated" involvement, the teacher engaged in some physical gestures, maintained close proximity to the child, or acknowledged the child's statements and responded. "Elaborated" also was coded if the teacher was engaged with the group, was asked and answered complex questions, or solicited active participation from all group members, including, but not exclusively, the target child. The highest scale point was "intense." This was coded when the teacher hugged or held the child; restated the child's statement, thus acknowledging and providing answers to the child; engaged the child in conversation; or played interactively with the child. In group situations, "intense" was coded if the teacher engaged in a conversation meant to include all group members, including, but not exclusively, the target child.

Using the frequency of these behaviors, we created a summary code called "responsive teacher involvement" that represented the sum of the proportion of simple, elaborated, and intense adult involvement divided by the total units of when the child was within 3 feet of a teacher.

Peer Play Codes. We used the Revised Peer Play Scale (Howes & Matheson, 1992) to measure the children's engagement with peers. The scale has seven points. The first 2 points measure solitary play and peer play that is not interactive: (1) solitary play with proximity to peer without interaction, and (2) parallel play when the target child and a peer are within 3 feet of each other and engaged in the same activity but do not acknowledge each other. The other five scale points capture interactive peer play: (3) parallel play with eye contact; (4) simple social play; (5) complementary-reciprocal play; and two levels of pretend play—(6) cooperative social pretend (the target child and another child enacting complementary roles), and (7) complex social pretend play (the target child and a peer demonstrating both social pretend play and metacommunication about the play). Complementary-reciprocal social play, cooperative pretend play, and complex pretend play are competent forms of play with peers (Howes & Matheson, 1992). The peer play scale points were mutually exclusive and the highest possible observed scale point was recorded in each interval. From the coded peer play, we created a measure of the proportion of the interactive play that was competent play by summing time in complementary-reciprocal play, cooperative pretend play, and complex pretend play.

Complexity of Child's Engagement with Learning Materials Codes. We also used a scale that captures the complexity of the child's play with materials (Rubenstein & Howes, 1979). The first 3 coding categories are fairly low in complexity: (1) "carry/mouth," (2) "manipulate," and (3) "functional" (using the toy or objects in a functional manner, e.g., pushing a truck). The fourth and fifth categories represent more complex activity: (4) "creative," using the object in a goal-directed manner within some larger creative context (e.g., using a shovel to make a sand castle) or for systematic experimentation (e.g., novel use of an object to solve a problem); and (5) "dramatic," a child's use of an object as if it were something else in the service of pretending (e.g., using a block as a pot for cooking). From the coded cognitive activity, we created a measure of the proportion of the complex play by summing the time the child spent at levels 4 and 5 and dividing by the total number of units of activity.

Teacher Engagement with Children in Activities Codes. In each snapshot, we coded the content of the engagement the teacher had with a child and an activity. For this recording, the teacher was not required to be within 3 feet of the child. These codes informed us of the nature of an observed interaction the teacher had with the child regardless of proximity. More than one coding category could be recorded in each snapshot.

The following categories were coded: conversation, language play, facilitate peer interaction, positive management, and negative management. "Conversation" was coded when the teacher talked with the children in a positive manner. "Language play" was coded when the teacher engaged in some form of language play with the child or whole group of children, for example, using rhyming games, reading one-on-one, or having a social conversation. "Facilitate peer interaction" was defined as the teacher's trying to promote the child's interaction with other children; for example, helping children to start a game, placing children in proximity to one another, or helping them solve a conflict. "Positive management" was defined as the teacher's verbally intervening, redirecting the target child, or reminding the child of the rules for behavior; for example, verbal intervention, redirection, preventive intervention, or issuing a reminder to the child. "Negative management" was coded if the teacher handled the child's problem or misbehavior in a harsh or negative way, such as putting the child in time-out, yelling, criticizing, scolding, threatening, or employing sarcasm or physical abuse.

Activity Codes. Finally, we created coding categories for children's activities. This set of codes captured the activity that the teacher had set up for the children. These categories were: (a) creative activities, including fantasy play, blocks, and open-ended art; (b) language arts, including looking at or reading books to self, being read to, listening to a story (e.g., on record, tape, or video), music, and large-group activities (e.g., circle time); (c) didactic learning activity, including teacher-modeled art projects or teacher-directed drill and practice of school skills, which generally occurred in teacher-led group contexts; (d) fine-motor activity, including playing with small objects usually called manipulatives, such as puzzles or interlocking blocks; (e) gross-motor activity, including running or dancing; (f) hanging out, including standing or sitting with others, such as talking and laughing with teachers and/or peers; (g) routine activities, including transitioning to the next activity, grooming activities, meal time, and snack time, and so on; and (h) being unoccupied, including when a child is not engaged with any other person, any object, or any specific activity (e.g., child aimlessly wandering around or staring into space). During each snapshot, the observer selected only one activity that best fit what the child was doing. For analysis, each child received a score for the proportion of time involved in these activities.

Global Ratings

Attachment Q-Set. To examine the relationships between individual teachers and children, we used the Attachment Q-Set (AQS) (Waters, 1995). Following the naturalistic observations, the observers took the 90 behavior descriptions that serve as items in the AQS (e.g., "this child turns to the teacher when she is upset") and sorted them into nine piles of 10 items each. In this way, the observers described the teacher–child relationship according to the 90 behavior descriptions. Each particular behavior was given a 9-point score corresponding to very characteristic (behaviors in pile 9) to very uncharacteristic (behaviors in pile 1). The item scores for each child–teacher relationship were correlated with an ideal child–teacher relationship (Waters, 1995). These became the children's security scores. Scores can vary from –1.0 to 1.0. A higher score indicates greater security.[9]

Classroom Interaction Scale. The Classroom Interaction Scale (Arnett, 1989) is a 26-item, 4-point rating scale completed by the observer for the head teacher in the classroom at the conclusion of the observation period.[10] It yields three scores: sensitivity (warm, attentive, and engaged); harshness (critical, threatens children, and punitive); and detachment (low levels of interaction, interest, and supervision). Scores from this instrument have been found to predict teachers' involvement with children and the children's social competence (Howes, Phillips, & Whitebook, 1992) and attachment security (Howes & Hamilton, 1992).

Early Childhood Environment Rating Scale. The Early Childhood Environment Rating Scale (Harms & Clifford, 1980) has been widely used in child development research (Helburn, 1995; Phillips & Howes, 1987; Whitebook, Howes, Phillips, & Pemberton 1989). This scale comprehensively assesses the overall day-to-day quality of care provided for children.[11] ECERS items are rated on 7-point scales, with a 3 indicating barely adequate quality, a 5 indicating good quality, and a 7 indicating excellent quality. An average item score is calculated for each classroom.

Notes

Chapter 1

1. Our field does not have common nomenclature for programs serving young children. I use the term *early childhood education*, or *ECE*, to include community-based child care and preschool programs designed to both care for and educate children too young for kindergarten.

2. The use of the words *I* and *we* in this book is deliberate. I, Carollee Howes, have written the book and, consistent with the principle of using the active voice, will use *I* in that form. I also will use *I* when it is clear to me that I am responsible for the analysis. In other cases I will use the word *we* to recognize that I was part of a larger team that collaboratively designed, implemented, and created an understanding of the project and the programs.

3. These community advocates formed two advisory boards. Board members were Vickie Ansley, Yvonne Barnes, Ruth Beaglehole, Carrie Blackhaller, Jan Brown, Deb Cassidy, Richard Cohen, Ethel Carr, Carol Cole, Sharon Davis, Carol Phillips Day, Alice Walker Duff, Kit Kollenberg, Von Langston, Kelly Maxwell, Karen Ponder, Barbara Richardson, Sue Russell, Tina Roemer, Beverley Morgan-Sandoz, Wendy Parise, Lucy Roberts, Patricia Wesley, Diana Jones Wilson, and Talitha Wright.

4. All names of programs are pseudonyms.

5. Research partners who conducted observations and interviews were Jennifer Schexnayder, Esmeralda Nava, Jolena James, and Eva Shivers in California, and Gisele Crawford in North Carolina.

6. The members of the research team were Carollee Howes, Richard Clifford, Sharon Ritchie, Gisele Crawford, Carol Cole, Jolena James, Esmeralda Nava, Kay Sanders, Eva Shivers, Alicia Soto, Holli Tonyan, and Alison Wishard.

Chapter 2

1. These elements are drawn from Rogoff's description of focus.

2. As described in Appendix A, the programs asked for feedback sessions from our observations. The research team provided feedback, and the program directors perceived that the feedback changed practices.

Chapter 3

1. The more recent publication of an analysis of seven large-scale studies of ECE classrooms suggests that having a BA degree in ECE may not be sufficient to produce a learning environment that promotes children's pre-academic success (Early et al., 2007).

2. Test of comparison: F (2, 66) = 4.06, p = .02.

3. Test of comparison: $\chi(8)$ = 17.35, p = .03.

4. M = 5.67 (SD = .75; range 5.41–6.35).

5. Sensitivity: M = 3.58 (SD = .38; range 3.22–3.82); harshness: M = 1.49 (SD = .36; range 1.36–1.79); detachment: M = 1.26 (SD = .35; range 1.0–1.63).

6. We lost children in the follow-up study by design. Only children from California were represented in the first- and second-grade follow-up sample. No parent invited to participate refused permission although some moved away. Eleven of the twelve programs were represented in the kindergarten sample. Children from Nickerson, an after-school program, participated at the onset as first graders, but not as kindergartners. The children seen at all three longitudinal time points were similar to the other children in the longitudinal study in sex (χ^2 (1) = .03, ns), ethnicity (χ^2 (3) = 2.20, ns), and living in difficult life circumstances (χ^2 (1) =. 99, ns).

7. There were no overall differences in these measures across programs: F (4, 150) = .57, p = ns, partial eta squared = .02.

8. Reliability coefficients calculated for young children between the ages of 5 and 6 years were between .79 and .84.

9. Reliability coefficients calculated for combined Hispanic normative groups equaled .93 for young children between 5 and 6 years of age.

10. Calculated reliability coefficients for children between 4 and 6 years of age ranged from .92 to .96.

11. PPVT/TVIP; M = 93.9, SD = 12.8, range = 66–127.

12. W–J Applied Problems; M = 106.5, SD = 14.8, range = 79–151.

13. PPVT/TVIP; first grade: M = 89.6, SD = 17.1; second grade: M = 87.6, SD = 16.8.

14. W–J Applied Problems; first grade: M = 114.7, SD = 11.9; second grade: M = 116.4, SD = 16.7.

15. The STR has shown excellent psychometric properties across a number of student and teacher samples (Pianta & Steinberg, 1992).

16. The CBR ratings of aggression toward peers, exclusion from peer activity, withdrawn/asocial behavior, anxious/fearful behavior, victim of aggression, prosocial with peers, sociability with peers, domineering with peers, and distractible behavior reflect the quality of the child's behavior with peers within the classroom setting. A score of 5 reflects that the category was very characteristic of the child, a score of 3 indicates that the category was somewhat characteristic of the child, and a score of 1 means that the category was not very characteristic of the child during the observation. We used a principal components factor analysis with varimax rotation (accounting for 85% of the variance) to reduce these ratings to three composite measures of the child's observed behaviors with peers: anxious with peers (withdrawn, anxious, and excluded); aggressive with peers (dominant and aggressive), and prosocial with peers (prosocial, sociable, not withdrawn).

17. An average of 4.22 on a 5-point scale of positive teacher–child relationships and a mean of 1.97 (again, 5-point scale) on conflictual teacher–child relationships.

18. Children's scores on peer aggression (M = .26, SD = .42) and peer anxiety (M = 1.32, SD = .39) were in the low range, while their scores on peer prosocial were in the high range (M = 3.59, SD = .34).

19. Positive: first grade; M = 4.15, SD = .64; second grade: M = 4.04, SD = .62.

Chapter 4

1. The figures in this chapter and subsequent analyses have as their denominator the 170 children who were observed in their programs. Thus, the figures represent the proportion of children served by programs or teachers who articulated the practice. Each of the 170 children participated in the research project in one of two periods of data collection. At each data collection point, approximately 25% of the children from each program's classrooms were selected. The classrooms were selected because they served toddler and preschool children. That is, if a program had only one preschool classroom serving 16 children, four children were selected. If instead the program had three classrooms, two serving preschoolers and one serving toddlers, and each classroom had 16 children, 12 children were selected from the program. In the first period children (half girls and half boys) were randomly selected from all the children in the classroom. Six months later children were randomly selected from only the children in the classroom whose parents had given permission for them to be in the longitudinal study, extending beyond the time the children were in the programs. There were no differences between these two data collection times in the demographic characteristics of the children and in the behaviors observed. Therefore, the two time periods were collapsed for analysis. Children were paired with their primary teachers. We randomly selected the children, and then the research partner of the program selected a primary teacher for each child. The primary teacher was the teacher that a child was most likely to go to when he/she was distressed or wanted to share experiences. Teacher practices described in these figures are from the child's primary teacher. Program practices described in these figures are the practices of the program in which the child was enrolled.

Using teacher–child pairs as the unit of analysis means that we assigned all of the scores for the particular child, teacher, and program to the pair, rather than to the individual teacher or child. Each pair thus has a unique combination of scores. Using teacher–child pairs as the unit of analysis reflects a theoretical orientation to the mutual construction of relationships and experiences. I assume that every teacher constructs a unique relationship with every child in the classroom because the behaviors that the child contributes as well as the behaviors that the teacher contributes shape the nature of the relationship (Howes & Ritchie, 1999). I further assume that the nature of the teacher–child relationship *and* the characteristics of the child (e.g., timid or bold) make the experiences of each child in the classroom unique and independent of every other child (Crockenberg, 2003).

2. This unit of analysis means that only about half of the teaching staff who were observed with children and interviewed was included in this analysis. The teachers dropped were all assistant teachers who did not serve as primary caregivers for any children.

Chapter 5

1. We conducted tests of similarities and differences in interpersonal interactions across larger cultural communities using multivariate analysis of covariance. We used a multivariate approach because most of the outcome measures were not independent. We used child's age and gender as covariates because many of the outcomes were related to both age and gender, yet sample sizes, and indeed the major concerns of this study, precluded using them as terms in the analysis. We dropped four teachers from this analysis because they were outliers. The dropped teachers were the White man and Chinese woman

teachers at El Peace, the Japanese American teacher at South Central, and the African American teacher at Coast.

2. Tests of comparison: $F(7, 155) = 16.82$, $p < .001$; Scheffe = .05.

3. To make these comparisons, we used a multivariate analysis of covariance using teacher as the unit of analysis and the five groups defined by larger cultural community as covariates, as well as a bonferroni adjustment for multiple comparisons. Tests of comparison: multivariate $F(4, 147) = 19.92$, $p < .001$; $\eta^2 = .28$.

4. Tests of comparison: $F(3, 151) = 44.72$, $p < .001$; $\eta^2 = .47$.

5. Tests of comparisons: $F(3, 151) = 5.04$, $p < .002$; $\eta^2 = .09$.

6. Tests of comparisons: $F(3, 151) = 27.42$, $p < .001$; $\eta^2 = .35$.

7. Tests of comparison were made using multivariate analysis of covariance with education level of the teacher in the teacher–child pair, child age, and child gender as covariates, and a bonferroni adjustment for multiple comparisons.

8. Tests of comparison: multivariate $F(44, 572) = 55.58$, $p < .001$; $\eta^2 = .81$.

9. Tests of comparison: multivariate $F(16, 600) = 2.43$, $p < .001$; $\eta^2 = .38$.

10. Tests of comparison: $F(4, 150) = 16.29$, $p < .001$, $\eta^2 = .34$; Scheffe = .05.

11. Tests of comparison: $F(4, 150) = 23.44$, $p < .001$, $\eta^2 = .39$; Scheffe = .05.

12. Tests of comparison: $F(4, 150) = 18.18$, $p < .001$, $\eta^2 = .32$; Scheffe = .05.

13. Tests of comparison: $F(4, 150) = 8.99$, $p < .001$, $\eta^2 = .19$; Scheffe = .05.

14. Tests of comparison: $F(4, 150) = 49.51$, $p < .001$, $\eta^2 = .84$; Scheffe = .05.

15. Tests of comparison: $F(4, 150) = 91.55$, $p < .001$, $\eta^2 = .56$; Scheffe = .05.

16. Tests of comparison: $F(4, 150) = 12.39$, $p < .001$, $\eta^2 = .25$; Scheffe = .05.

17. Tests of comparison: $F(4, 150) = 37.68$, $p < .001$, $\eta^2 = .50$; Scheffe = .05.

18. Tests of comparison: $F(4, 150) = 98.03$, $p < .001$, $\eta^2 = .72$; Scheffe = .05.

19. Tests of comparison: $F(4, 150) = 27.09$, $p < .001$, $\eta^2 = .42$; Scheffe = .05.

20. Tests of comparison: $F(4, 150) = 60.92$, $p < .001$, $\eta^2 = .29$; Scheffe = .05.

21. Tests of comparison: $F(4, 150) = 10.40$, $p < .001$, $\eta^2 = .42$; Scheffe = .05.

22. Tests of comparison: $F(4, 150) = 11.00$, $p < .001$, $\eta^2 = .23$; Scheffe = .05.

23. Tests of comparison: $F(4, 150) = 4.39$, $p < .001$, $\eta^2 = .10$; Scheffe = .05.

24. Tests of comparison: multivariate $F(21, 414) = 4.23$, $p = .001$; $\eta^2 = .17$.

25. Tests of comparison: $F(4, 150) = 3.88$, $p = .01$, $\eta^2 = .07$; Scheffe = .05.

26. Tests of comparison: $F(4, 150) = 3.17$, $p = .03$, $\eta^2 = .06$; Scheffe = .05.

27. Tests of comparison: $F(4, 150) = 6.21$, $p = .001$, $\eta^2 = .10$; Scheffe = .05.

28. Tests of comparison: $F(4, 150) = 9.60$, $p = .001$, $\eta^2 = .16$; Scheffe = .05.

29. Tests of comparison: multivariate $F(15, 444) = 25.41$, $p = .000$; $\eta^2 = .46$.

30. Tests of comparison: $F(4, 150) = 5.18$, $p = .002$, $\eta^2 = .09$; Scheffe = .05.

31. Tests of comparison: $F(4, 150) = 34.95$, $p = 000$, $\eta^2 = .41$; Scheffe = .05.

32. Tests of comparison: $F(4, 150) = 35.83$, $p = .000$, $\eta^2 = .67$; Scheffe = .05.

33. Tests of comparison: $F(4, 150) = 22.88$, $p = .000$, $\eta^2 = .31$; Scheffe = .05.

34. Tests of comparison: multivariate $F(6, 298) = 3.77$, $p = .001$; $\eta^2 = .07$.

35. Tests of comparison: $F(4, 150) = 4.73$, $p = .003$, $\eta^2 = .09$; Scheffe = .05.

Chapter 6

1. One of them is not African American and thus was not included in the sample of teacher–child pairs used for analysis.

2. Following the multivariate analysis of covariance, with age and gender covaried, described in Chapter 5, we compared the pairs of African American teachers and African American children with the pairs of African American teachers and Latino/a children.

3. In subsequent years, the core of the research team that worked on this project has worked with several more early childhood programs, originally with African American children and families as participants and now with Latino children and families, and found similar patterns of practices and challenges.

Chapter 7

1. Following the multivariate analysis of covariance described in Chapter 5, we compared the 29 Latino/a teacher–Latino/a child and 12 Latino/a teacher–other-than-Latino/a child pairs, again using multivariate analysis of covariance with age and gender as covariates. There were no significant differences between matched and unmatched pairs.

Chapter 8

I am particularly grateful to Gisele Crawford and Richard Clifford for their insights regarding meaning of race within the North Carolina programs and larger cultural communities.

Chapter 9

1. Of the children in this project who came from difficult circumstances, 83% were from this larger cultural community.

2. Following the multivariate analysis of covariance reported in Chapter 5, we compared the 16 pairs of Latino/a teachers and Latino/a children with 16 pairs of Latino/a teachers and other-than-Latino/a children. There were no significant differences.

Chapter 10

1. The sample for the Wishard and colleagues publication included all of the ECE programs described in this book plus 10 more from the same geographic area but not selected by community advocates.

2. In 2005, the National Center for Early Development and Learning (NECDL), the early childhood research center that funded this project through the U.S. Department of Education's Office of Educational Research and Improvement, ceased to exist. In 2006, the U.S. Department of Education, through the Institute of Educational Research and Improvement, awarded the early childhood research center component to the leadership team of the NECDL. The new research center, the National Early Childhood Research Center (NCRECE), has continued this work. The NECDL was housed at the University of North Carolina; NCRECE is housed at the University of Virginia.

Appendix A

1. In brief, the chronology of the collection phase of the project was as follows: (1) researchers identified advocates within the selected communities to serve on Los Angeles

and North Carolina advisory boards; (2) the research team and advisory boards developed collaborative definitions of quality; (3) advisory boards nominated exemplary programs; (4) researchers gathered information on nominated programs, including site visits; (5) researchers and advisory boards made consensus decisions on participating early childhood programs; (6) programs agreed to participate; (7) the researchers were engaged in multiple methods of gathering data within programs and there were periodic meetings of the advisory boards; (8) during this same period, researcher teams met weekly (and often bicoastally) for ongoing analysis of data, to capture observations about the data that were outside of the scope of the predetermined questions and responses, to note possible emerging patterns, to suggest synthesizing themes, and to raise questions, with these sessions taped, transcribed, and stored electronically; and (9) researchers wrote detailed case histories of each program, completed quantitative data analysis, and continued to gather data on a randomly selected sample of children as they moved through kindergarten to second grade.

2. Sarita Santos, Sharon Ritchie, Jolena James, Gisele Crawford, and Alicia Soto began data collection for the longitudinal sample. Special thanks need to be given to Alison Wishard and Kay Sanders, who took time out of their Ph.D. programs to complete the longitudinal sample data collection, compensated only by love, not salaries.

3. The term *snapshot* refers to a procedure where the observer takes a virtual snapshot by looking and listening to a child for a very short period of time and then recording the child's activities and behaviors.

Appendix B

1. Geographic constraints made it impossible to have focus groups in North Carolina.

2. Inter-coder reliability for segmentation was Kappa = .98.

3. Inter-coder reliability for content category codes ranged from Kappa = .74 to Kappa = .89.

4. Inter-coder reliability for content category codes ranged from Kappa = .86 to Kappa = .95.

5. Inter-coder reliability for most salient response ranged from Kappa = .74 to Kappa = .89.

6. Eight observers were trained to an 85% exact agreement criterion on each item prior to data collection. Because observations took longer than a month to complete due to differences in classroom, program, and researcher's schedules, monthly inter-observer reliability checks were conducted throughout data collection. Median inter-observer reliability for exact item placement was Kappa = .84 (range, Kappa = .79 to .93).

7. The term *snapshot* refers to a procedure where the observer takes a virtual snapshot by looking and listening to a child for a very short period of time and then recording the child's activities and behaviors.

8. The children observed at Time 1 were randomly selected from the classroom (two girls and two boys from each classroom at the site). The children observed at Time 2 were randomly selected (again two girls and two boys per classroom) from children who had received parental permission to participate in the longitudinal study. There were no differences between the demographic characteristics of the children or the behaviors observed

at Times 1 and 2. Therefore, data collected at the two time periods were collapsed by averaging the scores from Time 1 and Time 2.

9. Observers were trained to an 85% exact agreement criterion on each item prior to data collection. Monthly inter-observer reliability checks were conducted throughout data collection. Median inter-observer reliability for exact item placement was Kappa = .87 (range, Kappa = .79 to .96).

10. Median inter-observer reliability was Kappa = .85.

11. Inter-observer reliability on the ECERS ranged from Kappa = .82 to Kappa = .96, median = .89.

References

Abbott-Shim, M., Lambert, R., & McCarty, F. (2000). Structural model of Head Start classroom quality. *Early Childhood Research Quarterly, 15*, 115–134.

Ahnert, L., & Lamb, M. E. (2003). Shared care: Establishing a balance between home and child care settings. *Child Development, 74*, 1044–1050.

Ahnert, L., Rickert, H., & Lamb, M. E. (2000). Shared caregiving: Comparisons between home and child-care setting. *Developmental Psychology, 36*, 339–351.

Arnett, J. (1989). Caregivers in daycare centers: Does training matter? *Applied Developmental Psychology, 10*, 514–552.

Azmitia, M., Cooper, C. R., Garcia, E. E., & Dunbar, N. D. (1996). The ecology of family guidance in low-income Mexican-American and European-American families. *Social Development, 5*, 1–23.

Baker, J. A., Dilly, L. J., & Lacey, C. L. (2003). Creating community-oriented classrooms: Nurturing development and learning. In C. Howes (Ed.), *Teaching 4- to 8-year olds: Literacy, math, multiculturalism, and classroom community* (pp. 157–172). Baltimore: Brookes.

Ball Cuthbertson, B. E., Burr, B. F., Fuller, B., & Hirshberg, D. (2000). *Los Angeles County needs assessment*. Berkeley: University of California.

Barnett, S., Yarosz, D., Thomas, J., Jung, K., & Blanco, D. (2007). Two-way and monolingual English immersion in preschool education: An experimental comparison. *Early Childhood Research Quarterly, 22*, 277–293.

Barnett, W. S., Hustedt, J. T., Friedman, A. H., Boyd, J. S., & Ainsworth, P. (2007). The state of preschool 2007: State preschool yearbook. Rutgers, State University of New Jersey, National Institute for Early Education Research.

Bowlby, J. (1982). *Attachment and loss: Vol. 1. Attachment*. London: Hogarth.

Bowman, B., Donovan, M. S., & Burns, S. (Eds.). (2000). *Eager to learn: Educating our preschoolers*. Washington, DC: National Research Council.

Bracken, S. S., & Fischel, J. E. (2006). Assessment of preschool classroom practices: Application of Q-sort methodology. *Early Childhood Research Quarterly, 21*, 417–430.

Bredekamp, S. (1987). *Developmentally appropriate practice in early childhood programs*. Washington, DC: National Association for the Education of Young Children.

Bredekamp, S., & Copple, C. (Eds.). (1997). *Developmentally appropriate practice in early childhood programs* (Rev. ed.). Washington, DC: National Association for the Education of Young Children.

Bretherton, I., & Munholland, K. A. (2008). Internal working models in attachment relationships: Elaborating a central construct. In J. Cassidy & P. Shaver (Eds.), *Handbook of attachment* (2nd ed., pp. 102–130). New York: Guilford.

Brice-Heath, S. (1988). Language socialization. *Black Children and Poverty: A Developmental Perspective, 42,* 29–41.

Bronfenbrenner, U., & Morris, P. A. (1998). The ecology of developmental processes. In W. Damon & R. M. Lerner (Eds.), *Handbook of child psychology: Vol. 1. Theoretical models of human development* (pp. 993–1028). New York: Wiley.

Brooks-Gunn, J., Rouse, S. E., & McLanahan, S. (2007). Racial and ethnic gaps in school readiness. In R. C. Pianta, M. J. Cox, & K. L. Snow (Eds.), *School readiness and the transition to kindergarten in the era of accountability* (pp. 283–306). Baltimore: Brookes.

Bryant, B., Clifford, R. M., & Peisner, E. S. (1991). Best practices for beginners: Developmental appropriateness in kindergarten. *American Educational Research Journal, 28*(4), 783–803.

Burchinal, M. R., Peisner-Feinberg, E., Bryant, D. M., & Clifford, R. (2000). Children's social and cognitive development and child care equality: Testing for differential associations related to poverty, gender, or ethnicity. *Applied Developmental Science, 4,* 149–165.

Buriel, R., & Hurtado-Ortiz, M. T. (2000). Child care practices and preferences of native- and foreign-born Latina mothers and Euro-American mothers. *Hispanic Journal of Behavioral Sciences, 22,* 314–331.

Cauce, A. M., & Domenech-Rodriquez, M. (2002). Latino families: Myths and realities. In J. Contreras, K. A. Kerns, & A. M. Neal-Barnett (Eds.), *Latino children and families in the United States* (pp. 3–26). Westport, CT: Praeger.

Chang, H. (1993). *Affirming children's roots.* San Francisco: California Tomorrow.

Chavez, L. (1989). Hispanic children and their families. In R. S. Delgado & J. Stefancic (Eds.), *The Latino/a condition: A critical reader* (pp. 106–109). New York: New York University Press.

Clifford, R. M., Barbarin, O., Chang, F., Early, D., Bryant, D., Howes, C., et al. (2005). What is prekindergarten? Characterisitics of public pre-kindergarten programs. *Applied Developmental Science, 9*(3), 126–134.

Coll, C. G., Lamberty, G., Jenkins, R., McAdoo, H. P., Cunic, K., Wasik, B., et al. (1996). An integrative model for the study of developmental competencies in minority children. *Child Development, 67,* 1891–1914.

Collins, P. H. (1990). *Black feminist thought: Knowledge, consciousness, and the politics of empowerment.* New York: Routledge.

Copple, C., & Bredekamp, S. (Eds.). (2009). *Developmentally Appropriate Practice in Early Childhood Programs Serving Children from birth through age 8.* Washington, DC: NAEYC.

Crockenberg, S. (2003). Rescuing the baby from the bathwater: How gender and temperament (may) influence how child care influences child development. *Child Development, 74*(4), 1034–1038.

Dahlberg, G., & Moss, P. (2005). *Ethics and politics in early childhood education.* New York: RoutledgeFalmer.

Dahlberg, G., Moss, P., & Pence, A. (2007). *Beyond quality in early childhood education and care* (2nd ed.). New York: Routledge.

Daniels, D. H., & Shumov, L. (2003). Child development and classroom teaching: A review of the literature and implications for teaching teachers. *Applied Developmental Psychology, 23,* 495–526.

Delpit, L. (1988). The silenced dialogue: Power and pedagogy in educating other people's children. *Harvard Educational Review, 58,* 280–298.

Derman-Sparks, L. (1989). *Antibias curriculum tools for empowering young people.* Washington, DC: National Association for the Education of Young Children.

Derman-Sparks, L., & Olsen, J. (2010). *Anti-Bias Education for Young Children and Ourselves.* Washington, DC: National Association for the Education of Young Children.

Dickinson, D., & Smith, J. R. (1994). Long-term effects of preschool teachers' book reading on low-income children's vocabulary and story comprehension. *Reading Research Quarterly, 29,* 104–122.

Dodge, D. T. (1988). *The creative curriculum.* Washington, DC: Teaching Strategies.

Duncan, G. J., Dowsett, C. J., Classens, A., Magnuson, K., Huston, A., Klebanov, P., et al. (2007). School readiness and academic achievement. *Developmental Psychology, 43,* 1428–1446.

Dunn, L. M., & Dunn, L. M. (1997). *Peabody picture vocabulary test—revised.* Circle Pines, MN: American Guidance Service.

Dunn, L. M., Padilla, E. R., Lugo, D. E., & Dunn, L. M. (1986). *Test de vocabulario de images.* Circle Pines, MN: American Guidance Service.

Early, D., Maxwell, K. L., Burchinal, M., Alva, S., Bender, R. H., Bryant, D., et al. (2007). Teachers' education, classroom quality, and young children's academic skills: Results from seven studies of preschool programs. *Child Development, 78*(2), 558–580.

Early, D., & Winton, P. J. (2001). Preparing the workforce: Early childhood teacher preparation at 2- and 4-year institutions of higher education. *Early Childhood Research Quarterly, 16,* 285–306.

Farver, J. M., & Howes, C. (1993). Cultural differences in American and Mexican mother–child pretend play. *Merrill Palmer Quarterly, 30,* 344–358.

Fisher, C. B., Jackson, J., & Villarruel, F. (1998). The study of African American and Latin American children and youth. In W. Dammon & R. M. Lerner (Eds.), *Handbook of child psychology: Vol. 1. Theoretical models of human development* (pp. 1145–1207). New York: Wiley.

Fuligni, A., Howes, C., Lara-Cinisomo, S., & Karoly, L. (2009). Diverse pathways in early childhood professional development: An exploration of early educators in public preschools, private preschools, and family child care homes. *Early Education and Development, 20,* 507–526.

Fuller, B., Holloway, S. D., Bozzi, L., Burr, E., Cohen, N., & Suzuki, S. (2003). Explaining local variability in childcare quality, state funding, and regulation in California. *Early Education and Development, 14,* 47–66.

Fuller, B., Holloway, S. D., & Liang, X. (1996). Family selection of child care centers: The influence of household support, ethnicity, and parental practices. *Child Development, 67,* 3320–3337.

Galimore, R., Goldenberg, C., & Weisner, T. S. (1993). The social construction and subjective reality of activity settings: Implications for community psychology. *American Journal of Community Psychology, 21,* 537–559.

Garcia-Coll, C., Crnic, K., Lamberty, G., Wasik, B., Jenkins, R., Garcia Vazquez, H., et al. (1996). An integrative model for the study of developmental competencies in minority children. *Child Development, 67,* 1891–1914.

Genishi, C., & Goodwin, A. L. (Eds.). (2008). *Diversities in early childhood education.* New York: Routledge.

Genishi, C., Ryan, S., Ochsner, M., & Yarnall, M. M. (2000). Teaching in early childhood education: Understanding practices through research and theory. In V. Richardson (Ed.), *Handbook of research on teaching* (4th ed., pp. 1175–1210). New York: Macmillan.

Graue, M. E. (1992). Social interpretations of readiness for kindergarten. *Early Childhood Research Quarterly, 7*, 225–243.

Haight, W. L. (1999). The pragmatics of caregiver–child pretending at home: Understanding culturally specific socialization practices. In A. Goncu (Ed.), *Children's engagement in the world* (pp. 128–147). New York: Cambridge University Press.

Halgunseth, L. C., Ispa, J., & Rudy, D. D. (2006). Parental control in Latino families: An integrative review. *Child Development, 77*, 1282–1297.

Hamre, B. (2007). Learning opportunities in preschool and elementary classrooms. In R. C. Pianta, M. J. Cox, & K. L. Snow (Eds.), *School readiness, early learning and the transition to kindergarten*. Baltimore: Brookes.

Hamre, B., & Pianta, R. C. (2001). Early teacher-child relationships and trajectory of school outcomes through eighth grade. *Child Development, 72*, 625–638.

Harms, T., & Clifford, R. M. (1980). Early childhood environment rating scale. New York: Teachers College Press.

Hart, B., & Risley, T. R. (1992). American parenting of language-learning children: Persisting differences in family–child interactions observed in natural home environments. *Developmental Psychology, 28*, 1096–1105.

Hart, C. H., Burts, D. C., & Charlesworth, R. (1996). Integrated developmentally appropriate curriculum: From theory and research to practice. In C. H. Hart, D. C. Burts, & R. Charlesworth (Eds.), *Integrated curriculum and developmentally appropriate practice: Birth to age eight* (pp. 1–28). Albany: State University of New York.

Heath, S. B. (1983). *Ways with words*. Cambridge: Cambridge University Press.

Helburn, S. (1995). *Cost, quality and child outcomes in child care centers* (technical report, public report, and executive summary). Denver: University of Colorado.

Helburn, S. W., & Howes, C. (1996). Child care cost and quality. *The Future of Children, 6*, 62–81.

Hill-Collins, P. (1994). Shifting the center: Race, class, and feminist theorizing about motherhood. In E. N. Glenn, G. Chang, & L. R. Forcey (Eds.), *Mothering* (pp. 45–65). New York: Routledge.

Hoff-Ginsberg, E. (1991). Mother–child conversation in different social classes and communicative settings. *Child Development, 62*, 782–796.

Hofferth, S. L., Shauman, K. A., Henke, R. R., & West, J. (1998). *Characteristics of children's early care and education programs: Data from the 1995 National Household Education Survey.*

Hondagneu-Sotelo, P. (2001). *Domestica*. Berkeley: University of California Press.

Howes, C. (1988). Peer interaction in young children. *Monographs of the Society for Research in Child Development, 53*(1, Serial No. 217).

Howes, C. (1997). Children's experiences in center-based child care as a function of teacher background and adult child ratio. *Merrill Palmer Quarterly, 43*, 404–426.

Howes, C. (2008). Friendships in early childhood: Friendship. In K. Rubin, W. Bukowski, & B. Laursen (Eds.), *Handbook of peer interactions, relationships, and groups* (pp. 180–194). New York: Guilford Press.

Howes, C., Burchinal, M., Pianta, R. C., Bryant, D., Early, D., Clifford, R., et al. (2008). Ready to learn? Children's pre-academic achievement in prekindergarten. *Early Childhood Research Quarterly, 23,* 27–50.

Howes, C., & Hamilton, C. (1992). Children's relationships with child care teachers: Stability and concordance with maternal attachments. *Child Development, 63,* 879–892.

Howes, C., & James, J. (2002). Children's social development within the socialization context of child care and early childhood education. In C. Hart & P. Smith (Eds.), *Handbook of childhood social development* (pp. 137–155). London: Blackwell.

Howes, C., James, J., & Ritchie, S. (2003). Pathways to effective teaching. *Early Childhood Research Quarterly, 18,* 104–120.

Howes, C., & Matheson, C. C. (1992). Sequences in the development of competent play with peers: Social and social pretend play. *Developmental Psychology, 28,* 961–974.

Howes, C., Phillips, D. A., & Whitebook, M. (1992). Thresholds of quality: Implications for the social development of children in center-based child care. *Child Development, 63,* 449–460.

Howes, C., Pianta, R., Bryant, D., Hamre, B., Downer, J., & Soliday-Hong, S. (2008). *Ensuring effective teaching in early childhood education through linked professional development systems, quality rating systems, and state competencies: The role of research in an evidence-driven system* (National Center for Research on Early Childhood Education White Paper). Charlotte, VA: University of Virginia.

Howes, C., & Ritchie, S. (1998). Changes in child–teacher relationships in a therapeutic preschool program. *Early Education and Development, 4,* 411–422.

Howes, C., & Ritchie, S. (1999). Attachment organizations in children with difficult life circumstances. *Developmental Psychopathology, 11,* 254–268.

Howes, C., & Ritchie, S. (2002). *A matter of trust: Connecting teachers and learners in the early childhood classroom.* New York: Teachers College Press.

Howes, C., & Shivers, E. M. (2006). New child–caregiver attachment relationships: Entering child care when the caregiver is and is not an ethnic match. *Social Development, 15,* 343–360.

Howes, C., Shivers, E. M., & Ritchie, S. (2004). Improving social relationships in child care through a researcher-program partnership. *Early Education and Development, 15,* 57–78.

Howes, C., & Spieker, S. (2008). Attachment relationships in the context of multiple caregivers. In J. Cassidy & P. R. Shaver (Eds.), *Handbook of attachment theory and research* (2nd ed., pp. 317–332). New York: Guilford Press.

Howes, C., & Stewart, P. (1987). Child's play with adults, toys, and peers: An examination of family and child-care influences. *Developmental Psychology, 23,* 423–430.

Howes, C., & Wishard, A. G. (2004). Revisiting sharing meaning: Looking through the lens of culture and linking shared pretend play through proto-narrative development to emergent literacy. In E. Zigler, D. G. Singer, & S. J. Bishop-Josef (Eds.), *Children's play: The roots of reading* (pp. 143–158). Washington, DC: Zero to Three.

Isenberg, J. P., & Jalongo, M. R. (Eds.). (2003). *Major trends and issues in early childhood education.* New York: Teachers College Press.

Jackson, J. F. (1993). Multiple caregiving among African-Americans and infant attachment: The need for an emic approach. *Human Development, 36,* 87–102.

Johnson, D. J., Jaeger, E., Randolph, S. M., Cauce, A. M., Ward, J., & NICHD ECCRN. (2003). Studying the effects of early child care experiences on the development of children of color in the United States: Towards a more inclusive research agenda. *Child Development, 74,* 1227–1244.

Kagan, L. S., & Kauerz, K. (2007). Reaching for the whole: Integration and alignment in early education policy. In R. C. Pianta, M. J. Cox, & K. L. Snow (Eds.), *School readiness and the transition to kindergarten in the era of accountability* (pp. 31–48). Baltimore: Brookes.

Kessler, S., & Swadener, B. B. E. (1992). *Reconceptualizing the early childhood curriculum: Beginning the dialogue.* New York: Teachers College Press.

Kirk, R. E. (1995). *Experimental design.* Belmont, CA: Wadsworth.

Kochanska, G. (2002). Committed compliance, moral self, and internalization: A mediational model. *Developmental Psychology, 38,* 339–351.

Kontos, S., Howes, C., Shin, M., & Galinsky, E. (1995). *Quality in family child care and relative care.* New York: Teachers College Press.

Kontos, S., Hsu, H.-C., & Dunn, L. (1994). Children's cognitive and social competence in child care centers and family child care homes. *Journal of Applied Developmental Psychology, 15,* 87–111.

La Paro, K. M., & Pianta, R. C. (2000). Predicting children's competence in the early school years: A meta-analytic review. *Review of Educational Research, 70,* 443–484.

Ladd, G. W., Birch, S., & Buhs, E. S. (1999). Children's social and scholastic lives in kindergarten: Related spheres of influence. *Child Development, 70,* 1373–1400.

Ladson-Billings, G. (1999). *The dream helpers: Successful teachers of African American children.* New York: Teachers College Press.

Lamb, M. E. (1998). Nonparental child care: Context, quality, and correlates. In I. E. Siegel & K. A. Renninger (Eds.), *Handbook of child psychology: Vol. 4. Child psychology in practice* (pp. 73–133). New York: Wiley.

Lamb, M. E. (1999). Nonparental child care. In M. E. Lamb (Ed.), *Parenting and child development in "nontradtional families"* (pp. 39–55). Mahwah, NJ: Erlbaum.

Lee, J., & Walsh, D. (2005). Introduction to the special issue: Unpacking quality in early childhood programs. *Early Education and Development, 16,* 403–404.

Liang, X., Fuller, B., & Singer, J. D. (2000). Ethnic differences in child care selection: The influence of family structure, parental practices, and home language. *Early Childhood Research Quarterly, 15,* 357–384.

LoCassle-Crouch, J., Konold, T., Pianta, R., Howes, C., Burchinal, M., Bryant, D., et al. (2007). Observed classroom quality profiles in state-funded pre-kindergarten programs and associations with teacher, program, and classroom characteristics. *Early Childhood Research Quarterly, 22,* 3–7.

Lubeck, S. (1985). *Sandbox society: Early education in Black and White America.* Philadephia: Falmer Press.

Lubeck, S. (1998). Is DAP for everyone? A response. *Childhood Education, 74,* 299–301.

Maccoby, E. E., & Jacklin, C. N. (1987). Gender segregation in childhood. In E. H. Reese (Ed.), *Advances in child development and behavior* (pp. 239–288). New York: Academic Press.

Mashburn, A. J., Pianta, R. C., Hamre, B. C., Downer, J. T., Barbarin, O., Bryant, D., et al. (2008). Measures of classroom quality in pre-kindergarten and children's development of academic, language and social skills. *Child Development, 79*, 732–749.

Meisels, S. (1999). Assessing readiness. In R. C. Pianta & M. Cox (Eds.), *The transitions to kindergarten: Research, policy, training, and practice* (pp. 39–66). Baltimore: Brookes.

Miller-Jones, D. (1988). The study of African-American children's development: Contributions to reformulating developmental paradigms. In D. Slaughter (Ed.), *Black children and poverty: A developmental perspective* (pp. 75–92). San Francisco: Jossey-Bass.

National Association for the Education of Young Children. (2005). NAEYC Governing Board approves new early childhood performance standards and accreditation criteria. Retrieved February 27, 2009, from http://www.naeyc.org/accreditation/050415.asp

Neuman, S., & Roskos, K. (1992). Literacy objects as cultural tools: Effects on children's literacy behaviors in play. *Reading Research Quarterly, 27*, 203–225.

New, R. (2005). Section 1 Commentary: Legitimizing quality as quest and question. *Early Education and Development, 16*, 445–448.

NICHD ECCRN. (1996). Characteristics of infant child care: Factors contributing to positive caregiving. *Early Childhood Research Quarterly, 11*, 269–306.

NICHD ECCRN. (1997). Child care in the first year of life. *Merrill Palmer Quarterly, 43*, 340–361.

NICHD ECCRN. (2002). Structure > process > outcome: Direct and indirect effects of caregiving quality on young children's development. *Psychological Science, 13*, 199–206.

NICHD ECCRN. (2003). Social functioning in first grade: Associations with earlier home and child care predictors and with current classroom experiences. *Child Development, 74*, 1639–1662.

Orellana, M., Reynolds, J., Dorner, L., & Meza, M. (2003). In other words: Translating or "para-phrasing" as family literacy practices in immigrant households. *Reading Research Quarterly, 38*(1), 12–34.

Peisner-Feinberg, E. S., & Burchinal, M. R. (1997). Relations between preschool children's child-care experiences and concurrent development: The cost, quality and outcome study. *Merrill Palmer Quarterly, 43*, 451–478.

Peisner-Feinberg, E. S., Burchinal, M. R., Clifford, R. M., Culkin, M. L., Howes, C., Kagan, S. L., et al. (2001). The relation of preschool child care quality to children's cognitive and social developmental trajectories through second grade. *Child Development, 72*, 1534–1553.

Phillips, D. A., & Howes, C. (1987). Indicators of quality in child care: Review of research. In D. A. Phillips (Ed.), *Predictors of quality child care* (pp. 1–20). Washington, DC: National Association for the Education of Young Children.

Phillipsen, L. C., Burchinal, M. R., Howes, C., & Cryer, D. (1997). The prediction of process quality from structural features of child care. *Early Childhood Research Quarterly, 12*, 281–303.

Pianta, R. C. (1998). *Enhancing relationships between children and teachers*. Washington, DC: American Psychological Association.

Pianta, R. C. (2003). *Standardized classroom observations from pre-k to 3rd grade: A mechanism for improving access to consistently high quality classroom experiences and practices during the P–3 years*. New York: Foundation for Child Development.

Pianta, R. C. (2007). Early education in transition. In R. C. Pianta, M. J. Cox, & K. L. Snow (Eds.), *School readiness and the transition to kindergarten in the era of accountability* (pp. 3–11). Baltimore: Brookes.

Pianta, R., Hamre, B., & Stuhlman, M. (2003). Relationships between teachers and children. In W. M. Reynolds & G. Miller (Eds.), *Handbook of psychology: Vol. 7. Educational psychology* (pp. 199–234). New York: Wiley.

Pianta, R. C., & Howes, C. (Eds.). (2009). *The promise of PreK*. Baltimore: Brookes.

Pianta, R., Howes, C., Burchinal, M., Bryant, D., Clifford, R., Early, D., et al. (2005). Features of pre-kindergarten programs, classrooms, and teachers: Do they predict observed classroom quality and child–teacher interactions? *Applied Developmental Science, 9*, 144–159.

Pianta, R. C., Mashburn, A. J., Downer, J. T., Hamre, B., & Justice, L. (2008). Effects of web-mediated professional development resources on teacher–child interactions in pre-kindergarten classes. *Early Childhood Research Quarterly, 23*, 431–451.

Pianta, R. C., & Steinberg, M. (1992). Teacher–child relationships and adjusting to school. In R. C. Pianta (Ed.), *Beyond the parent: The role of other adults in children's lives* (pp. 61–80). San Francisco: Jossey-Bass.

Polakow, V. (2007). *Who cares for our children? The child care crisis in the other America.* New York: Teachers College Press.

Powell, D. R. (1989). *Families and early childhood programs.* Washington, DC: National Association for the Education of Young Children.

Powell, D. R., & Stremmel, A. J. (1989). The relation of early childhood training and experience to the professional development of child care workers. *Early Childhood Research Quarterly, 4*, 339–355.

Raver, C., Jones, S. M., Li-Grining, C. P., Metzger, M., Champion, K. M., & Sardin, L. (2008). Improving classroom practices: Preliminary findings from a randomized trial implemented in Head Start settings. *Early Childhood Research Quarterly, 23*, 10–26.

Reilly, J. S. (1992). How to tell a good story: The intersection of language and affect in children's narratives. *Journal of Narrative and Life History, 2*(4), 355–377.

Richman, A., Miller, P., & Levine, R. (1992). Cultural and educational variations in maternal responsiveness. *Developmental Psychology, 28*(4), 614–621.

Ritchie, S. (2003). Community-oriented classroom practices: Developing positive teacher–child relationships. In C. Howes (Ed.), *Teaching 4- to 8-year olds: Literacy, math, multiculturalism, and classroom community* (pp. 25–46). Baltimore: Brookes.

Ritchie, S., & Howes, C. (2003). Program practices and child–caregiver relationships. *Journal of Applied Developmental Psychology, 24*, 497–516.

Ritchie, S., James-Szanton, J., & Howes, C. (2003). Emergent literacy practices in early childhood. In C. Howes (Ed.), *Teaching 4- to 8-year olds: Literacy, math, multiculturalism, and classroom community* (pp. 56–74). Baltimore: Brookes.

Rogoff, B. (2003). *The cultural nature of human development.* New York: Oxford University Press.

Rogoff, B., & Angelillo, C. (2002). Investigating the coordinated functioning of multifaceted cultural practices in human development. *Human Development, 45*, 211–255.

Rogoff, B., Matusov, E., & White, C. (1996). Models of teaching and learning. In D. R. Olson & N. Torrance (Eds.), *The handbook of education and human development* (pp. 388–414). Oxford: Blackwell.

Roosa, M. W., Morgan-Lopez, A., Cree, W. K., & Specter, M. M. (2002). Ethnic culture, poverty, and context: Sources of influence on Latino families and children. In J. Contreras (Ed.), *Latino children and families in the United States* (pp. 27–44). Westport, CT: Praeger.

Rubenstein, J., & Howes, C. (1979). Caregiving and infant behavior in daycare and homes. *Developmental Psychology, 15*, 1–24.

Rubin, K. H., Bulowski, W., & Parker, J. (1998). Peer interactions, relationships, and groups. In W. Damon (Series Ed.) & N. Eisenberg (Vol. Ed.), *Handbook of child psychology: Vol. 3. Social, emotional, and personality development* (5th ed., pp. 619–700). New York: Wiley.

Sameroff, A. (1983). Developmental systems. In W. Kessen (Ed.), *Handbook of child psychology: Vol. 1. History, theories, and methods* (4th ed., pp. 237–294). New York: Wiley.

Sanders, K. E., Deihl, A., & Kyler, A. (2007). DAP in the 'hood: Perceptions of child care practices by African-American child care directors caring for children of color. *Early Childhood Research Quarterly, 22*, 394–406.

Shivers, E. M., Howes, C., Wishard, A. G., & Ritchie, S. (2004). Teacher-articulated perceptions and practices with families: Examining effective teaching in diverse high quality child care settings. *Early Education and Development, 15*, 167–186.

Shonkoff, J. P., & Phillips, D. A. (Eds.). (2000). *From neurons to neighborhoods.* Washington, DC: National Academy Press.

Slaughter, D. T. (1988). Black children, schooling, and educational intervention. In D. T. Slaughter (Ed.), *Black children and poverty: A developmental perspective* (pp. 75–92). San Francisco: Jossey-Bass.

Slaughter-Defoe, D. T. (1995). Revisiting the concept of socialization. *American Psychological Association, 50*, 276–286.

Spodek, B., & Saracho, O. N. (Eds.). (1990). *Early childhood teacher preparation.* New York: Teachers College Press.

Stipek, D., Feiler, R., Byler, P., Ryan, R., Milburn, S., & Salmon, J. M. (1998). Good beginnings: What difference does the program make in preparing young children for school? *Journal of Applied Developmental Psychology, 19*(1), 41–66.

Stipek, D., Feiler, R., Daniels, D., & Milburn, S. (1995). Effects of different instructional approaches on young children's achievement and motivation. *Child Development, 66*, 209–223.

Storch, S. A., & Whitehurst, G. J. (2002). Oral language and code-related precursors to reading: Evidence from a longitudinal structural model. *Developmental Psychology, 38*, 934–947.

Suarez Orozco, C., & Suarez Orozco, M. (1995). Migration: Generational discontinuities and the making of Latino identities. In L. Romanucci-Ross & G. A. DeVos (Eds.), *Ethnic identity: Creation, conflict, and accommodation* (3rd ed., pp. 321–347). Walnut Creek, CA: Alta Mira Press.

Tamis-Le Monda, C. S., & Bornstein, M. H. (2002). Maternal responsiveness and early language acquisition. *Advances in child development and behavior, 29*, 89–127. New York: Academic Press.

Tamis-LeMonda, C., Bornstein, M. H., & Baumwell, L. (2001). Maternal responsiveness and children's achievement of language milestones. *Child Development, 72*(3), 748–767.

Tonyan, H. A., & Howes, C. (2003). Exploring patterns in time children spend in a variety of childcare activities: Associations with environmental quality, ethnicity, and gender. *Early Childhood Research Quarterly, 18*, 121–142.

Uribe, F. M. T., LeVine, R., & LeVine, S. (1994). Maternal behavior in a Mexican community. In P. M. Greenfield & R. R. Cocking (Eds.), *Cross-cultural roots of minority child development* (pp. 41–54). Hillsdale, NJ: Erlbaum.

U.S. Census Bureau. (2004). *North Carolina Quickfacts.* Retrieved February 27, 2005, from http://quickfacts.census.gov/qfd/states/37000.html

Washington, V. (1988). Historical and contemporary linkages between Black child development and social policy. In D. T. Slaughter (Ed.), *Black children and poverty: A developmental perspective* (pp. 93–105). San Francisco: Jossey-Bass.

Waters, E. (1995). Appendix A: The attachment Q-set (version 3.0). *Monographs of the Society for Research on Child Development, 60*(2–3, Serial No. 244), 234–246.

Whitebook, M. (1999). Child care workers: High demand, low wages. *Annals of the American Academy of Political and Social Science, 563*, 141–146.

Whitebook, M., & Bellm, D. (1999). *Taking on turnover.* Berkeley, CA: Center for the Study of Child Care Employment.

Whitebook, M., Howes, C., Phillips, D., & Pemberton, C. (1989). Who cares? Child care teachers and the quality of care in America. *Young Children, 46*(4), 5–47.

Whitehurst, G. J., Arnold, D. S., Epstein, J. N., & Angell, A. L. (1994). A picture book reading intervention in day care and home for children from low income families. *Developmental Psychology, 30*, 679–689.

Winsler, A., Diaz, R. M., Espinoza, L., & Rodriguez, J. L. (1999). When learning a second language does not mean losing the first: Bilingual language development in low-income, Spanish-speaking children attending bilingual preschool. *Child Development, 70*, 349–362.

Wishard, A., Shivers, E., Howes, C., & Ritchie, S. (2003). Child care program and teacher practices: Associations with quality and children's experiences. *Early Childhood Research Quarterly, 18*, 65–103.

Woodcock, R. W., McGrew, K. S., & Mather, N. (2001). *Woodcock–Johnson III: Tests of achievement.* Itasca, IL: Riverside.

Woodcock, R. W., & Munoz-Sandoval, A. F. (1996). *Batería Woodcock Muñoz revisada: Pruebas de Aprovechamiento.* Itasca, IL: Riverside.

Yelland, N. (Ed.). (2005). *Critical issues in early childhood education.* Berkshire, UK: Open University.

Index